Robert Heller is one of the country's leading authorities on management. He was the founding editor of *Management Today* and took it rapidly to the position of Britain's leading management magazine. He is the author of many acclaimed and bestselling books, including *The Naked Manager, The Supermanagers, The Age of the Common Millionaire, The Super Chiefs, The Fate of IBM* and, with Will Carling, *The Way to Win*. His most recent book is *Goldfinger: How Entrepreneurs Get Rich by Starting Small*. He writes a monthly newsletter with Edward de Bono, *Letter to Thinking Managers,* and is a frequent visitor to management groups all over the world. He lives in North London.

In Search of European Excellence

THE 10 KEY STRATEGIES OF
EUROPE'S TOP COMPANIES

Robert Heller

HarperCollinsBusiness
An Imprint of HarperCollinsPublishers

HarperCollinsBusiness
An imprint of HarperCollins*Publishers*
77–85 Fulham Palace Road,
Hammersmith, London W6 8JB

This paperback edition 1998

1   3   5   7   9   8   6   4   2

First published in Great Britain by
HarperCollins*Publishers* 1997

ISBN 0 00 638812 4

Printed and bound in Great Britain by
Caledonian International Book Manufacturing Ltd, Glasgow

CONTENTS

ACKNOWLEDGEMENTS

This book could not have been contemplated, let alone completed, but for my good fortune in knowing so many of the thinkers who have charted, directed, and inspired the course of the real revolution that is overtaking the theory and practice of management. First and foremost (as all the other writers and speakers would agree) is Peter Drucker. Thanks to Management Centre Europe, I have been privileged to chair seminars at which Peter has expounded his latest, luminous thinking. They have added profoundly to the years of education which I have derived from his friendship and his remarkable writings.

The Drucker seminars also introduced me to C.K. Prahalad of the University of Michigan, Sir Peter Bonfield (then chief executive of ICL), and the inimitable Mike Kami, among other brilliant minds. I owe each of them a great deal for their penetrating insights. I am also indebted to MCE and to the admirable Jenny Webb and Karen O'Donnell for my encounters with Rosabeth Moss Kanter of the Harvard Business School and Barry Stein: anybody who is concerned with the performance of large organizations must rely on their seminal work.

Equally, Peter M. Senge of MIT is the indispensable guide to the learning organization and mastery of the business system, while Manfred Perlitz of the University of Mannheim is a most penetrating analyst of global trends. I have also been fortunate to work with thinkers whose thoughts about thinking have influenced me greatly – in particular Mark Brown of Innovation Centre Europe and, of course, Edward de Bono, my partner in the monthly *Letter to Thinking Managers*, which has been a major source for these pages. Michael Goold, Andrew Campbell and Marcus Alexander showed me their work in progress on *Corporate Level Strategy* and kindly allowed me to quote from it. David Benjamin sent me his very valuable notes on innovation.

References to books on which I have gratefully drawn, are in the notes. I owe a particular debt to the works by William H. Davidow and Michael S. Malone on the virtual corporation; and Michael Hammer and James Champy on reengineering. My knowledge of Total Quality Management rests largely on my interviews for my book *The Quality Makers*. I am extremely grateful to its progenitor, Sven-Erik Gunnervall of Norden Publishing, and to my interviewees – especially, for this book, to Bernard Fournier and Dennis Kennedy, respectively the managing directors of Rank Xerox and Honeywell (UK), Claus Møller of TMI, and Jacques Horovitz of MSR.

The above by no means completes the list of invaluable sources, who include Philip Sadler, formerly of the Ashridge Management College, Bill Ramsay of Templeton College, and Constantinos Markides of the London Business School. Chloe Cox and Alan Mossman introduced me to their own work on organizations and that of Robert Fritz. Peter Wickens was my source on the human resources breakthroughs at Nissan UK. David Bundred of Lucas Industries let me use his brilliant paper on modern purchasing. Interviews with Ryazuburo Kaku, Sir Derek Birkin and Ben Rosen, respectively chairmen of Canon, RTZ and Compaq, Ricardo Semler, the driving spirit of Semco, and Ben Tregoe of the Kepner-Tregoe management consultancy produced valuable insights and material.

Many other practitioners and teachers of management have influenced my thinking – and the practice of managers all over the world. It has been fascinating to see the real-world reflection of the theories of key figures such as the late W. Edwards Deming; Igor Ansoff, the father of modern thought on corporate strategy; Jay W. Forrester of MIT; David P. Norton, a prime mover of the balanced scorecard; Gary Hamel, co-author of rich insights with C. K. Prahalad; Kasra Ferdows; Robert H. Waterman, Jr; and Shin Taguchi. These teachers, like those mentioned earlier, do not inhabit ivory towers.

Their cause of real reform has been joined by leaders of action both among businessmen and consultants. I have been fortunate to see the results in many remarkable cases, including the work of two successive CEOs of SmithKline Beecham, Bob Baumann and Jan Leschly: of Pasquale Pistorio and Murray Duffin at SGS-THOMSON; Sir David Simon at British Petroleum; Alastair Cumming at British Airways; Feargal Quinn of Superquinn; Hal Rosenbluth of Rosenbluth International; Tony Gilroy of LucasVariety; and Gérard Van Schaik at Heineken. I am particularly grateful to Ben Heirs of Heirs Associates for the fascinating account of his pathfinding work with the latter company.

In this field of contemporary history, I cannot praise too highly the work of the journalists, several credited in these pages, who have produced such excellent material for the leading publications: in the United States, *Fortune*, *Business Week*, the *Wall Street Journal*, *The New York Times* and the *Chicago Tribune*; in Britain, the *Financial Times*, *The Times* and the *Independent on Sunday*. From the academic world, the *Harvard Business*

Review has always been a rich source of information and ideas, while in consultancy, the *McKinsey Quarterly* is unique – its interviews with General Pagonis and Jay Forrester are outstanding contributions.

My close association with the Kalchas Group, the British strategic consultancy, has produced a constant flow of ideas: I must thank Michael de Kare Silver in particular for asking me so many questions, and providing so many answers himself. Working for the editors of *Management Today, Worldlink* and *Business Solutions* has also been highly productive for me. The whole book arose out of a highly constructive dialogue with Bob Garratt and Lucinda McNeile of HarperCollins, who suggested that I should turn my attention from the American companies that largely featured in my earlier book, *The Leadership Imperative*, and survey the imperatives at work in Europe. I am grateful to them and to my excellent editor at HarperCollins, Juliet van Oss, for her patient midwifery. And I have been very lucky to have had the help of four excellent secretaries: Elli Petrohilos, Devon Scott, Anne MacKenzie and Pathika Martin.

INTRODUCTION

New managers and new methods are transforming world business in the struggle to win the new century's management wars. The winners will succeed, not only by virtue of their developed strengths, but by default. Those managements that stick with the ways in which they have always managed won't be around to witness their own defeat. They and their companies will be history.

Europe is being reshaped by this invisible revolution, the most sweeping economic change since the triumphs of post-war recovery. Unification has been galloping ahead, not through the halting impact of politicians and political treaties like Maastricht, not even through the limping progress towards a single currency, but through the decisive actions of business leaders. Restructuring, expanding, forming alliances and forging ahead into the former Soviet Bloc, they are redrawing the map of Europe in a wave of dynamic moves.

Yet in public perception, Europe still lags behind America and Japan (and even the upstarts of Asia) in industrial might, technological prowess and management ability. Look at even the international editions of business magazines, and European companies rate little mention. Europe's lower esteem stems largely from the management lag – from its seeming backwardness in exploiting the new technologies and philosophies of organization and achievement.

Even catching up confronts the Europeans with a considerable task. Seizing the lead demands far more – creating a powerful answer to the American and Japanese gurus and their followers. This evolving European version of New Century Management is described in this book. The Europeans can meet this challenge; though they did miss the chance to strike back when former wonders of US business were faltering and even failing on all sides.

What do Caterpillar Tractor, Digital Equipment, Fluor and IBM have in common? All suffered calamitous setbacks in the eighties, and all were among the heroes of the stupendously bestselling *In Search of Excellence*.[1] But very few of the stars – all of them Americans – that were praised by Tom Peters and Robert H. Waterman, Jr. shine in today's business firmament. In the nineties, new names are leading new companies in new ways, and obeying the imperatives of a dramatically changed environment.

But the companies are still American. Compaq and Eckhard Pfeiffer, Intel and Andy Grove, Bill Gates and Microsoft, Scott MacNeally and Sun Microsystems have risen on the tide, not only of new technology, but of the new management ideas. The two streams flow together: fast change can't be managed by old methods. Moreover, the imperatives have also been recognized in old-line companies like General Electric and Coca-Cola. GE's Jack Welch and Coke's Roberto C. Goizueta are outstanding among chief executives who have recognized what Peter Drucker has named 'the new realities'.

Those realities are equally clear to the best of Europe's new breed of managers, leaders of change who are perfectly capable of matching America's best. I have identified ten key strategies with which Europe's revolutionaries have set off in search of their own brand of excellence. The old reactionaries are still in the majority, and too large a majority at that. But their ascendancy in all other respects is rapidly draining away as the new leaders act decisively in the following ten intertwined arenas of corporate renaissance:

1 Devolving leadership – without losing control or direction.

2 Driving radical change – in the entire corporate system, not just in its parts.

3 Reshaping culture – to achieve long-term success.

4 Dividing to rule – winning the rewards of smallness while staying or growing large.

5 Exploiting the 'organization' – by new approaches to central direction.

6 Keeping the competitive edge – in a world where the old ways of winning no longer work.

7 Achieving constant renewal – stopping success from sowing the seeds of decay.

8 Managing the motivators – so that people can motivate themselves.

9 Making team-working work – the new, indispensable skill.

10 Achieving total management quality – by managing everything much better.

European leaders who have grasped these ten vital renaissance strategies are determined not to follow in the footsteps of those who took great companies and led them into the ranks of the once-great. In his later book, *The Frontiers of Excellence*,[2] Waterman tackles this issue, painfully raised by the high fall-out rate of the original *Excellence* heroes. He calls the question 'irritating and tough'. It lies at the heart of management: 'Why do some great companies, like IBM, stumble badly while others . . . remain vibrant?'

He praises one company as a vibrant example, the heroic pioneer of an approach which truly is central to the new management: the self-managed team concept. This company's strategic success, he notes, has much to do with its relentless drive to make self-direction a management reality. Its strength springs from the raw ability to out-innovate the competition, both with new products and through cost advantages won by the enormous productivity gains of self-directed work. This company's system gives people everywhere the control they need to feel and be their personal best.

Such praise stands in vivid contrast to another corporate portrait which appeared in *Fortune*: 'the ultimate hierarchy – to be unkind, an inwardly pointed pyramid of anal-retentive order-takers loathed by competitors and retail customers alike'.

The two companies are one and the same: Procter & Gamble. The second (and later) description appeared in *Fortune* in March 1994. In this portrait, P&G's success had rested on over-charging for its products. High internal costs and falling market shares had now forced P&G to redesign 'the way it develops, manufactures, distributes, prices, markets and sells products', turning the company 'upside down'.

Waterman's own explanation for the feet-of-clay syndrome (which plagues all authors who select corporate paragons) is that great companies 'lose their edge' – his moral being, 'Learn from the best while they're good and move on'. The trouble with that lesson is that the best are never as good as they seem. The truth is that IBM was already deeply flawed when *In Search of Excellence* was written: root-and-branch problems never spring up overnight. As for P&G, the deep faults identified by *Fortune* co-existed with the virtuous management lauded by Waterman.

The camera can lie. Outsiders focus on what they want to see and miss the larger picture. But it's equally easy for insiders to ignore the obvious, and for big companies in particular to shelter from their failings behind their size. The competitive disadvantage of large scale has been obvious for decades. Even though the leviathans have remained rich and powerful, mass has slowed them down and given openings to the new and nimble. Now European managers have come to see that sheer scale, the last bastion of the big, has ceased to offer either competitive advantage or even simple protection.

Today, managements whose minds and deeds are stuck in the *status quo* are obsolescent, weak and failing. In the next few years, they will be obsolete – and failed. Renewal and nimbleness have become paramount necessities for the large and established. For the younger business, staying new and agile is equally imperative. But managers are in luck. New tactical and strategic technologies are available, just in time to give management the new essentials: information, speed, control and excellent outcomes.

This technology includes that of the seismic revolution in information and communications: mankind has moved from mainframes to the Internet in a blink of history's eye. But the new management technology is really dominated by the application of *thought*, not solo, but teamed with other brains. The hard technology of product and process provides the tools, which far surpass those available to previous generations. The soft technology of managing people applies the hard tools in order to create breakthroughs.

On each of the ten vital renaissance strategies, examples of effective, progressive top managements abound to enlighten and encourage. There are also many examples of top people who haven't displayed either the courage or the commonsense to alter profoundly or dismantle the apparatus which protects their own importance (and self-importance). Corporate high-life creates cosy chairs in which over-cosseted bosses try to manage the unmanageable by remote control. It can't work – which makes it far from surprising (to everybody but the bosses) if their companies don't work well, either.

All these inoperative companies, though, were originally created or recreated by highly successful businessmen, who for decades had managed their offspring through all the vicissitudes of growth, transition and challenge. Their business genes are still vigorous, widespread and effective. To revitalize Euro-managing, to find European excellence, those genes need only to be allied with the new knowledge about what makes people and organizations work effectively and enjoyably; and then to be applied to a changed and changing social, political, economic and technological climate.

If this is done – and it's a great test – management has a grand opportunity to build success that not only matches but outdoes the past. Managers are awakening to this opportunity at all levels, in companies of all sizes. By finding the right answers to the ten searching issues explored here, in company after company, internal revolution is stirring and advancing to match and expedite the external changes of a single and greatly enlarged Europe.

This book is about the companies and the managers who are seeking to create the European future – Finnish, British, German, French, Dutch, Swiss and many cross-border combinations: Anglo-Dutch, Franco-Italian, Swiss-Swedish-German. Some of the subjects are owned outside Europe, by Americans and Japanese. But that, too, is part of the new European order. Competition has become global, and players in the global wars must battle for opportunity and supremacy in the vast European market.

In a global economy the challenges and the changes are universal. Europe has started from well behind the Americans and Japanese – so its companies must run much faster and fight much harder. A new kind of excellent company is emerging in consequence: fast on its feet, flexible, adventurous, responsive and constantly improving and mutating. A new breed of excellent managers is rising to meet that challenge. This is how they can – and must – win the management wars.

ONE

The Devolution of Leadership

The making of ABB

A brave new Europe must eventually mean a bold new form of European company. The lines of this paradigm's development are already clearly etched. Euroco will build global market strength, if necessary aided by shrewd acquisitions in the world's key sectors and markets. It will exploit these global strengths by slashing costs (eliminating surplus capacity, taking out working capital) to achieve the lowest cost structure in all its discrete businesses.

Euroco will also astutely diversify and concentrate sources of production (probably moving into East European production on a significant scale). Finally, and most important, the new European company will drive forcefully for organic growth. The prescription is clear, logical and feasible.

Most major groups are working towards at least some of the prescribed aims. But one group above all has set the new pattern: Asea Brown Boveri (ABB). 'The verdict is clear,' wrote the *Financial Times* in 1995. 'For the second year running, and by a substantially increased margin, top European business men have named ABB, the Swedish-Swiss engineering multinational, as the company for which they have the most respect.' The vote for ABB is undeniably a tribute to the success of Percy Barnevik, the bearded architect of the combine, in articulating and executing his vision of the new European corporation.

Neither ASEA, its Swedish half, nor Brown Boveri, the Swiss component, previously had anything like the respect of ABB and its nearest also-rans: Nestlé, British Airways, BMW, Shell and Marks & Spencer. The compelling Barnevik vision is that of a group which, like Shell and Unilever, is transnational in ownership. However, it goes beyond these models in creating separate global businesses that seek their own destinies under the minimum of central control.

Famously, Barnevik reduced two head office establishments that totalled 6,000 employees to a mere 150. Almost a third of the departed went into new service companies, set up quasi-independently to provide HQ functions on a contractual, profit-making basis. The appeal of the vision and the forceful action taken to implement Barnevik's ideas have brought him innumerable invitations to address seminars, plus many prestigious interviews (including one with the *Harvard Business Review*) as well as the accolade of his peers.

In the early years, Barnevik's peers applauded despite the low profitability which characterized what he describes as a period of consolidation. Recently, however, ABB has sprung forward. In 1995, the group reeled off major achievements: net income up 73 percent to $1.3 billion; margins up from 8.2 percent to 8.7 percent en route to the 10 percent target for 1997; operating profit after depreciation up 25 percent; and revenues 14 percent higher at $33.9 billion – meaning that ABB had added over $16 billion of sales to those of its first year.

The growth achieved also vindicates Barnevik's wider management philosophy. One of its pillars is true multinationalism. His executive board has eight members: three are Swedes and two Swiss. The others come from Germany (which was by far Brown Boveri's biggest bastion), America (where Barnevik made two critical acquisitions during the consolidation period) and Denmark. Promoting cross-border cooperation is one area where Barnevik, who generally discourages central intervention in the interests of local autonomy, does interfere.

'The thing I watch is when, say, a German manager has to appoint someone, he very often will come up with a German. It is not because of nationality and language, but because he usually knows that person better. I tell him to go and interview candidates in other countries. Maybe it will make him think that it could be useful to have, say, an Italian or an American on his senior staff.'

The polyglot nature of European business is a source of great potential strength. But the way in which trans-European companies traditionally organize by separate countries is inimical to utilizing this strength to the full. Often, the subsidiary based in France, Germany or the UK is resolutely French, German or British in character and personnel, despite its overseas ownership and control. The advantages in pride and cohesion have increasingly been offset by the diseconomies. Global markets and economies of scale require the imposition of broader control and direction.

Other multinationals are now emulating ABB by building businesses whose remits are global, reducing the power of the national companies and making them subservient to the wider grouping. Few, however, have started on this road as early as Barnevik, or have taken the logic to its inescapable conclusion – that international businesses must be run internationally.

ABB's results have deeply impressed Pierre Bonelli, chief executive of the Sema Group consultancy. At a panel discussion on technology organized by *The Wall Street Journal Europe* in early 1996, Bonelli endorsed the view of ABB as the model for the future – a company whose global culture has no national base. 'In Europe, you need a networked company . . . a nationless company.' This strengthens, rather than weakens, a group's technological prowess: in 1995, a poll of 100 chief technology officers across Europe voted ABB the best manager of technology and innovation.

The 1995 deal with Daimler-Benz, merging AEG's railway equipment business with ABB's, sought to exploit this global culture: it would make ABB the world's largest supplier, seeking to operate across frontiers in an industry traditionally bounded by them. To make such ambitions work, however, Barnevik has created an organization that, at first sight, seems unmanageable. Its business 'segments' cover power generation, power transmission and distribution, industrial and building systems, transportation equipment and financial services. That's only five in all – but over 5,000 profit centres report to the divisions.

Barnevik argues that the key to managing the unmanageable lies in people rather than systems and organization charts. How well people, singly or in groups, create and follow up initiatives makes the critical difference. 'The real challenge,' as Barnevik puts it, 'is creating an entrepreneurial atmosphere in what can easily amount to a big bureaucratic company.' Obviously, that drive can never be wholly successful. But ABB's results and real-life cases do encourage the belief that bureaucracy can be beaten back by determined individuals.

In Canada, for example, a new CEO, Paul Kefalus, found sales stagnating on his arrival in 1994. In James Moore's account in *The Death of Competition*,[1] he didn't turn to improved products and processes to boost the business. Instead, he turned to the customers. What were their strategies? How could ABB work with them to help achieve their strategic aims? For those customers who were prepared to back this approach, Kefalus formed small expert teams drawn from all relevant ABB units – producing, for example, a system of remote-controlled robots for a mining company.

The dozen-plus partnerships formed with major customers have helped to increase Canadian sales significantly. The acid test of Barnevik's ideas is that the group continues to lead, not by reputation, but by results: the reward of allowing managers to manage, and of having individual initiative count for more than the organization – the exact opposite of the centralized, bureaucratic and prescriptive European tradition.

In 1996, Barnevik became chairman in a move that consolidated two separate boards and made ABB at board level what it had long been operationally – one company. Barnevik stresses that point: 'The combined board creates a strong signal of unity inside and outside the company. It is an important symbolic and practical change.' In creating the unified, stateless company, ABB has shown the way to the rest of Europe.

Down the organization

The famous line about heavyweight boxers maintains that the bigger they are, the harder they fall. The creation and enlargement of ABB, mainly by merger and acquisition, shows total disregard for this theory – though it certainly seemed to apply to many gigantic corporations in the early years of the 1990s. Two of the greatest industrial corporations in the US, and thus the world, General Motors and IBM, made unprecedented losses, and the two largest securities firms, Salomon on Wall Street and Nomura in Japan, were humbled by scandal.

In Europe, Italy's three leading European groups, Fiat, Pirelli and Olivetti, have all been suffering; Daimler-Benz, the cynosure of German heavyweights, made the country's largest-ever losses; Crédit Lyonnais, France's largest bank, ran up the biggest bad debts ($25 billion) in banking history; Britain's grandest industrial company, ICI, split itself into two under pressure, while the most lauded British investment bank, S.G. Warburg, lost its direction and independence.

One link in these events is clear – the gap between the aims of big company organizations and what actually happens. Organizational form and organizational behaviour are not one and the same thing. The whole of Percy Barnevik's strategy at ABB has been built on the belief that, if you sincerely want results, you get them by organizing accordingly. The proof of that pudding is easily found: can employees in your organization answer a few simple questions about the business? For example:

1 If cost reduction is an objective, what improvement projects are they currently working on?

2 Do they understand the identity and nature of the competition?

3 Have they met with their management in the past six months?

4 Do they understand how their job contributes to cost and profit?

These questions are tests, not of the employees, but of the management. Unless every one of your employees can answer all the chosen questions, it isn't just communication that has failed. Even in a sophisticated and highly organized business, penetrating questions should get positive answers, not for their own sake, but to generate and guarantee progress. That's a matter of *process*: companies with higher productivity are based on more effective processes, which must include the process of management itself.

That process embraces the future, the philosophy, and the dynamic of the firm. The future demands careful planning for improved results and strong follow-up to ensure that the plans, modified by feedback, are implemented. The philosophy consists of the guiding and driving principles, the shared values, which inform the processes. The dynamic is the will and the methodology for taking action that are exemplified so strongly by ABB, and which are the crucial, missing element in many European organizations.

From the beginning Percy Barnevik set ABB's businesses ambitious targets for profitability; overall, they achieved a 25.2 percent on stockholders' equity in 1995, up from 20.5 percent the previous year. Both numbers were higher than the 1995 figures for Philips (17.9 percent) and vastly greater than the Siemens result (8.7 percent). Barnevik's demanding ways work. Expect the target to be achieved, and work back from the target to what must be done to hit the mark.

In my observation, this isn't news to most managements. They know what to do, and even how it should be done: the failure lies in actually doing it – or rather, not doing it. The action mode involves pressure for short-term performance. This has its dangers, and has been widely excoriated as the root of Britain's industrial under-achievement – while the Continentals (and the Japanese) are praised for their longer vision. But poor short-term performance makes long-term achievement much more difficult.

At its most elementary level, the thought is enshrined in Geneen's Law, which holds that hitting the first quarter's budget targets is all-important: miss them, and you never catch up in the next three. Many managers have confirmed this truth, which comes from Harold S. Geneen of ITT, history's most determined exponent of MBB (Management by

Budget), and is based on many years of tough (very tough) experience in the field.

Inquisitorial quarterly insistence on bottom-line financial performance is a feature of many US-owned operations in Europe. In many cases (as at Geneen's ITT), it generates a pattern of behaviour among managers which is marked by fear and ambition, in roughly equal quantities. Notoriously, one consequent temptation is to boost profits by devices like postponing investment or cutting back on the marketing spend. The emphasis on profit is misleading in itself, and so is the obsession with one quarter or one fiscal year.

The task is to manage to achieve short-term success while building (and never jeopardizing) achievement in the middle and long terms. It is no use squeezing higher figures out of operating managers quarter by quarter if the rising profits conceal (and are part-financed by) a decline in competitive power in the businesses concerned. Nemesis inevitably awaits. The object of the corporate exercise is to create value over time. How much value has each business added over the past five years? How much value will be added over the next five?

These financial outcomes will depend on a host of key non-financial factors such as the likely rise or decline in the market sector; the market share that the business has now and expects to attain; the room for price increases, or, quite possibly, the prospect of price cuts. It would be astounding if ambitious targets – or even modest ones – could be reached without heavy contributions from new products or services. What successes and results are the latter expected to generate?

There are other penetrating questions. How do the projected non-financial trends, and the conseqent financial ones, compare with the present? How do they relate to the past? Historic trends in sales, gross profit margins, operating expenses and margins, capital turnover and returns both on sales and capital are commonly ignored by managers. Fixated on forecasts, and conditioned by being judged against forecasts (that is, budgets), rather than on year-to-year growth, they don't use the past as a guide to the present and future.

Looking back, though, encourages the long view. If you are managing for continuous high performance, this isn't an optional exercise. What managers do must be consistent with what they want to achieve. Equally, the company must be organized with consistency to enable things to get done. Thus, clear responsibility is essential: divided responsibility makes a nonsense of decentralization. In a sensible set-up, ultimate control is exercised by the leader, and execution, as at ABB, is decentralized to people with the power to act – the processes and paraphernalia of organization must not get in the way.

Neither must reorganization. The series of upheavals through which many companies have passed in the last decade have left a trail of insecurity, confusion and career destruction. The aim of constructive change programmes is to combine the flexibility and speed of response that competition (and human satisfaction) demand with the control and discipline that are essential to mobilize all the company's material and human resources in the same cause.

It is necessary, before embarking on change programmes at all, to establish how the company truly rates in technology, productive efficiency and customer satisfaction – not in the eyes of its own management, but in those of the most interested parties: the employees, the customers, and the suppliers. How far have reality and central perception diverged?

The bad examples reflect a familiar pattern that many managers will recognize – and with some pain:

- 'Initial management thrusts have wrought great change in your organization, but as attention has shifted to other priorities, old behaviours have reasserted themselves. There is a word for this phenomenon in manufacturing – snapback.'

- 'You have tried to make changes through training or other interventions and found that you have had little or no lasting impact, despite using some of the best internal or external trainers or consultants.'

- 'Staff seem really motivated to behave in a particular (and you think productive) way, yet for much of the time they actually behave in very unproductive ways.'

The writers of that passage, Chloe Cox and Alan Mossman, observe that 'If you have chronic problems with organizational or individual behaviour, the chances are that the underlying structures of your organization do not support the behaviour you want – they cause the unwanted behaviour you are getting.' Action managers concentrate on 'resolving behaviour', which gets from A to B; in contrast, the structures created and recreated by the corpocrats encourage 'oscillating behaviour', which moves backwards and forwards between A and B.

The management thinker Robert Fritz, in his book *Corporate Tides*, describes precisely what happens in these circumstances. The desire to change leads to changes being introduced, which creates a big yearning for stability, which produces an even greater need for changes – which only produces another contradictory oscillation. Within this context, the gains from individual improvements are lost, simply because the wrong behaviours are being supported by the system. Remove that support, and the behaviours can change marvellously.

That's why the very same matrix structures (organizing by product, region and function) that are a recognized cause of grave troubles in Western companies work fine at Japanese groups like Canon – because the processes and behaviours within Canon's matrix are simply superior and more dynamic. It's also why the apparently cumbersome structure at ABB has been able to deliver. All systems can be dynamized, even the monthly figures: hard-driving companies update the expected annual results *every month*, and always look four quarters ahead, adding a new one every quarter.

Continuous cost reduction should be equally dynamic and progressive. At the Italian aerospace group Alenia, managers are made to specify what cost cuts have been included in their budgets through improved quality processes, and precisely how the cuts will be achieved. Such hard-nosed approaches are better than experimenting with softer means such as appraisal systems.

That's not to denigrate soft means: they, too, can have the required element of dynamism. Mostly, they don't. For example, a common appraisal system rates people on a scale from one to five, which means 'outstanding'. Four is the rating for 'highly effective, three for 'effective'. In one European organization, typically enough, fixed percentage bonus rates were attached to the ratings: 5 percent for effective, 10 percent for very effective and 15 percent for outstanding. The highly demotivating result was that hardly anybody scored more than three: too many higher scores would have bust the payroll budgets.

It's a Herculean struggle to achieve a progressive one-for-all group culture against such organizational impediments. Few corporate errors outdo, for sheer futility, stifling the firm's own energies. Time and again, that's precisely what organizing centralists do. But hard-driving Barnevik-style decentralizers are coming into their own. Their approach is far the better way to build global market strengths and capitalize on them by achieving optimum efficiencies, organic growth and collective dynamism. And that's the only approach that makes sense for the new Europe – and the new European company.

The shared strategies of ICL

The global accounting and consultancy firm, Ernst & Young, when it set out to analyse 'management practices that impact performance', found one universally beneficial practice which may well hold the key, not only to better performance, but to resolving the biggest demotivator of all: mismatch between people and the organization. The 'Best Practices Report', compiled with the American Quality Foundation,[2] says flatly that:

> Widespread understanding of the strategic plan by people inside and outside the organization has a broad beneficial impact. The two groups whose understanding showed the strongest impact on performance are middle management . . . and customers . . . Most organizations said that their middle management partially understands the strategic plan; increasing that understanding from partial to full is a strategy to gain competitive advantage – with positive impacts on profit, quality and performance.

Very few organizations, inside or outside Europe, have acted on this insight at all. Even fewer have lived its lesson more thoroughly than Britain's ICL, praised during Sir Peter Bonfield's reign as chief executive as the best-managed and financially most successful of truly European computer companies. Bonfield understood that when a board has handed down a vision from on high, people must be motivated to interpret and implement the vision. This impelled him to institute a 'Directors' Programme' for a hundred of his managers and their top teams.

Was the Programme a form of management development? Or a planning device? Or was it both? The aim was to involve all senior managers in implementing the vision, with these three objectives:

1 To enable delegates to articulate the . . . vision for the 1990s in relation to their business and personal responsibilities.

2 To enable them to demonstrate confidence in working across boundaries and initiating new teamwork practices.

3 To enable them to produce evidence of an Implementation Plan in support of specific areas of the corporate strategy.

In this three-part process, the managers, group by group, were exposed to a five-fold process:

The Challenge.

Our Response.

Adding Value and Measuring Progress.

Managing Change Effectively.

Building Team Implementation Plans.

The challenge in business terms was to build on the successes which ICL had won by pioneering the open systems market, especially in retailing, local government, manufacturing and logistics. In human terms, the task was to prepare and equip managers and their teams thoroughly to respond to the challenge. This was not just a one-way process. Mark these searching questions:

1 What are your personal areas of concern in relation to achieving the vision?

2 What is the rationale behind each of the board's areas of concern, and on which do you think the board should expect each part of the business to make its greatest impact?

3 In relation to the main areas of concern in your group, what are the critical business problems that underlie them and that need to be addressed and solved?

In other words, these people were asked, not simply to implement orders from above, but to address the strategic issues directly and critically themselves. The managers were being asked both to understand the strategy and to contribute to its refinement and realization. The organizers understood that the organization might get in the way of the vision and of individual initiatives, so the managers were asked to set aside 'all current constraints imposed by ICL policies and practices' and to 'design an ideal system for solving your critical business problems'.

Moreover, they were required to re-enter 'the real world of ICL, as you experience it' and to 'compare your ideal system with its equivalent' in the company: 'In terms of basic tasks, where are the important gaps?' They were told to 'ignore the espoused cultural values and norms' and to describe the actual ones – setting aside systems and structures, and concentrating on 'behaviour, norms and values', giving specific examples and anecdotes. Thus the programme recognized the gap between top management and middle managers, but sought to close the chasm.

Most important, the exercise wasn't simply an exercise in motivation – an all too common failing. As Thomas S. Robertson wrote in the *Business*

Strategy Review, published by the London Business School, 'pursuit of the holy grail [whether it is empowerment, cultural change, leadership or anything else] absorbs resources – time, funds and energy – and has a high opportunity cost if managers would have a better pay-off from pursuing activities with clearer bottom-line potential ... the most common response to the holy grail is lots of rhetoric and very little committed action.'

This is a sure route to demotivating managers.

The ICL approach plainly overcomes both of Robertson's objections. But this issue goes far beyond such vital matters as motivation and ending the alienation of middle managers from the organization. If the firm is pursuing inappropriate strategies, or implementing appropriate ones badly, disaster must follow. ICL's history, as well as demonstrating the virtues of sharing strategy, has recently shown what happens if the wrong one is being shared.

In 1995, the company moved from the previous year's operating profit of £58.3 million to a loss of £31.2 million. There was also massive reorganization, involving the loss of 1,300 jobs, retreat from the PC business and retrenchment to almost exclusively a service and software operation. That all cost another £152 million, making a total loss of £188.3 million. Plans to emphasize and reinforce ICL's independence from its 85 percent owner, the Japanese Fujitsu, by returning to the stock market had to be postponed indefinitely. What had gone wrong?

Over-dependence on public sector orders hadn't helped, as that fount of wealth became less copious. But ICL had also bet heavily on a light that failed. In 1991, ICL bought the personal computer business of Nokia, the Scandinavian electronics group, as the gateway to major expansion of its European presence in a crucial market. Intelligently enough, the merger was handled like a reverse takeover: Nokia managers moved into key positions at ICL, rather than the other way round. But the purchase didn't answer the always burning strategic question: why should the customer buy an ICL computer rather than anybody else's?

In a crowded PC marketplace, ICL lacked any differentiator: its poor but deserved reward was a miserable 2.1 percent of the market. Another miserable figure was its 1 percent return on the software and systems business, which now accounts for the entire group turnover. By the time these results were announced, Bonfield had been elevated to the plum job of managing director at British Telecom; but did ICL's strategic setback invalidate his approach – and the Best Practices Report?

The answer must be no. Sharing in strategy will improve performance everywhere. Not sharing strategy will damage performance – and the firm. Bonfield had made significant strides away from the blunderbuss management which relies on old weapons and ways, and removal of this self-erected obstacle had worked magically on ICL's peformance and survival. It isn't a question of 'sometimes the magic works, and sometimes it doesn't'. Rather, sometimes you need to find a new magic.

That can always be discovered where ICL found half its former successful strategic initiatives: from the people down the line. Ask them to contribute frankly and freely, and the ideas will pour forth. They may well be uncomfortable for top management. Some will probably be iconoclastic, challenging the mind-set of the corporation and the rules by which it lives. Above all others, those ideas are the ones you want.

Breaking the rules

'Break all the rules' was the advice of that giant of customer service, the late Sam Walton. It was the tenth and last of the great man's commandments, the foundation of the unexampled growth of Wal-Mart to become the world's largest retailer. The rules mostly concern fellow employees (Walton set the fashion by calling them 'associates' or 'partners'). He advised that you should share, communicate and celebrate success with your partners, motivate, appreciate and listen to them.

All European managers, even if they are only paying lip service, would agree with the retailing sage on those points, as they would with his emphasis on commitment, control of expenses and exceeding customers' expectations. But few organizations obey the rule-breaking rule. Walton's incitement to anarchy doesn't mean lack of control; Wal-Mart's own control systems are superb – effective control is the essence of successful retailing. But, as he sensed and practised, great businesses need to combine regularity with improvisation, order with elements of spontaneity and disorder. This is essential when the exercise of initiative and innovation will determine the difference between success and failure – between growth tiger and pussy cat.

In their hearts, managers know this to be true. They prove it every time a crash development programme is required, or an urgent problem has to be solved, or a new business has to be launched. The almost invariable response is to set up a group that is often expressly exempted from obeying the rules – written and unwritten.

All companies, and much managerial thinking, are governed by rules.

The first are the formal, written regulations which lay down what managers and other employees can, can't and must do. The second variety are the informal rules, 'the way we do things round here', which can be even more restrictive than the formal restraints. The third variety is made up of mind-sets – the ways in which people think about the external world and the relationship of the business to that world.

The culture of control operates most obviously and most restrictively via the first variety of rules. The cultural brakes are just as restrictive with the second, unwritten variety. But the mind-set rules govern what the organization does in ways that are extremely powerful and wildly erratic: sometimes restrictive, the collective mind-set can also run wildly out of control. All companies have unfounded myths, spoken or unspoken, about themselves: these, too, are part of the mind-set.

The shared mind-set operates in its most powerful and influential mode at the top management level. Both the rules and the beliefs may be founded in deep error, and may contribute to even worse mistakes. If you break the rules and look at the company, say, from an aggressive competitor's viewpoint, the truth can shock the myths to destruction. For instance, do you still believe in economies of scale? Small competitors have shown that, in fragmented and competitive businesses, the economic advantages available today through placing large orders are much less significant, even to a giant. Certainly the savings are nothing like great enough to offset vastly higher costs of overheads, advertising and bureaucratic delays.

The extent to which internal rules build unneccessary delay into the system creates the case for what is known as 'time-based competition', in which every process is analysed, taken apart and reassembled to eliminate excess time. That is not the norm of business conduct. But in unconventional times and situations, conventional behaviour doesn't stand a chance: you must dare to be different.

To have that courage stimulated, every top management needs a wider vision, the ability to see the wood as well as the trees, the power to rise above the rules and the grinding, often numbing pressures of day-to-day and week-to-week operations. Top managers need to be acutely sensitive to trends, especially when an imminent sea-change threatens the whole strategy. Ideally those qualities should be possessed by the chief executive. In reality, they are seldom owned either by the leader or by anybody else at the top.

Companies easily develop an all-embracing internal view which governs external actions to a potentially fatal degree. Internal rules and corporate myths stem from what Peter M. Senge of MIT calls a 'mental model'. With that mind-set uppermost (and often enshrined in a financial model), managers, from the chief executive downwards, can't and won't see the company's setbacks, even a collapse into loss, as a failure of the system. To their minds the system might need tightening up, by reorganization, redundancies and other cost-cutting – but radical changes in the cultural rules won't be thought necessary.

When crisis intervenes, that complacency is shattered. In writing about his cat, drowned in a murderous attempt on a goldfish bowl, the poet Gray noted that 'one false step is ne'er retrieved'. By the same token, one radical breaking of rules must lead to others. Unduly conservative and rule-bound systems and sub-systems won't survive the crisis pressures. Companies may even discover that their vaunted strengths, like the meticulous quality inspection of Mercedes-Benz cars, are actually weaknesses.

Dedication to top quality has its virtues, but also its vices. The traditional German excellence of product isn't quality as in Total Quality Management. Quality in the typical German sense had come to mean the highest specification, irrespective of need or even technology. Overengineering had become a national pastime, and to challenge the engineers was like assaulting an established religion.

All companies breed shibboleths as well as rules. For instance, purchasing departments pride themselves on their ability to drive down supplier prices. That disobeys the rules of total quality: the famous fourteen points of W. Edwards Deming, the founding father of TQM, abjured companies not to award business on the basis of price alone. The issue, however, is whether you can maintain that commitment in markets where price-cutters have changed the economics.

Pressure on prices puts pressure on costs, which in turn pressurizes in-house manufacturing. The easy response is to go off-shore. When even the Japanese have turned heavily to other Asian suppliers in search of lower costs, it's hardly surprising that Western firms have done likewise. At the same time, they have hammered suppliers on prices – and the suppliers in turn have hammered *their* suppliers.

However, there is a third course of action, which is more challenging, but far more constructive – cutting down internal manufacturing costs to competitive levels by adopting the new rules of manufacture. By simplifying processes, reducing numbers of components, breaking the rules and changing habits, an organization that thought itself efficient can find staggering economies. The savings, however, should never be ends in themselves. Unless the lower costs are deployed as elements of an effective, redesigned marketing and economic strategy, the cost benefits will be squandered.

The assault on manufacturing costs is ideal territory for one of the project groups which are the management model for the future. The excellent phrase 'hot groups' is used by Harold J. Leavitt and Jean Lipman-Blumen, who note that the groups 'do great things fast'. Writing in the *Harvard Business Review*,[3] they point out that most successful executives have at some time experienced what these groups are like. 'Lively, high-achieving, dedicated', the groups 'completely captivate their members, occupying their hearts and minds to the exclusion of almost everything else'.

The members, from three people to never more than thirty, show characteristics that are always the same: 'vital, absorbing, full of debate, laughter and very hard work'. Such groups can't operate in a culture of rigid rules: as Leavitt and his co-author write, they 'are not easily domesticated. Neatly organized institutions usually stifle them'. Hot groups require:

1 Openness and flexibility.
2 Independence and autonomy.
3 A policy of putting people first.
4 'The search for truth'.

The first qualities demand 'easy, informal access across hierarchical levels and across departmental, divisional and organizational boundaries'. The second mean that managers must leave hot groups 'alone for reasonable periods of time' – even though giving them plenty of 'elbow room' is anathema to controllers and administrators, who 'exist to make sure that everybody in the organization abides by the rules'. To put people first, you need to break a mighty rule, to reverse the 'logic of traditional organization design'. That logic runs as follows: 'First, define the task with great care; then, break it down into individual-sized pieces; and, finally, select people with skills and aptitudes appropriate for each piece.'

As Leavitt and Lipman-Blumen remark, 'Hot groups do not prosper in such settings.' Where do they seem to prosper? The fourth answer is 'in organizations that are deeply dedicated to seeking truth': in other words, where fact-based management rules. It should reign everywhere. The hot groups should eventually get reabsorbed into the rest of the company, along with the successful rule revisions and removals, and the passion for truth, on which the triumphs of, say, cutting costs and development time have been built.

Hot-group lessons have the power to change the company's business culture permanently – and that power should be used. One important example is cracking the widely found rules against cannibalization. The threat of losing high-priced, high-profit business by introducing lower-priced products has deterred innumerable managers from making down-market moves. But in today's conditions, the alternative to eating your own children is to see them devoured by somebody else.

After a hot group has successfully forced through a crash programme, such lessons should change the way the company does business: if rules like non-cannibalization remain sacred after their irrelevance has been demonstrated, the company deserves to fail. To avoid that, there must be a catalyst or catalysts outside the hot group team. Actually, any company is full of catalysts – people all the way down the line, right down to workers on the shop, office or factory floor. If they are encouraged to speak out, and are listened to, their free-of-charge recommendations can be as potent and far-reaching as the expensively purchased advice of outside consultants.

People must be able to say what they mean. That is basic to breaking the rules. It must apply at all levels. Boards of directors commonly embrace the new ideal of 'customer service' but remain resolutely out of touch with both the customers and the front-line employees who confront them. Only those in contact with the customer really know what's going on – for instance, whether high prices are adversely affecting sales.

Listening to such information doesn't just mean hearing. It means acting on what you hear, if what's heard makes sense. The manager has the right and duty to challenge the challengers. But they should only be overridden by fiat if you can't, by experiment, test what is right.

In new technology companies like ICL, the opportunities for fatal ossification come especially thick and fast: miss the technology or the market by months, and you may be behind for years. The plunge of its German rival, Nixdorf, from computer star to fallen idol, for example, took only a couple of years. The same process, though on a longer timescale, is also overtaking industries of less advanced technology. The process is driven by two forces: the quickening rate of change in customer-driven markets, and the widening of competition as truly global markets develop. Proprietary positions have become more vulnerable, not just in computers, but across the board.

The rules have changed accordingly. Even where most of the rules still stand, they may not be enough. Instead of rules, management needs principles – broad codes of behaviour which accept and accommodate the constancy of change.

There are eight basic principles for all managers which are, or should be, familiar to all modern production managers. The eight all imply continuous change and challenge:

1 Constantly improve non-financial performance measures.
2 Analyse and simplify all processes.
3 Launch many quick-fix, fast-payoff projects simultaneously.
4 Commit fully to a very few long-term, big improvement programmes.
5 Always include quality in the latter.
6 Concentrate improvement projects in areas where the pay-offs are biggest.
7 Have high targets, reasonable expectations.
8 Trust, train and educate – all the time.

There is also a ninth principle, which I gleaned from Shin Taguchi, son of the famous Japanese inventor of the Taguchi method, who introduced a highly technical way of engineering quality into the earliest (and – see the sixth point above – most cost-effective) processes. The ninth principle is: 'We need to THINK HARD.'

That hard thinking must extend to the rules, the way things have always been done. Any European company being honest with itself will find that some of those things don't need doing at all and that all others can be done better – some within the rules. But more and more, Walton's Tenth is the rule that counts. Break all the rules.

The salvation of SGS-THOMSON

Here's a surefire recipe for corporate mayhem. Take a volatile combination of French, Italian and British components in a high-tech industry dominated by the Americans, and try to make sense of a three-way merger that is losing $200 million a year, and is spread across most industrialized countries.

The prospects when SGS-THOMSON merged in 1987 to create a viable European contender in semiconductors looked deeply flawed. It

seemed hopelessly outgunned by the non-European competition. Even in
Europe, the company was outranked (nearly two-to-one) by the National
Fairchild combination.

Tricky political issues arose at once, for instance, where to locate the
group HQ. France won, though the site was almost on neutral territory,
near the Swiss border. The fundamental question was trickier still. How
could you motivate a diverse management to lead an equally diverse
workforce in so challenging a situation?

The task proved far more feasible than it sounds, thanks to the development of a common language – that of Total Quality Management
(see Chapter 10). SGS-THOMSON is now Europe's biggest semiconductor
business, after annual compound growth of 19 percent, as performance
improved on every parameter, from front-end yield to customer satisfaction. Without question, the work of the management led by Pasquale
Pistorio (who came from Motorola) has been crucial to this spirited performance – but all his executives pay tribute to TQM.

TQM's contribution was needed for strictly technical purposes. Without far higher standards of quality, the new company could never stay
in the game – let alone satisfy its management's urge to rise from sixteenth
in the world semiconductor league to a top ten spot. That has now been
achieved as part of a spectacular piece of wealth creation. Floated off as
a quoted company in December 1994, SGS-THOMSON has continued to
grow powerfully since flotation; the shares have quadrupled in only two
and a half years, during which sales have risen by 78 percent to $4.12
billion and profits by 73 percent to $625.5 million.

None of this could have been achieved without adopting a new,
transforming corporate life style that wasn't associated with any particular
nationality. TQM greatly facilitated the evolution of a genuinely combined
company. With Masaaki Imai's book *Kaizen*[4] as its gospel, and with continuous improvement in performance and customer satisfaction as its
goal, the group reduced defects from 500 per million parts in 1987 to 15
– and that's only one indicator of all-round advance. The uniform life
style wasn't French, Italian, or British. It was that of a new culture built
by a new, unified management.

Pistorio's team refused to accept that their blended culture was at
any disadvantage compared with the homogenous competition – especially from Japan. Murray Duffin, chief architect of TQM at SGS-
THOMSON, says that 'the idea that cultural differences create competitive
advantage is absolute rubbish. Everything that works in Japan works
in other countries.' Pistorio's own contribution was immense, not least

through insisting that other managers emulate his conversion (after two readings of *Kaizen*) to Imai's ideas.

The starting point was a fascinating exercise. It compared the attitudes required for TQM with the opinions of 250 managers, assembled in workshops, on what behaviours were needed in order to make personal progress in the company. Sometimes the behaviours matched. But the mismatches included six deadly characteristics. In effect, people felt they were prisoners of an inimical culture which stressed these killers:

1 Emphasis is above all on 'making the numbers'.

2 Don't be a bearer of bad news.

3 Don't dissent.

4 Don't raise human resources issues.

5 Promotion is not by merit.

6 Place personal or group goals above corporate ones.

With one exception, there is no reason why anybody would defend any of these behaviours. That exception is No. 1: the bottom line. Many top managements love to rule by numbers: like painting by numbers, it won't produce a great picture. Often this erroneous regime is deliberate. Sometimes it's a consequence of inattentive managerial behaviour – and inattentiveness was the problem at SGS-THOMSON. Top management had to change its own behaviour before it could hope to activate significant change in others

There is nothing complex involved. Pistorio's personal recipe for leadership is simple – a diet of common sense, trust in people, never asking others to do anything you wouldn't do yourself, the ability to work with and through others, and total dedication to the task in hand. His colleagues note that he displayed a great deal of energy, refused to play office politics, and showed them total loyalty.

He also backed highly unconventional initiatives. One head of department, instead of automatically taking charge at all meetings of a committee set up to raise efficiency, surrendered the chair and its powers to juniors, who took the top spot in turns. He found to his delight that people lost their fear of exposing problems. Being temporary boss, moreover, faced them with the necessity to take and implement decisions, knowing that the team decision – reached by consensus – would prevail.

The results? The same small number of people now handle a workload that has multiplied almost eight times in the last few years. Similar successes have been achieved in many hundreds of cases. The scale of the quality activity as at April 1995 sounds almost intimidating: 51 active programmes per 1,000 employees; 541 completed, and twice as many active or new; 7,594 people participating in teams and spending 42,271 hours on the process; three suggestions per employee per year.

The measured savings from continuous improvement had by then exceeded $100 million, but that's almost irrelevant compared with the overall strength of the turnround. It has plainly passed beyond turnround to the creation of a new and powerful organic advance. That has been achieved, quite simply, because it was the object of the entire exercise. Improvement programmes that are conceived solely in terms of processes and products may well achieve lovely results: sharp falls in defects, delivery times, etc. But these gains won't achieve their full value unless they are means to an end – and a highly ambitious end at that.

Another example from SGS-THOMSON shows what micro-improvements underlie these macro-advances. The company was installing a costly machine to manufacture a new device. The industry norm is a start-up period of 50 to 60 days. The 'champion team' that tackled the task was given half this time as a target: 28 days. By working 12 hours, seven days a week on the first and third stages, and two shifts seven days a week on the second stage, the team was making the first product in 17 days, four ahead of schedule. The total time to full production was a brilliant 24 days.

The decisions on that punishing work schedule were taken by the team itself. The members needed external leadership to launch the project, but 'built-up leadership' is what achieved the results. Although the build-up takes time ('it took four years to get to that point'), the payoff is worth its expenditure. As the manager in ultimate charge adds, the organization becomes both 'stable and flexible' and 'hidden talents rise up'.

In many companies internal talent gets held down under the water, instead of being allowed to swim powerfully towards ambitious corporate objectives. Why that suppression occurs is the most important question in management. Answer it correctly, and correct the causes, and you have the answer to almost everything else.

Motivating the motivators

The team led by Pasquale Pistorio at SGS-THOMSON had one advantage over established managements. These men were new to the corporation, able to think and act in new ways. They acted like the classic outsider

– the man head-hunted to fill the top spot vacated by an axed chief executive.

The effective outsider exploits the leverage which his unfamiliarity provides. Bob Baumann, an American from outside both pharmaceuticals and toiletries, came to Britain to head what was to become, under his highly successful aegis, SmithKline Beecham. One of Europe's first companies to retaliate to the *défi Americain* by challenging the Americans on their home ground, Beecham had run out of momentum. To restore the lost drive, Baumann was head-hunted after his predecessor's abrupt departure (a typical combination of events). He has described his subsequent *modus operandi*:

> I went round to the top 20 people that reported to me, that is, not just those reporting to me directly but also the people a little bit down below. At the same time, I went to ten or so people on the outside who dealt with the company . . . and I asked them all the same five questions:
>
> 1 What do you see as the basic goals of this company?
>
> 2 What do you see as the strategy for achieving those goals?
>
> 3 What do you see as the fundamental issues facing the company?
>
> 4 What do you see as the culture of the organization?
>
> 5 Do you believe the company is organized in a way that is appropriate to support its goals, strategy and culture?

The five key questions were backed by supporting enquiries: for example, on the second question, he asked, 'How is the company going to go about getting to those goals? Are these the right approaches, the right strategy for the company? And if they aren't, how would you change them?' By getting such keen questions answered, Baumann gained a strong grasp of the company's perceived situation, an excellent insight into key individuals and a platform for his own priority – engendering strategic change.

The thrust of his questioning was to empower and communicate, to share and encourage, to build a new cooperative, collaborative culture – in other words, to achieve what SGS-THOMSON has also shown to be within reach. But is reaching for the outside appointee the only means to this end? If so, most of Europe's companies are condemned to lack of success: for every board that hunts an outside head, scores promote insiders – possibly a time-server taking his turn, occasionally a man who, like an ideal new product, will surpass predecessors by being both different and better.

The need for external replacement of corporate chieftains in time of travail reflects a double malfunction of the system. If that system worked properly, outsiders would never be required. First, underperformance or worse occurs because the system fails to evolve the right top management or to motivate that management towards achieving the right results; second, this same failure to develop the company's most valuable human resources results in the absence of internal heirs.

This dual failure is demonstrated by the fact that no company deliberately adopts a policy of invariably appointing its chief executives from outside. The unmistakeable signal sent to able insiders would be highly demotivating, while the chances of developing a coherent long-term strategy and culture would wither away. The outside appointment is not a plan, but an accident waiting to happen.

Too many companies, alas, fail on this count. Often, under a variety of strange banners, their top managements have sought to align the entire company behind the 'vision'. Yet the vision obstinately remains just that: a dream. My own work in many companies has discovered the common cause – a yawning, deeply demotivating gap between top management perceptions and the far more significant perceptions in the market and workplaces. Either top management doesn't know what people think (other managers, other employees, suppliers and customers), or management knows, but takes no action.

As noted, this is highly demotivating. In contrast, asking people the key questions and acting on their answers is a hugely motivational force. Writing in *Business Strategy Review*,[5] Baumann argues in favour of applying his approach at lower levels of management – say, a new senior brand manager. This appointee might start by asking the people who work for and with him (and other interested parties): 'How effective do you think the overall brand has been – its penetration, market share, success, profitability and so on?' Then he might go on to ask, 'What do you think the future goals for the brand are?'

To that question, being a highly experienced manager, Baumann knows the all-too-likely answer. Those asked won't have a clue. 'Sales may say they have no targets, and manufacturing may say they always have too much stock.' These are typical of the answers I've heard myself. These people know the business intimately, but their many positive ideas are negated by poor management. The job of real motivators is to eliminate the negatives and substitute the positive, with the aid of the colleagues who have helped them to uncover these unacceptable truths. That happens continuously under the TQM regime at SGS-THOMSON.

Queries like Baumann's five master questions aren't once-for-all. They need asking and answering continually as markets, economic conditions and results evolve. The process of deeply involving others in questions, answers and solutions will always pay dividends, and it has to start at the top – with the very senior managers who hold the motivating power.

These senior managers have not been exercising that power effectively. The survey evidence points to massive demotivation, among both other managers and the workforce. The unhappiest of all workers in Europe are the British, according to International Survey Research. It found in 1996 that motivation and commitment were even lower than in the 'confrontational and destructive industrial relations climate' of the mid–1970s – before Lady Thatcher made herself the heroine of European capitalism.

Employees in Italy, Spain, France and Belgium were little better satisfied. Europe's most contented workers were in Denmark, Norway, Austria, Ireland and – top of the heap – Switzerland. All are small countries, a fact which indicates that the mass employment economies, and the large-scale companies mainly located within them, have a steeper hill to climb to match the best attainable standards of motivation.

It can be done. But top managers won't win the minds and hearts of managers or workforce if the summit's commitment to building a change culture is distrusted – and if job fears are all too real. The counter-productive results of this were shown by the disappointing economic aftermath of the Thatcherite reforms. They certainly ushered in an era of remarkable industrial peace, in which strikes were few and amazingly far between, but that's not an end in itself. There's no merit in a strike-free company that markets poor value and obsolescent products, or is ineptly managed and provides inadequate training and information. To put it another way, the object and motivation of top management should be to add value for customers, employees and shareholders alike by developing and exploiting state-of-the-art products and processes. None of that will be achieved without the excellent training and communication that are common to all well-motivated organizations.

These elements define the quality of management needed to win a golden European future. Many companies have conspicuously lacked that quality in the past, not just over short periods, but from decade to decade. It isn't suprising that these long-term failings are not seen by their perpetrators, who are naturally blind to their own mistakes. Nor is it surprising when the errors are gleefully exposed by those who follow. Incoming managements are happy to uncover the failings of their predecessors – and the outsider, having no stake whatsoever in the previous horrors, is often happiest of all.

To break the logjam, companies may need the outsider as a fresh force to pull in information and ideas from others (*à la* Baumann), to reject a history of resisting change from outside, and to shatter the bureaucratic mould in which people only know what others are thinking down the corridor, if there. In one multinational HQ in Europe, a consultant finished one interview and found that his interviewee didn't know the next man he was seeing – in an office a few doors away.

In this same company, the senior management only became aware of their leader's plans for its future and their own careers inadvertently, during discussions at a seminar designed, of all things, to improve their leadership abilities. The paramount requirement of motivational leaders is to achieve a framework in which people know and respect each other, in which both motivator and motivated, leader and 'led', can operate effectively and in comfort together.

Down the postwar decades, however, managements have created demotivating organizations. All the surgery and medicaments of the eighties and early nineties, the years of corporate crisis, were supposed to turn thinking and actions outwards and to bring down excess size. But the corporate patients, instead of being healed by their treatment, were often sickened by the side-effects.

In early 1996 the Institute of Management issued a survey conducted among 1,300 respondents in middle management. To quote the *Financial Times*, it painted 'a picture of overwork, stress and insecurity. These problems are particularly intense in organizations where there have been repeated rounds of redundancies.' How are these people supposed to act as motivators, as effective agents of change, or to help lead their companies into the forefront of global competition? How can they realize visions focused on the long-term improvement of goods, services and added value by innovation and initiative?

They can't, of course. But overwork, stress and anxiety can be converted into voluntary and self-fulfilling commitment by humane leadership. Like Baumann and Pistorio, each chief executive must find the approach that best suits their purposes. One hero, for instance, personally conducts eight hundred performance reviews a year. Assuming that he works three hundred days, that's eight every three days. The task seems to stretch the bounds of possibility, as he initially thought himself. But the personnel department 'walked me through the paperwork from Argentina and Pakistan and so forth, and I realized they were right'.

They were right for at least one very good reason. Those eight hundred personally conducted reviews must give the chief executive what Baumann derived from his questioning of other managers: a strong grasp of the company's perceived situation, an excellent insight into key individuals and a platform for his own priority. The reviews also show the leader's commitment to the company and its people – and develop and motivate leadership lower down.

That model is necessary for the new environment, which is increasingly intolerant of the command-and-control style. As C.K. Prahalad of the University of Michigan insists, today opportunity management is as important as operations management, companies that fall behind stay behind, and customers demand, not only to be satisfied, but to be surprised. His colleague Gary Hamel, of the London Business School, is equally insistent that 'numerator' management – aiming to boost revenues – is the proper objective, not 'denominator' management, which merely seeks to cut costs.

Opportunity and numerator management alike demand the unleashing of talent and energy below the top in order to generate new business and new profits. As Prahalad says, 'a firm's capacity for organic growth is the ultimate test of top management's value added'. That's the acid test, all right. And only by motivating the real motivators, those who implement the strategies (and should help in their formation), will that test be passed.

TWO

Driving Radical Change

The dwindling of the giants

In one industry at least, Europe has never had to bow the knee to the Americans, far less the Japanese. Its drugs industry has been led by the three bastions of Basle, Hoffman La Roche, Sandoz and Ciba, buttressed by British leaders like Glaxo and Wellcome, and fortified by the German chemical conglomerates. In the mid-nineties these powers began to unite, but the common theme of their mergers wasn't that more and better new drugs that would flow from their combined R&D – it was fewer jobs.

At Glaxo-Wellcome, the toll was 7,500; at Novartis, formed by marriage between neighbours Sandoz and Ciba, the target was a 10 percent cut. The reductions were greeted with enthusiasm by investors, even as European politicians wrestled with the stubborn, colossal and rising numbers of unemployed. Both the eighties and nineties have seen massive reductions in operations and employment among European companies anxious to boost efficiency and profitability, from Philips to VW, Fiat to IBM Europe.

In the same period, US giants also downsized with heavy cutbacks. The Americans, however, have begun to question whether true productivity was actually advanced by the lay-offs. Low morale and poor cooperation, both engendered by cuts in jobs and pay, can more than offset the savings in employment costs that so delight investors. Many of the businesses in which jobs were lost might have generated rapid organic growth – and cash – if they had been managed better.

Indeed, losses in jobs and monetary losses often go together. I have suspected a chain of cause and effect ever since analysing a *Fortune* listing, taken from among the largest 500 US companies, of the biggest job creators – and cutters – of the 1981–91 decade. In manufacturing, half of the ten greatest employment cutters had financial deficits in 1991, while two others had *negative* growth in earnings per share over the decade. The European performance differed only in timing.

The job-losers' figures look even dimmer when compared to *Fortune*'s ten biggest gainers in manufacturing employment. Seven of the ten showed annual gains in earnings per share that started at 6.6 percent and ran up to 49.9 percent. A similar tale is told in services, which in 1994 accounted for 65 percent of EU employment, up from 54 percent in 1980. In virtually all cases, the service is provided by people, and the more the service company grows and prospers, the more men and women it must hire.

Europe's giant service companies, however, have, been paying the price of previous, often state-owned, inefficiency. On the way to partial privatization, for example, Deutsche Telekom expects to enter the new millennium with 60,000 fewer workers than in 1995. The massive job losses in telecommunications have also arisen from the ineluctable technological pressures to which British Telecom is still reacting. But elsewhere, the obvious question is which came first, the chicken or the egg – the bad business or the big lay-offs?

The predominance of cars and steel in the ranks of losers, and of food and drink among the winners, might suggest that irresistible forces are responsible for driving employment up or down. That has some truth. But Europe's car and steel companies (like their American rivals) notoriously sharpened their beds of nails by across-the-board failure to compete effectively with Japanese rivals. The excess jobs were not the cause of underperformance; the lack of competitiveness created the excess jobs. Eliminating the excess by no means guarantees that a new trend of dynamic long-term performance will develop.

After all, these are the same companies – and usually much the same managements – which allowed surplus jobs to swell in the first place by losing competitive prowess in their core businesses, and which simultaneously failed to achieve powerful expansion in new activities. This failure is unlikely to be corrected against the backdrop of retrenchment. The cost-saving mind-set sits uneasily with the innovatory, forward-looking thrust that is the essence of the competitive response.

This is especially true in pharmaceuticals. In this industry, as a McKinsey man told *Business Week*, 'Just cutting costs is not enough. Long-term, it's still an innovation game.' One of the game's significant European players, David Barnes, the head of Zeneca, has observed further that 'Lowering their cost base and doing less R&D is a temporary fix.' It's one to which the giants quickly become addicted. Germany's Hoechst, having bought Marion Merrell Dow for $7.2 billion, promptly planned a 10 percent cut in spending on R&D: the idea was to save money by dropping dud projects and concentrating on likely winners.

The cut in spending, though, will do nothing to cure the basic inefficiencies that generated all those duds. Worse, cutbacks can create inefficiencies. It's an ominous sign for Germany's future, to take an startling example, that only 425,000 apprenticeships were available in mid–1996, down from 681,000 as recently as 1992. The highly-trained workforce has always been the bedrock of German industrial strength; the reductions will do nothing to make companies more competitive against Asians with lower wage and social security costs.

These cost differentials are not the cause of Asian superiority in products, innovation and speed-to-market. After the painful demonstration of this truth at one multinational subsidiary, where heavy cutbacks had been counterproductive, the local management had the sense to reverse engines. Instead of concentrating on the cost of labour, the company completely changed its deployment. Workers in small teams were empowered to organize their own work with modern methods: 'We now see,' said one of the reformed managers, 'that the productivity available is really extraordinary.'

Here, internal revolt, in the form of subnormal productivity, conveyed a message that management was fortunately able to hear. In most cases, plants, products and jobs which could have been made viable are condemned to death by top managements who are often applauded for their 'rationalizing' efforts – which frequently don't achieve their ends. Consultants Wyatt & Co looked at 450 major companies that downsized in 1991 and 1992. Two-fifths of the shrinkers didn't even succeed in cutting their costs. Less than half improved their profits. Two-thirds of those aiming for higher productivity were disappointed.

'Rationalizing' means closing plants. 'Down-sizing' means closing jobs. 'Dumb-sizing' (the name with which sceptical Americans have rechristened downsizing) means that the wonderful baby of growth has been thrown out with the bathwater of wasteful employment. The truly rational course is to develop valuable plants, not shut them, and to increase valuable employment, not fire valuable people. Creating new jobs by creating new businesses is today's real challenge for Europe's giants – and it's one that isn't being met.

Management's leading powers

There was once a wise old lawyer whose clients included several members of the most exclusive male clubs. Every now and then, one of the clients would call in to say he wanted a divorce. The lawyer's answer was always the same: 'Don't do it, dear boy. You'll only do it again.'

That's roughly the advice which should have been heeded by many downsizing companies. Slashing employment and costs can become a bad habit. A survey conducted by the Kepner-Tregoe consultancy found that, even among companies counting their slashing a success, over a third intended to axe again within twelve months. The reason is simple, according to T.Quinn Spitzer, K-T's chief executive: 'Most cost-cutting actions do not remove work, only the people who do it.'

The work still has to be done, and the absence of the removed people may well increase real costs and reduce effectiveness. The result can be a depressing exercise in chasing your own tail: depressing not only in terms of workforce morale, but also financially. In manufacturing, Philips, for example, has suffered several rounds of job cuts, but the loss of thousands of jobs hasn't repaired the electrical giant's lacklustre profit performance.

The issue isn't cutting costs, but *managing* them by linking the costs to an effective strategy. As noted, the American evidence in *Fortune* magazine demonstrates that the companies which shrink most are outperformed by those which expand. If a business is growing organically, raising its sales and profits, employment will also rise (preferably at a slower rate). If it's cutting employment, capabilities are usually being reduced in reaction to ebbing profits and markets, and the cutbacks may diminish the very strengths on which future dynamism depends.

'Change management' has a powerful appeal to management in the nineties. But it doesn't just mean traditional restructuring, altering the form of the organization, while reforming the roles and cutting numbers. What really pays off is the deeper kind of change: reshaping the organization's whole being so that people's behaviour will alter in ways that benefit the customers and hence the company.

You often find the same managements involved in both change approaches, the negative and the positive, at the same time. In 1994 one financial services company mounted its first-ever effort to change a culture which nobody loved. As the change seminars for senior management unfolded over four weeks, large managerial job cuts were announced in the regional organization. They would be followed, it was announced, by twice as many losses at head office. A negative effect was immediately obvious, since those who were going to lose head office jobs by the year-end hadn't been identified.

On a far larger scale, IBM, in Europe as in the US, has been guilty of the same mistake. The job losses damage morale as people see their colleagues, some of them friends, shown to the exit. The promise that further, unidentified losses will follow makes managers worry about being next. Insecurity is the greatest enemy of effectiveness, which promptly suffers. But there's an even more pernicious and more widespread error: *if the two forms of organizational change don't go hand-in-hand, neither will provide the full desired benefits.*

The supporting evidence is overwhelming. In 1987 I published a book entitled *The State of Industry*.[1] It was based on seventeen interviews with British companies, mostly represented by their chief executives, which had ridden out of severe recession at the start of the eighties. At the time, they were apparently riding high. Most had cut back on superfluous employees, facilities and products. All had adopted outward-looking and competitive strategies.

In just seven years after publication, four of the companies had been taken over – two of them (including Jaguar) after awful results – while two (Courtaulds and ICI) have been split in twain. Of the other 11, only three managed to survive the period without significant setback: the gasses group BOC, drug manufacturer Glaxo, and Vauxhall Motors, the British subsidiary of General Motors. The failure ratio is about as bad as the notorious undoing of the hero companies in *In Search of Excellence*.

In over half the companies, the change process hadn't gone far enough. The managements hadn't combined far higher ambitions with much lower costs. Cutbacks in employment, whether enforced by recession or technological change, should never be conducted in isolation. They must be combined with rethinking the entire business system, and all its subdivisions, to establish new and more productive methods of working in all functions. That way, the slimmer labour force can build a larger future.

The ultimate test for leaner organizations is what they can achieve through organic creativity. That means utilizing all the talents within the organization by the application of genuine team management under the pressure of stretching targets. This is unquestionably a spreading and highly effective mode that raises a crucial question: why does the ultimate *ad hoc* operation, the crash programme launched to turn round a desperate situation, so often work so well? So much better than the routine work of the organization on continuing processes?

It is because the principles and pressures are entirely different from those of conventional management. The crash programme has (a) a clearly defined purpose and (b) a tight deadline which imposes (c) a strict order of priorities for (d) a dedicated, specially selected team which carries no passengers and (e) improvises as it goes along towards (f) an objective whose success or failure will be clearly known.

The contrast with how things operate in most companies is acute, to judge by the common complaints in all six areas. Managers say that they have no objectives, or conflicting ones; fuzzy deadlines; no clear priorities; incompetent and over-promoted colleagues; rigid and irrelevant procedures; and opaque standards of success and failure. Reshuffles and firings won't resolve these difficulties, and neither will top-down dictation unless it has full bottom-up support.

Consider these key questions:

1 How fast do decisions get taken and policies executed? Are the processes involved under constant review and continuous reform?

2 Are managers and others praised and rewarded for innovative ideas turned into successful action? Is innovation an organizational and individual priority?

3 Are the measurement and reward systems aligned to business objectives, and are the measures presented in a simple form that everybody can understand?

4 Does the assessment of managers include the productivity of their people – and the latter's upward assessment of their bosses?

5 Are there clear and ambitious goals for the business, and does everybody agree with the aims – and have clear and ambitious goals for themselves?

6 Can individuals make a real difference to outcomes, and are they encouraged to do so?

7 Are mistakes treated as opportunities for learning – and not as occasions for punishment?

8 Does everybody contribute to the strategic thinking of the organization?

9 Is the company deeply committed to outdoing the competition in all important and measurable ways, and does it insist on continuous

improvement on all important measures (notably those affecting the customer)?

Too many organizations can't honestly answer 'Yes' to all nine questions. Even worse, the questions simply never get asked. That's especially tragic because implementing the change from 'No' to 'Yes' is relatively simple and inexpensive under all nine headings. That's also true of cutting down the number of levels through which decisions must pass. The benefits are obvious and immediate – and immediacy is vital.

Of course, total change takes time and can't happen overnight. Often, change programmes are given – and require – very long time-horizons. As Charles Miller-Smith, imported from Unilever to galvanize ICI, told *The Sunday Times*, the drive for 'cultural change' is 'not a one-year job', but 'a ten-year long march' – which you then repeat. It is essential, however, to achieve fast, overnight improvements which are measurable and recognized, not just because of the impact on morale, but also because nobody knows what will happen in three years' time – let alone ten.

The future is a series of presents running in sequence. The longer you delay in achieving evident transformation, the greater the danger of creating a widening gap between rhetoric and reality. The rhetoric-reality gap means there is a divergence between what management wants to happen (or, still worse, says is happening) and real results in the real world. If you find yourself explaining away the gaps, either belittling their importance or blaming them on circumstances beyond your control, you are treading on highly dangerous ground. That way lie complacency and arrogance, the deadly enemies of success. That's why recognizing the gaps and acting to close them is so important. The present management must act like an incoming group, facing up to unsatisfactory outcomes, assuming that internal faults are to blame, and acting swiftly to eradicate them.

As a case study of what happens when self-delusion takes over, Porsche is the perfect example. Management sat by and watched for ten years while sales of its sports cars, once world leaders, fell from over 50,000 a year to just 14,300 in 1993.

The underlying failure was basic: over-reliance on the increasingly ancient 911 as new model development languished. The new chief executive, Dr Wendelin Wiedeking, not only tackled the 911 problem, he also went for structural change – a new board, reduction of the first six management layers to four, and reform of the world sales organization. In the process, a third of the managers were fired or redeployed. Yet none of this drastic action, with 2,000 jobs lost overall, could be effective without deeper and wider change in the operational philosophy.

By early 1994, the revamped 911 was taking 30 percent fewer man-hours to make than in mid–1991, but 85 man-hours was still 70 percent higher than the rival Japanese norm. Wisely, in 1991 the Porsche management had turned to Japan for help, using a team headed by a man who formerly held the top engineering post at Toyota. Workers responded enthusiastically after early doubts. But Porsche management was still not out of the mental wood. In early 1994 it was half-expecting a less cooperative attitude once the urgency of crisis was spent.

The doubters should have listened properly to their own production director, who told the *Financial Times* that 'we have to use the crisis to change things, not just saw off heads'. The company needs to change, not 'things', but 'everything'. Even continuous improvement, which Wiedeking sought to implant permananently before the crisis momentum was lost, isn't enough by itself. Rather, you have to adopt the attitude expressed by Michael Bloomberg of Bloomberg Financial Markets.

Bloomberg's business is a thorn in the side of Reuters, Europe's ace global provider of financial information. The giant's dominance didn't worry Bloomberg a bit: 'Whenever you see a business that's done the same thing for a long time, a new guy can come in and do it better. I guarantee it.' The 'new guy' mentality is precisely what I recommended in Chapter 1, but the newness must be shown by better behaviours as well as better business ideas. Companies setting out on long-range cultural change programmes too often forget that attitudes are much harder to change than conduct. Bloomberg's ideas on conduct are highly effective – but they would be anathema in most of Europe:

1 No private secretaries, not even for the boss.

2 No private offices, and all partitions made of glass.

3 No job titles, even on business cards.

4 No entrance from the lifts to two of the three head office floors – so that people are forced to mingle.

5 No sales commissions, but instead bonus certificates which give employees a share in revenue growth that adds 25 to 100 percent to salary.

6 No signing powers for non-payroll cheques and contracts for anybody save the chief executive.

The last point ensures that the chieftain knows about everything that's happening. There's more than a hint of autocracy. But that has its uses – something which mustn't be overlooked in the wholly justified enthusiasm for participation and empowerment. The right person at the top can make a massive difference even to a large organization.

Although leadership has to come from top managers, they also have to recognize that having ideas isn't their sole prerogative, nor even that of their brightest and best subordinates. Spend time in any large organization, talking to people at all levels, and you find, as noted earlier, a wealth of practical insight that never gets translated into action – because the structure precludes it. The truth about organizational change is that getting the structure and the numbers right is the first step, and very important; but animating the structure to achieve the right actions by rightly motivated people is vital.

For any organization, and any organizational change, the central purpose is to create so thriving and developing an organic activity that the organization can provide excellent, well-paid employment for all its people. It's no easy task to harness their energies right through the corporation, including the shopfloor. That demands a painful act – the abdication of power.

Fortune once enumerated five kinds of power that top managers can exercise over their subordinates:

1 Rewarding, by word, pay or promotion.

2 Punishing, by word, discipline, demotion, or expulsion.

3 Exercising authority – either specific (i.e. the power of 'signing-off' on a decision), or tacit (if the boss doesn't like it, nothing happens; if he does, it does).

4 Deploying expertise – the greatest expert has the most powerful say in the area concerned.

5 'Referent power' – the reverence paid to a leader, for whatever reason, by others in the organization.

Fortune thought that the last two powers had waxed as the first three automatic – even autocratic – powers had waned. That waning must become increasingly apparent as horizontal, product- or project-based teams cut across both functional and national boundaries. That's now happening at many companies, and rightly so. But team groupings, carried to their logical conclusion, depower the centre. Its remaining and fundamental role is to exercise and delegate a sixth power: the power to lead people in chosen and supported directions that will safeguard and enhance their futures.

That power involves the choice of both the ends and the means ('the new way we do things round here') that will optimize contribution and generate satisfaction internally – and also externally, where the customers live. As service quality experts stress, and as the correlation of new job creation with increases in profits suggests, the external and internal go hand-in-hand, just like the two forms of organizational change: cutting costs and building the business.

'Hollowing the corporation' (by hiving off all possible activities to outside contractors), 'rationalizing' (by hiving off whole businesses) and 'downsizing' or 'right-sizing' (by hiving off employees) are all ugly euphemisms. There are plenty of others. The *Guardian*, looking at the American scene, found that, if there's a 'volume-related production schedule adjustment', then workers are 'dejobbed', 'dehired', 'unassigned'; 'involuntarily severed', 'surplused', offered 'career alternative enhancement'; they're 'non-renewed', 'delayered', or undergo 'a skill-mix adjustment'.

Ill-used, the euphemisms add up to a total process known as 'deconstruction'. If it turns to destruction, which can happen all too easily, the results are hollow indeed. But use the sixth power properly in the interests of all the people, by using all of the people, and you should never need to use the euphemisms.

The hollowness of Marks & Spencer

In 1996 Marks & Spencer achieved two contradictory distinctions: the retailing king was voted Britain's best-managed company for the second year running – and a television documentary pilloried the firm for alleged indirect use of Third World child labour and ripping off would-be suppliers. Both these charges went against the corporate grain, for benevolence towards suppliers and insistence on high ethical standards are keystones of an M&S economy built around the supplier relationship.

Long before anybody articulated the strategy of concentrating on 'core competencies', M&S had brought the methodology to near-perfection. None of the goods bearing the M&S chain's omnipresent St Michael label are made in its factories; it has none. Its garments are designed, the cloth purchased, and the manufacturing methods laid down by the retailer. There is two-way traffic: M&S will accept ideas and improvements suggested by its suppliers. But the tune is called by the paying piper.

In principle, the philosophy differs little from that of electronics companies like Sun Microsystems, whose enormous success, like that of M&S, demonstrates the huge potential of opting out. The workstations and Internet champ no longer runs its own distribution, makes its own chips, services its own machines, or manufactures its own components. All it does is design chips, software (to brilliant effect with Java, the key to the Internet) and workstations, which others make and Sun markets. It has truly 'hollowed out' the business.

Many European corporations, mostly to a much lesser extent, are seeking to minimize both assets and overheads by playing this sophisticated game of pass-the-parcel: not only do they 'out-source' central services (like information technology) that can easily be purchased from others; they also, Sun-like, farm out some of their production. Some writers use the term 'modular' to describe out-and-out out-sourcers, like athletic shoemaker Adidas – or like one maker of computer tape drives which has multiplied sales 100 times, and employment twentyfold, without building a single plant.

M&S has been a manufacturer without factories ever since the founder, Michael Marks, decided to sell all goods at the fixed price of a penny. This created a need for guaranteed supplies of guaranteed quality at guaranteed cost. His successors have precisely the same need.

Since everything M&S sells – clothes, furnishings, food and drink and financial services, etc – is sold under its own St Michael brand, it can't hide behind its suppliers. Instead, it is forced to work closely with them in associations, some many decades old, that are demanding, but essentially cooperative. As one executive claims, 'We do share a sense of common purpose.' This model, in which customer and supplier work in harness to create shared success, is not only the key to M&S's past success; it's the evolving pattern of business economics.

The control of supply, all the way from design to quality, is crucial to the ability of M&S to exploit the environment in which the customer is served – Place, one of M&S's four basic Ps: Product, Place, Processes, People. Nothing, not even hollowing out a company, can remove these basic necessities. The business must sell the Product that customers want, in the Place where they want it, via Processes that deliver smoothly and efficiently in a seamless operation – and that all depends on People.

The M&S philosophy is that, even if the first three Ps are exactly right, all can come to naught if your people get it wrong. Conversely, an effective performance by one person can appease a dissatisfied customer, despite defective performance on the three other counts. The People dimension is one where M&S, with its special brand of benevolent paternalism, has long enjoyed a competitive advantage. It is also the one which puts management under most strain – a stress which out-sourcing may only intensify.

Can you have effective people policies if, at the extreme, you choose, like Sun, to be almost 100 percent 'horizontal' – buying in virtually every manufacturing item, and most corporate services, from outside suppliers? Like digital watches before them, personal computers have become a 'Mickey Mouse' business: the labels and the advertising are different, but the contents of products purporting to come from different manufacturers are to all intents and purposes identical. 'Makers' like this must rely almost wholly on people who are not in their employ.

The problem will become more general as the proportions of manufactured items bought-in from outsiders continue to rise universally. The tendency to disband in-house service departments in favour of outsiders is becoming widespread. The consequence is that, whereas M&S has total control over the interface with the customer, and exploits it with practised professional care, many out-sourcers hand over aspects of their customer franchise to outsiders. The potential disadvantage is obvious.

Significantly, few leaders have wholeheartedly followed Sun. Of the ten most admired British corporations in *Management Today's* 1993 poll, only M&S is truly 'horizontal', in that it sells exclusively its 'own' products, but makes none. Two others are stores groups. But the rest of the top ten included Cadbury Schweppes, Unilever, Smiths Industries, Whitbread, Rentokil and GKN, all of which are highly – and vertically – committed to products and production alike. The same would be true of any similar most-admired list in Continental Europe, the US or Japan.

The new hollow companies are in a new game – and a hazardous one. One danger lies in the fact that they can only preserve their strength and high, often fabulous sales per employee so long as they set the pace, either by value or technology. By definition, though, they risk seeing the technological lead passing to component and peripheral makers – in PCs it has already passed, notably to Intel and Microsoft. Like this almost omnipotent pair, many component firms now have stronger customer franchises than the systems suppliers who are their hosts.

The M&S strategy is the exact reverse. It has made its brand stronger than that of any supplier. In such circumstances the power over supplies is potentially overbearing: hence recurrent stories, especially at times when sales and profits are sluggish, of suffering suppliers being squeezed by mighty supermarket chains. The hollow manufacturer, in contrast, comes dangerously close to being a private label wholesaler: the danger being that one day the retailers will not only squeeze the hollow middleman, but cut him out with their own brands.

The extreme form of vertical integration, in which companies sought to make every component themselves, and provide all their own services, has receded into the mists of industrial history. Will the hollow corporation go the same way? Will horizontal disintegration be the fate of the firm that not only separates out key functions, but places many outside the firm?

The M&S example has long taught the vital importance of doing precisely the opposite – breaking down the boundaries between functions and uniting them. In its operations, design, purchasing, logistics, manufacturing and marketing are as fully integrated as its fused strategies on Product, Place, Process and People. Seen in the light of its long and immensely successful experience, hollowness is not a wondrous new management principle: it's a new way of approaching old necessities. In this new world, the function of managers isn't only to manage their own people. They must manage relationships with suppliers – and with customers – to achieve the best outcomes for their own businesses.

That can only be done by maximizing the results won throughout the entire business system. In many ways, the M&S methods for achieving this optimization were brilliant precursors of today's fashionable 'virtual' companies, which seek to break down the frontiers between themselves and the outside world. As the huge sales of M&S clothing have long demonstrated, value holds the key. It is highly probable that elements of virtuality will be required to win that value – and the future.

The virtues of virtual corporations

In 1993 the British transport and logistics group, NFC, was thrilled when a US subsidiary won an order from a major furniture company. To break into the fast-growing market for supplying home offices and small businesses, the company established a new venture, Turnstone, that would take its orders over the phone. The selling proposition – for which the NFC firm's capabilities were indispensable – was that the happy customers would get the furniture of their desire *within five days*.

The offer isn't simply an example of highly efficient customer service.

The efficiency is only a consequence of something that sounds much grander: the venture was established as an example of *The Virtual Corporation*. That's the title of a book, co-authored by William H. Davidow and Michael S. Malone,[2] that describes its subject thus: 'To the outside observer, a virtual corporation will appear almost edgeless, the interface between company, supplier and customers permeable and continuously changing.'

Turnstone's task was to deliver products 'produced instantaneously and customized in response to customer demand' with the intimate aid of partner/suppliers. Such a company doesn't stop at its own boundaries. Virtuality goes beyond the now familiar importance of regarding the ultimate customer as the starting point for the business system. Every supplier, it is now argued, should be regarded as part of your company.

Even that doesn't broaden the concept enough. If you subscribe to the theory of virtual corporations, you believe, to quote *Business Week*, 'in a single entity with vast capabilities [that] will really be the result of numerous collaborations assembled only when they are needed'. In this concept, the future of the business is determined, not simply by its own strengths ('key competencies', in the jargon), but by its shifting alliances with outside partners.

In a business that's run according to the precepts of virtuality, the company does far more than make brilliantly fast deliveries of customized orders. It embraces a whole mass of techniques and trends to change processes and practices, but not in isolation. You have to tackle the system in the round. And you need the full resources of the information revolution for that purpose. The virtual corporation is inevitably built around and sustained by its data processing systems.

The gains available even at the lower, more technical end of the virtuality spectrum are by no means negligible. For example, what about a 25 percent rise in sales, and a 67 percent improvement in stockturn, leading to 25 percent larger gross profit? These results for a jacket and trouser maker cited by Davidow and Malone flowed from giving all members of the supply chain instant access to retail and wholesale data on sales, orders, and inventories. Response can thus be instant – and instantly profitable.

Davidow and Malone also cite a carpet retailer whose costs fell by 13 percent after accepting a supplier's offer to meet orders daily – and, what's more, deliver direct to the customer. The retailer needed some considerable persuasion. That's generally the case, as the Swiss chemical giant Ciba found in trying to get a German intermediate supplier to collaborate on quality. The Swiss met with a flat '*Nein*', maintained over two years. Then the supplier capitulated, not to the force of reason, but to the fact that all its customers were making the same demand.

The old ways are more than systems; they are states of mind. Very few managers find it natural or comfortable to rethink: that is, to challenge the intellectual (and emotional) bases of the way they operate, even though rethinking offers large, and often cheap, scope for improvement.

As with Ciba's German supplier, though, the day-to-day pressures of the management task are forcing companies into new and radical modes, facilitated by their information technology systems. For every company, quickness of response is now of the essence: it should govern every process and the provision of every product and service. And it can't be won through the traditional adversarial relationship between supplier and manufacturer.

That tradition is 'dead', says David Bundred, a senior executive with LucasVarity. He believes that strategic sourcing, networking supplier relationships and managing partnerships are the future. One by one, the planks of the old purchasing policies, marked by constant wars, with price as the *casus belli*, have been ripped out – because today, customers want the 'variety, velocity, quality and cost-competitiveness' that can only be provided through collaboration.

The new demands of VVQC are revolutionizing not only external relationships, but internal ones. That's because 'openness, equality and partnership have to extend to functions within companies', as Bundred says. In some cases, the internal and external partnerships are formed willy-nilly. As noted above, there are advanced products (PCs being an acute example) which contain nothing but bought-in components, and where alternative component suppliers may simply not exist. In other cases, the competitive advantages of cooperation are simply too great to ignore.

The issue for managers is not whether they desert the old guard and join the revolution. Rather, it is whether they move forward by progressive steps, responding to the current and future pressures, or take a truly bold plunge into the future. Davidow and Malone naturally favour the braver course. All employees, they say, will have 'to revise the way they deal with one another and with the outside world' – a tall order if ever there was one – for 'the virtual corporation to appear here, now'.

It's beginning to happen. Companies are greatly shortening response times and achieving extraordinary customer-led variations in what was once standard mass production. As managements adapt to the new necessities, using the tools of the IT revolution, the very nature of management is changing. Just as the Ford-style assembly line has been outdated by developments like self-managed, flexible manufacturing cells, so hierarchical order-and-obey management has been overtaken by flexible, cellular working in changing, self-directed groups.

Virtual employees will be virtual self-managers, relying on IT instead of middle management for the rapid transmission of messages back and forth. The universal pressures are intensifying to an either–or degree: either companies adapt to the new imperatives of virtuality, or they will be overwhelmed. The challenge can't be met by simple downsizing. Such cutbacks, however swingeing, are self-defeating unless they march in step with adoption of the new processes.

Is the virtual corporation anything more than the apotheosis of Bundred's purchasing revolution? Davidow and Malone claim that virtual managers will go well beyond those bounds: they will have the ability to master the information tools of today – and tomorrow. 'Further increases in computer power enable us to predict the future, to predict behaviours, to perform simulations, and to take virtual walks through design.' The dream is that manufacture, testing, and distribution of goods and services will be pulled together into a simultaneous, instantaneous whole.

The problem for most managers is to identify their own futures in this glorious vision. Obviously, a manufacturer who can (like Toyota today) produce a new car to detailed customer specification within 72 hours has a serious competitive advantage over one who takes 72 days – or even seven. In high-tech electronics, too, state-of-the-art manufacture and the quickest responses are obligatory; otherwise, you're out of business.

The virtuality doctrine argues that nobody is exempt. Sooner or later, the smartest competitor will learn to deliver a markedly better product or service cheaper and faster. Against such competition, laggards – costlier, slower and deficient in quality – can't long survive. Indeed, that's why several Western industries have slumped in the face of Japanese competition.

Europe's future economic power depends on its ability to participate fully in the further stages of the manufacturing revolution led by the Japanese. For the Asian lead to continue would be deeply anomalous, given that the fundamental information technologies, still exploding along an exponential growth curve, are dominated by the US. But that only intensifies the problem for Europe, which in most industries leads neither in technology nor in its application.

Europe is, however, making some progress towards the ideals of virtual management, in which, say Davidow and Malone, the corporation 'is going to employ its customers as co-producers in everything [and] find itself increasingly customer-managed'. In practice, Japanese companies were the first to form customer-supplier alliances. But leading Western companies are now working hard at integrating internal computer systems with external suppliers of information – including even the individual customer.

While much of the virtuality thesis concentrates on the new technologies that make these advances possible, Davidow and Malone argue that 'simple organizational innovation will be as important to the virtual engineering process as all of the computer power we can bring to bear'. The Japanese successes in world markets were largely won in the mind, not the laboratory. It's the willpower to take advantage of invention, innovation and intelligence, and the understanding of the human role in exploiting change, that are crucial.

The facts of the virtuality trend are self-evident and surely decisive. But decision-makers must surmount some uncomfortably high hurdles. Take the supplier-customer relationship, where collaborative intimacy is basic even to neo-virtuality. Exchange of sensitive information and the relegation of price in priority are wholly foreign to traditional, secretive, untrusting and price-dominated ways of doing business.

Similarly, conditions where empowered workers can individually decide to respond to customer needs – the new working methods presuppose responsiveness and creative input at all levels – can never be achieved in a multi-layered command hierarchy. Virtuality is advocating a socio-political revolution in both inter-company and customer relationships and within the firm. That sounds, and to an extent is, idealistic.

The pragmatic Bundred sees the difficulties and the time-lags. Speaking to a conference on purchasing, logistics and supply, he introduced a sour note of reality: 'I have to say from personal experience that the old system is a long time dying, and the corpse has a habit of sitting up and hitting me.' He was referring to purchasing people who still put price first and foremost.

They can't be blamed entirely. They are prisoners of corporate systems which are geared to an epoch in which manufacturers made unchanged products in enormous runs on inflexible production lines, buying in only basic materials and standard components. They generally made the more complex components in-house, often as a deliberate counterweight to external suppliers. Whether in-house alternatives existed or not, companies liked to have several alternative sources, playing off one against another, and eliminating the risk of dependence. That still sounds entirely logical to most managers. Incorrect policies often do have the at-first-sight semblance of sense. Yet real supplier partnerships are slowly being constructed, despite the odds against them,

Just as relationships of trust are likely to develop externally, so they will between managers and others inside the organization. That should happen out of sheer necessity, as managers make the transition to lean, adaptive, information-based organizations. But will top management be prepared to relax its control to the necessary extent? The answer is that political and economic revolutions create their own dynamism. The forces of virtuality are hard at work within organizations which, in all outward respects, appear to contradict the thesis.

Look, for example, at the compulsions on car-makers, no matter how hidebound their hierarchies may be in other ways. Today they are forced to depend utterly on single sub-assemblies produced by a sole supplier who may well have conceived the design, and whose quality and reliability are crucial to the model's success. In company after company, industry after industry, the practical necessity of velocity, value, quality and cost-competitiveness is forcing *de facto* partnerships of the kind that virtuality demands.

The breakdown of hierarchy and the emergence of project-based teamwork are likewise being urged on by events. Ask any assembly of managers if they have recently been involved in project groups, and half are likely to say yes. On the shopfloor, too, virtuality's responsive, self-managed teamwork is appearing. That's not because the theory attracts managers, but because irresistible practical improvements in costs, flexibility and productivity are available.

Competitive necessity, too, is forcing all managers and processes towards full, computerized participation in the knowledge-based reinvention of management. Is there an alternative to that reinvention? Obviously, the pace of change varies greatly from industry to industry and company to company. In the slower-moving areas, managers can go peacefully about their old business, confident that the old ways will see them out.

Their conservatism, though, is a fateful error, for the company that revolutionizes its supplier relationships will have lower costs, faster response times and happier customers. Other things (like making the right products) being equal, that must also mean higher profits. Or, as Bundred puts it, 'An open, honest relationship between equal partners in the supply chain is the only way of optimizing the performance of the supply chain.' Similarly, within companies 'the only way of achieving velocity in design and manufacture is to break down the old barriers and rebuild new relationships' by adopting 'simultaneous engineering'.

That means all functions working together in teams from the start and is 'about relationships', not technology. The denial of New Century Management is akin to the Luddite resistance to new machines. It is the psychology of management that's at stake here. The Luddites risk the same fate as the electronic watch pioneers in Switzerland. The pioneers abandoned the new-found territory, which was promptly occupied by rivals (of course, the Japanese).

There are moments in business history when dramatic change causes a break with the past – and when those who don't join the future are finished. Variety, velocity, quality and cost-competitiveness now apply to everything. As a result, the management game has new rules:

1 Expect upheaval: when analysing your Strengths, Weaknesses, Opportunities and Threats, also analyse those of your competitors – and of a hypothetical new competitor using new technology, new distribution, new pricing, etc.

2 Invest in any technology or methodology that promises (or threatens) to create significant change, so that, if and when the moment comes, you are not caught unprepared.

3 Create flexibility, so that the organization isn't locked into a *modus operandi* that can only be changed after long delay and at excessive cost, which you may not be able to afford.

4 When the moment of change comes, move fast: forget the past and move boldly into the new era.

5 Accept that pain may well result: better to make the sacrifice yourself than to be knifed by the competition.

6 Live by the ideals of virtuality, where quickness of response is of the essence, governing every process and the provision of every product and service.

The fact that much truly revolutionary activity is already in train has its flip side: the work is usually piecemeal and uncoordinated. One part of an organization may be striding forward, while others are stuck in the mud of the past. The task before top management is to create an overall context in which all the elements of virtuality are bound together. Only good and modern management, based on commonsense analysis, can open the gates to the virtual revolution.

The new need of Volkswagen

In January 1997, General Motors and Volkswagen finally buried the hatchet after the most acrimonious battle that even the strife-prone car industry has seen. The conflict began when VW, seeking a new and red-hot production director, poached José Ignacio López de Arriortúa from GM. The Spaniard had been imported into the US after stunning success with GM in Europe. The fighting only ceased after López had been forced out of VW – but the issues raised by the hostilities rumble on.

The primary bone of contention, which remained the subject of accusations, was whether López stole GM's secrets on being seduced back by VW. But behind the whole fierce saga lay another contentious issue: the conviction at both GM and VW that the futures of such vast manufacturers revolved around one man's indispensable services. To judge by the results, their faith had reason: what López had achieved at GM's Opel subsidiary he proceeded to emulate at VW.

A mere three months after arrival, López was already claiming spectacular wins for KVP2 – the gimmicky shorthand for Continuous Improvement Programme Squared. Over 200 workshops had either been completed, started or planned. The worker teams already trained, it was proudly announced, had improved productivity by an average 28 percent, and quality by 30 percent, reducing lead-times by 27 percent, stock requirements by 34 percent and workspace utilization by 34 percent. The indispensable man had evidently worked miracles – or had he?

Three years after those magic three months, according to the *Wall Street Journal Europe*, VW chairman Ferdinand Piëch and López were 'struggling to make the German auto maker leaner and meaner to match efficiency gains notched up by competitors ... but change is coming slowly to Wolfsburg and VW's five other western German facilities'. A consultant spoke more harshly: 'They've created an image of themselves as being white knights, but they haven't really bit the bullet in Wolfsburg.' Shamingly, that huge plant barely covers its own running costs.

Will the real VW please stand up?

The reality lies between the two extremes. Piëch and López have pushed VW firmly into profit while building its brand strength formidably. As the dust settled over the GM dispute, an automotive industry expert told the *Wall Street Journal* that 'They'll have the densest firepower of new products over the next 18 months. This should translate into superior and rising market shares.' The new armoury is based on a powerful strategy that by 1998 should see VW producing only four 'platforms' for all its models (against today's 16). That industry-leading strategy is expected to achieve pre-tax profits six times 1995's exiguous 1·3 percent.

The tiny margins reflect the uncomfortable fact that everything has taken far too much time – primarily because of failures in top-down leadership. VW exemplifies the paradox about Europe's great car companies. Like the Americans (owners of two of the European giants, Opel-Vauxhall and Ford), they put severe pressure on suppliers to improve quality and performance to Japanese levels – at a time when the mighty leaders palpably lagged behind those standards themselves.

They have, true, made significant gains from their low points. At VW, the assembly time on the new Polo is half the 28 hours taken for its predecessor – but the process still takes twice as long as it should. Assembly line efficiency has been rising by 15 percent annually – but this has created a surplus of workers who have been turned, perhaps uneconomically, to making more parts in-house.

That flies in the face of industry trends and of Piëch's own conversion to 'modular production', in which whole sub-assemblies are provided and maybe even fitted by the supplier. The delivery of entire cockpits, fully assembled doors, and so on helps to explain the Polo's radically shorter assembly time. But VW is no pioneer in these methods, which were adopted by other manufacturers years ago. Moreover, while the German company poured effort into getting higher quality and productivity from its blue-collar employees, the serried ranks of its bureaucracy remained untouched by the endeavour. Interdepartmental jealousies and 'smokestack' (vertical) organization have hampered the all-important productivity drive.

The dedicated project team, with its own devolved leadership, is foreign to this corpocratic culture. As a result, at a time when Japanese rivals had long entrusted new cars to independent and independently led product teams, and their evaluation to exhaustive market research, VW actually prided itself on a two-day session at which its directors drove all the new models before giving their approval. This exercise, which no doubt the bosses enjoyed hugely, was supposed to test the cars from the customers' viewpoint.

Such deep misunderstanding of the new necessities permeates VW's top-down leadership modes, which are symptomatic of a general European reluctance to join the management revolution. In the great corporations, the lure of top-down leadership remains strong – and in several respects the attraction is easily understood. Superb leaders resolve many difficulties for their subjects. They take all the decisions and all responsibility. They make all the rules. They assume all ultimate power. And in the process, they become indispensable – because they have created a potential vacuum that, by definition, nobody else can fill.

For many years nobody could fill the gap left by VW's true founder, Heinz Nordhoff, the man who led a brilliantly successful post-war rebellion against the Americans' infatuation with large cars and their insistence on the 'dominant design' in engineering – engine at the front driving the rear wheels. Ironically, Nordhoff happily aped the dominant design in management – man at the front driving everybody else. That style of leadership became ingrained at VW and elsewhere, which explains why the auto-hierarchs and others waited so long to carry through vital technological and management change.

In situations which cry out for new methods, the task of renewal can't lie in the hands of people who know only the old ways and are comfortable with those habits. Old dogs are unwilling to learn new tricks. This doesn't mean that they can't. It does mean, however, that they won't – unless the whole environment is changed so radically that only new tricks will work. So, in comes the indispensable concept of collective leadership, exercised all the way down the line.

Sharing the responsibilities

How the embattled leaders of VW must envy the freedom from past and present constraints of a greenfield company – like, say, the motor industry's Japanese transplants in the US and Europe. Nissan Motors in Sunderland is an instructive example. The north-east of England had never housed a car plant before, let alone one whose owners, being Japanese, took a radical approach to management. An all-British top management established a revolutionary environment in which new dogs happily learnt new tricks.

Peter Wickens, one of the original British directors at Nissan, now retired, gave an inspirational account of his company's wholly different approach.[3] The inspiration lies in the evidence that ordinary people can achieve extraordinary results – if, paradoxically, you treat them like ordinary people. The six essential steps sound very ordinary themselves:

1 Secure top-level commitment to change.
2 Involve the appropriate people in diagnosing the needed changes in detail.
3 Promote the need for change.
4 Plan the change process.
5 Develop the people.
6 Maintain and reinforce the change process.

Have any programmes for any management remedy ever been put forward without demanding top-level commitment? Naturally, that's what all consultants and in-house specialists demand for their specialities. Usually the demand is impractical, simply because top managers overwhelm themselves with so much operational detail (which they love) that there isn't enough time to commit more than words to customer satisfaction, quality, service, world-class performance, or any other noble cause. The way in which these dignitaries choose to work forces senior executives into MBLS: Management by Lip-Service.

Lip-service guarantees the failure of good intentions. The logical solution is to change the way in which top managers work. If you delegate operational matters, concentrate on things that only top managers can do, and demonstrate change by example, MBLS can be replaced by effective action. You forget the concept of going 'down' the organization. At Nissan, mentally there is no 'down': everybody is equal when it comes to achieving better performance.

The strength created at Sunderland, which rapidly equalled parent plants in Japan on specific measures of efficiency, showed itself in adversity. Expansion plans for the plant had been predicated on growth in the European market which it serves. When recession hit in the early 1990s, the fall in demand threatened the sustained employment which had seemed a plank of the success at Sunderland. Lay-offs became inevitable. How could they be achieved without damaging the hard-won ethos of the plant?

The answer was to use that ethos. Instead of management laying down the answer, the problem was handed over to the workforce, which was asked to come up with its own solution. The scheme submitted to management was reasonable and fair: in some respects, managers might have hesitated before proposing what the workers were actually prepared to accept. Obviously, the result couldn't have been achieved in a less productive atmosphere.

This demonstrates a general principle. By asking people for their opinions, and involving them in reaching solutions, you take a giant step forward in promoting change. As the redundancy issue showed, this isn't a matter of gung-ho morale-building; instead, systematic, planned progress is required. Wickens is enthusiastic (and so am I) about finding some quick, visible fixes: that is, obvious large improvements in limited but conspicuous areas – getting rid of reserved car parking spaces, or starting a manufacturing cell to service a single important customer.

The crucial point, though, is that corporate change is anything but a quick fix. Time, trouble and the Robert the Bruce Principle (if at first you don't succeed, try, try again) are all required. But people's energy and commitment may wane unless they see that change brings benefits. Their work towards getting those benefits will be the foundation of their personal development, which, of course, can never end, any more than change itself. The enemy of change is complacency: managers must be their own most severe critics – permanently.

That is the key to *kaizen*, the continuous improvement of processes, which goes hand-in-hand with the introduction of new ones that provide major gains. There's a crucial difference here between East and West. The American academic Lester B. Thurow points out that American firms spend two-thirds of their R&D money on product and a third on processes – a vice which European companies tend to share. The Japanese are exactly the other way round, and they have it right. Process holds the key, the *how* rather than the *what* of what you do.

The central process is that of management itself, which leads back to Wickens and the Nissan factory. The prime job of management at Sunderland is to facilitate. The 36 managers who looked after 4,000 employees at the time didn't operate in a multi-layered hierarchy, but as motivators who don't direct people, but 'empower' them.

That isn't, incidentally, a term that management expert Peter Drucker much cares for – he says that empowerment is as much a term of power and rank as the old ones it's supposed to replace. Instead, he prefers to talk about 'responsibility' and 'contribution'.

Here Nissan really does have the right idea: for instance, job titles aren't hierarchical, but generic: engineer, senior engineer, supervisor, administrative assistant, controller and so on describe the members of an effective team. Team is the key word, although the obvious and excellent merits of team management can, of course, be over-praised. In real life, team-based organizations don't run perfectly, or to everybody's satisfaction.

That includes the Japanese factory transplants like Nissan. But they do run visibly better – so much better as to prove that managing by real teamwork is no longer an option. It's a necessity: and the team includes everybody, inside and outside the company, who contributes to its success. For real teams, there'll be nothing to fear, especially from competitors who are still stuck in the old ruts.

The dominant designs, in engineering and management alike, are finally crumpling after a Japanese team-centred onslaught that respected none of the old rules. The intense pressures have forced irreversible change on all car companies. Yet Europe has been less responsive than circumstances demanded – with the rare exception of Rover, before its takeover by BMW. The fundamental principles applied at Rover used the watchwords 'Better, faster, cheaper'. Under that banner, management pushed home the belief that doing a thousand things 1 percent better outdoes a 1,000 percent miracle on a single process.

Pursuing continuous improvement, Rover, heavily influenced by its Honda partners, sought to maximize added value, with zero duplication and no workforce passengers. Managers saw that their business was about customers, not products; all activities had to contribute to delivering 'extraordinary satisfaction' to customers (including the internal customers for departmental work). Without planned progress to world-class performance, Rover couldn't hope to compete in a worldwide industry. That meant taking balanced, fact-based decisions founded on business realities and multifunctional teamwork.

That teamwork is the simple necessity imposed by complex tasks. You can't introduce modern 'simultaneous' or 'concurrent' development of a new car, for example, unless you have teams cutting not only across functions, but across the frontiers between customer and supplier. And if you can't achieve simultaneity, you will be beaten out of sight by those who can. Inexorably, even at VW, management is moving from fixed, vertical hierarchies towards fluid, horizontal teams.

As Peter Drucker has brilliantly expounded, however, different teams play different games – baseball, soccer, or tennis doubles. The three variations contrast markedly. Success won't come if you have the wrong team for the situation. The formations are as follows:

1 For repetitive tasks and familiar work, use the *baseball* organization. Every member has a fixed role and operates independently. This

doesn't mean separately – the pitcher needs the catcher, and there are double and triple plays when the ball whips from one fielder to another. But the team never operates with all members in unison.

2 For known tasks which require greater flexibility and responsiveness (like a new product team), the *soccer* principle is perfect. Orchestras and surgical teams, too, move in the same way. Everybody has a fixed role, again, and there is a fixed procedure (the orchestral 'score'); but no individual can play without the others, and the result depends on successful unison.

3 For tasks which require constant improvisation and need to maximize individual contributions, *tennis doubles* have to be played. This is (or should be) top management at work: the partners complement each other's strengths and weaknesses, and work together as individuals to achieve a combined effect. This isn't an orchestra, but a jazz combo.

The stages of management, as charted by Drucker, start with the baseball mode. The chief executive works through subordinates with fixed functional or line responsibilities that are seldom exercised in combination. That's the corpocracy in action, serving The Great Man. Today, the better top managements are playing jazz, with a genuine team in which the chief executive is first among equals. The team ranges freely within the agreed overall theme; but it never knows exactly what the final outcome will be.

The jazzmen depend heavily, however, on their colleagues: the soccer or orchestral players. All functional management is now shifting into the soccer, orchestral or operating theatre mode, in which specialized skills need to be combined, and sometimes supplemented. That's in order to deal with situations where experience is essential, but where adaptations to circumstances, and even experiments, are constantly required.

Does team-based management unhorse the leader in all organizations at all times? The crude answer is that sometimes only the force of a charismatic leader like López can cut through: to shake up the system, seismic shocks are necessary. In turnrounds, this argument is usually decisive. Nobody appoints a committee man to rescue a company in crisis. But turnrounds – and their leaders – are notoriously prone to either lapse or relapse, simply because the saviours have improved the performance without fundamentally improving the system.

The great organizers know how to turn functional and cross-functional teamwork into a way of life, avoiding waste and achieving synergies (internally and with external suppliers) through flexible and adaptive systems. If López had been such an organizer, GM wouldn't have needed the indispensable man so desperately: whatever system he left behind would have worked fine without him.

Inevitably, teamwork and collaboration would have dominated those workings. Both apply especially in the realm where López made his legendary reputation: purchasing, a key activity in which the Japanese have taught the whole Western car industry far-reaching lessons. López did have a team of dedicated followers, his 'warriors': but their name and style don't suggest the cooperative, mutually supportive way in which vendor and customer are now supposed to work.

In this new world, price is relegated, at most, to equal ranking with quality and reliability. In contrast, the wonder-man's contribution to GM in Europe was admired almost entirely in terms of cutting prices (other people's, that is). Exactly the same happened with VW, where López is credited with cutting purchasing and production costs at Wolfsburg by 40 percent, primarily by squeezing suppliers – achieved by samurai-style confrontation rather than the gentler Zennist approach.

In any event, purchasing, while critical, is only part of the pattern. Three years after VW gave the Spaniard untrammelled power to work his will, the company was still a high-cost producer in a low-cost world, still a top-down corpocracy in the age of bottom-up collaboration. Relying on one man, however brilliant, eventually leads to trouble – unless the talents of everybody else in the organization are mobilized and released in new ways that will outlive the peerless leader. Any system that hinges on irreplaceable people is plainly and deeply defective. It's far more important to reinvent the system than to hire The Great Man. Spread the responsibility and you raise the results.

THREE

Reshaping the Culture

The roots of LucasVarity

In June 1996, Lucas Industries, the leading British maker of automotive parts, agreed to merge with Varity Corporation, a main North American rival in braking systems. It seemed a genuine marriage – not made in heaven, certainly, but with solid earthly prospects. As the world's fifth largest supplier of automotive components, the combination could hope to guarantee its membership in the exclusive club (no more than 20 members) expected to dominate the industry in the millennium.

By the New Year, however, the marriage of true minds and hearts was looking more and more like an American *putsch*. Not a single Lucas director was left on the board. The future lay primarily in the hands of the ex-Varity chief executive, Victor Rice. The drive to reform the $6·8 billion LucasVarity, and thus to exploit what Rice called 'a huge opportunity to improve the working capital and overhead structure of this company', was in the care of another Varity graduate, Briton Tony Gilroy.

Lucas was clearly the junior partner. Yet it had once seemed to lead British industry in awareness of the formula for corporate success in the nineties. Strive to stay abreast of a changing sector, speed up your processes to meet the needs of a demanding market, change the organization and make it look outwards – to where the Japanese, your most formidable competitors, provide a clear example. Dr John Parnaby, then the Lucas Industries director in charge of manufacturing technology, stressed these needs as far back as 1987:[1]

> It has become clear that the right strategy is to use a total systems approach integrating the many elements of the simplifying methodologies of systems design and operation . . . This strategy leads to high levels of capability in three areas which have previously been the sole province of the Japanese: economic manufacture of high product variety, economic low-cost achievement of high product quality, and flexibility of

performance of people systems and factory machine systems
... Only in this way can the large gaps in performance be
closed.

Such gaps emerge in telltale figures like lead-times, inventory turns
and output per man, where the distance between actual and potential
performance – as revealed by their subsequent correction – can be huge.
Naturally, Lucas over many years poured effort into applying Parnaby's
prescription to its core automotive component business. Yet in the nineties, the gaps still loomed amazingly large.

Far from becoming superefficient, the company found so much
remaining slack that it could reduce manufacturing lead-times from 55
to 12 days, cut order-to-dispatch lead-times from 105 to 32 days, double
inventory turns, increase productivity by half and cut floor space requirements so greatly that two factories could be closed. As David Harvey of
the Business Intelligence consultancy observes,[2] 'a cynic might ask how
dire the performance ... was in the first place'.

For all its efforts, Lucas had not raised its performance to the best
Japanese standards. Consequently, it was still in vulnerable mode: short
of global scale, working at low 6 percent operating margins, generating
too little cash for its investment needs, and riding a profit-and-loss seesaw.
That is a deeply disappointing outcome in light of the benefits promised
when, in Harvey's words, 'organizations have discarded outmoded and
uncompetitive operational practices and adopted new ways of doing
business'.

The activity is called business process reengineering, or BPR, the
subject of a major Business Intelligence report. The problem at Lucas, as
now at LucasVarity, is that the requirement goes far beyond radically
improving specific operations. That narrower focus made consultants
Michael Hammer and James Champy the world's most famous reengineers. Yet in their book *Reengineering the Corporation*[3] they reach a
dismal conclusion:

> ... most companies that begin reengineering ... end their
> efforts precisely where they began, making no significant
> changes, achieving no major performance improvement ...
> Our unscientific estimate is that as many as 70 percent of
> organizations ... fail to achieve any results.

A McKinsey expert told *Fortune* in like vein that 'We did an audit of
client experiences with process reengineering. We found lots of examples

where there were truly dramatic impacts on processes – 60 percent to 80 percent reductions in cost and cycle time – but only very modest effects at the business-unit level . . .' The changes, it turned out, 'didn't matter in terms of the customer'. While Champy believes that reengineering results have improved since he wrote the book, there is still, he reckons, a 50 percent failure rate. Why?

Most reengineering (like, say, cutting Ford Motor's accounts payable costs by 80 percent through eliminating the invoicing stage altogether) consists of what might be called 'sub-projects': stand-alone process improvements that involve relatively low-level teamwork and initiative and are not linked to reengineering the entire business. These are the kinds of projects that have provided bread-and-butter (and sometimes plenty of jam) for consultants since time immemorial. The benefits are real, but limited by definition.

Even when whole business units have been put through the re-engineering wringer, the limits apply. In numberless cases spectacular results have been won in parts of corporations whose overall performance remained unsatisfactory. That's a fair summary of what happened at Lucas, and what will happen again at LucasVarity unless a much broader view is taken. The future rests ultimately on the group's overall ability to marry radical internal change with a transformed approach to the external customer.

The merger provides a far stronger platform for the effort. Certain benefits flow automatically: for instance, achieving across-the-board technological capacity – which neither side had before – in braking systems for all types of vehicle. But the required double transformation is far from automatic. The key lesson of the failed reengineers is that initiatives to reshape businesses and their cultures often founder because top managements, while preaching revolution, in practice never go beyond narrow reform.

That simply isn't good enough in the external conditions of today's markets. Nor will it meet the internal needs of the corporation. Old bad habits will reassert themselves unless an axe is taken to their roots. At Lucas too many opportunities for too many improvements previously went begging: Lucas, after all, lost money in one year of the nineties, as did Varity in two. The remedies won't work, unless the reengineers can reengineer the most crucial element of all: themselves.

Rewards of reinvention

The much-publicized backlash against business process reengineering in the nineties is scarcely surprising, given the disappointing results mentioned earlier. But the criticism can be taken too far. Rich improvements are still available in vast amounts from what Michael Hammer and James Champy, in *Reengineering the Corporation*, describe as (my italics) '*fundamental* rethinking and *radical* redesign of business *processes* to achieve *dramatic* improvements in critical contemporary measures of performance, such as cost, quality, service and speed'.

The need remains glaringly obvious – so much so that most managements have taken the point. But many yearn for much more. They want their companies to be 'lean, nimble, flexible, responsive, competitive, innovative, efficient, customer-focused and profitable'. Why, then, are so many of those same companies, according to Hammer and Champy, 'bloated, clumsy, rigid, sluggish, noncompetitive, uncreative, inefficient, disdainful of customer needs, and losing money'?

The reengineers can easily produce evidence to justify the insults. If they walk a customer request through all its stages, asking everybody concerned to deal with the proposal at once, bizarre discoveries follow – like an actual process which requires only 90 minutes, but gets elongated by the inefficiencies in the system to a whole week. This kind of ineffective system doesn't spring up overnight. Why don't the normal workings of the organization prevent the slow growth of organized structural incompetence?

Equally, if organizational sludge has accumulated, why can't insiders find the antidote? One simple reform works brilliantly across a great range of cases like that above. Entrust the task to one person, who handles the request from start to finish – and cease passing it to a different person for each stage. Have a back-stop to deal with the more complicated, but rare cases, for which, absurdly, the whole process has often been designed. But what kind of culture allows such poor design: and then does nothing to correct its pernicious results?

Again, the structure is to blame. The organization is probably split into departments, all of which insist on having their piece of the action (or inaction). The key lies in attacking the structure, and the culture which it breeds, by eliminating what Hammer and Champy call 'cross-organizational hand-offs'. If you don't entrust everything to a single individual, you empower 'case teams', groups 'who have among them all the skills that are needed' to satisfy the customer: 'Typically a case-worker-based process operates *ten times* faster than the assembly line version that it replaces.'

This is admirable, from both the company's and the customer's point of view. It certainly meets the criteria of being fundamental, radical and dramatic. But will the whole of the company perform similar wonders? It certainly won't with the kind of culture that fosters and persists in errors. As noted, rethinking and radical redesign of any individual process will very probably produce dramatic improvement in detail. Employee involvement and morale also benefit greatly from these projects. But lasting economic and employee benefits are lost if the results are submerged in an overall business system which is ineffective and stultifying.

Misled managements may actually worsen the system by misguided efforts to improve its parts. As Hammer and Champy observe, they try to 'fix' processes instead of changing them: instead of focusing on specific processes, they appoint task forces on 'issues' like empowerment, teamwork, innovation, and customer service. They ignore the fact that successful process redesign will trigger radical changes elsewhere in the business system. Nor do they involve people and their reward and recognition in the change.

They settle for minor results. They give up too early. They limit the scope of the reengineering effort in advance by premature definition of the problem. In sum, they let existing corporate cultures and management attitudes get in the way. Cultures resist change instinctively, because managers fear the unknown – and that principle runs right to the very summit.

Consultants know that, offered a 20 percent improvement in a particular process, chief executives will sign on the dotted line. Offer them a great 200 percent leap forward, however, and the sale becomes far more difficult – for that must involve drastic change. In *Fortune's* words, reengineers in effect ask, 'If we were a new company, how would we run this place? Then, with a meat axe and sandpaper, they conform the company to their vision'.

Managers are understandably none too keen on being axed or sandpapered themselves; or to accept that their established vision of the company has become irrelevant; or (to bring the issue down to earth) to incur huge six-figure monthly consultancy bills that threaten to become eternal – for the company will never run out of business processes to reengineer. But these concerns, while substantive, dodge the real issue, which is that the re-engineering idea, however labelled, is inescapable, but only partial.

Lower cost, better quality, improved service and greater speed – the targets of reengineering – only work their greatest wonders within the framework of a business which has itself been rethought to succeed in its changing markets and objectives. So reengineering isn't enough. Most of the companies surveyed by Business Intelligence, David Harvey found,[4] 'saw no alternative but to *reinvent* their organizations' (my italics).

'Reinvention' is not a technical term like reengineering. It was coined by a magazine writer to describe the American corporate shake-ups of the eighties and nineties. It struck a rich vein. It put a bright gloss on shabby facts. Some once-great business had become mired in stagnant sales, declining profits, lagging technology and waning competitive prowess. Now a management reared in obsolete traditions was expected to match, better still surpass, the achievements which Lucas's John Parnaby envied – those of the best performers in Japan.

The phrase 'reinvent' perfectly suited the situation and the public relations need. The corporation had been 'invented' by some founding genius. Now his heirs had to start, like him, from a blank sheet of paper. They might write off much of the inheritance, they might throw more of it away. The end-result would be a new corporation, reinvented, free of the lumber of the past and full of the virtues of renewed and reinvigorated management.

But reinvention has spawned at least as many disappointments as reengineering. The 'reinventors', too, have to struggle for success against the entrenched opposition of structures and cultures born in a period of lower competition and fewer challenges. The new message has to penetrate an organization full of unwilling ears. Even wide-ranging reorganization and rehabilitation can fail to shake the inertia of a major corporation. Yet the conventional wisdom of reinvention sounds thoroughly irresistible:

1 Give more autonomy to individual businesses.

2 Remake the culture.

3 Shift the emphasis from products to services.

4 Emphasize customer satisfaction.

5 Cut back employment.

6 Reduce other direct and indirect costs.

7 Share risk and gain expertise through partnerships.

Sadly, many a management, even if it understands the need for these Seven Steps of Reinvention, shows no sign of being able to achieve their true object: to change, not just the lead-times, stock-turns, and so on, nor even the organizational structure, but the total behaviour of those within the structure. The telltale evidence of failure lies in the large gulfs between words and deeds.

Check down through the company, and you find that the defects that brought low performance in the past have persisted despite the reinvention – and sometimes because of it. The reinventors tend to go back to the drawing board whenever confronted by clear evidence that the 'new' company works no better than the old. With each successive disappointment, external and insider comments on the reinventions become more grudging and guarded.

You can understand the growing lack of enthusiasm of people confronted by a whole string of often contradictory reinventions. Sometimes reforms intended to create a more responsive, dynamic system only create a costly, rigid and rudderless result. Sometimes new programmes are created only to lose impetus and die. Sometimes new structures are dismantled before people have become used to the change. It's the same pattern of cultural malfunction that was identified earlier in explaining the mismanagement of reengineering.

True reinvention is only available to companies which go beyond the boundaries imposed by fixed ideas to create a whole new framework for their business processes. These models, moreover, have truly reinvented themselves, not when the business was already in crisis, but by dealing from strength – and rebuilding on that strength, not on weakness.

In life assurance, for example, Sun Life was already king of its prime sector, selling through 'independent financial advisers'. Management still saw an urgent need to rebuild organizational capability to cope with fundamental change in a life insurance market moving from rapid growth to stagnation or worse. In addition to setting new business priorities, the management worked hard to communicate a new 'Sun Spirit', with a set of seven ways to deliver its 'commitment to industry excellence'. The spirited seven, which have an obvious fit with the Seven Steps of Reinvention listed above, were:

1 Putting the customer first at all times.
2 Taking individual responsibility to satisfy customer needs.
3 Maximizing opportunities for self-development.
4 Creating an environment of professionalism, integrity and fun.

5 Valuing teamwork as the means to attain our objectives.

6 Seeking continuous improvement in all our operations.

7 Taking pride in Sun Life.

The spirit infuses very detailed actions with hard, measurable objectives – superior solutions, superior service and superior satisfaction. The procedure of true reinvention follows much the same route in firms in very different industries: rethink and communicate to everybody the entire philosophy of the business and then radically improve all its processes in that light. They take what sounds like a simple decision – to listen to the customers and work back from their requirements: but that results in far-reaching corporate change.

Countless managers claim that they are 'putting customers first', becoming 'customer-led', and stressing 'customer care'. The vital difference is that Sun Life acted on what it heard: as a result, the key customers (those independent financial advisers) voted it 'company of the year' three times in a row. Equally important, the company sustained its effort. After ACHIEVE, the change programme begun in 1990 and finished in 1993, Sun Life launched into continuous improvement and then into Project NEW UNIVERSE, designed to improve radically all customer service processes for the markets of the millennium.

Shifting the company's whole emphasis, from marketing expenditure to giving customers value for money, was accompanied by specific process reengineering, clearly related to the new strategy, and designed to produce dramatic improvements in cost and speed. Going back to the beginning provides the only acceptable start-line. You then decide what, starting anew, you wish to achieve. And that search for desired outcomes holds the key to real success. As Hammer and Champy say, 'work is best organized around outcomes, not tasks'.

Outcome-centred reinvention *à la* Sun Life is a tall order for everybody, including top managers themselves. The commitment to a change in whose pains top management fully shares is indispensable. Without that sharing, any work on total quality, reengineering, reinvention or any other reform programme will fail overall. The push for change must start at the top for more than one reason.

First, only the top people, led by the chief executive, can turn a change programme into a way of life, by insistence, endorsement, recognition and, above all, by example. Second, the broader view that can't be expected from those in the frontline is brought into focus by those farther away. Their cardinal responsibility is to monitor, update and, if necessary, reform the overall business system or systems which comprehend all other processes.

Third, because the reasons why reengineering and reinvention fail are cultural, only the custodians of the culture can remove those obstacles. They alone can tackle the counterproductive dominance of organized hierarchies, functionally divided and vertically managed. Top-down executives still control the business world. But the top-down system is incompatible with the dramatic changes and pressures that have reshaped both markets and managerial requirements. That conflict has resulted in crisis – which can only be resolved by near-revolution.

Reinvention will fail if it stops short of the revolutionary change that's urgently required to accomplish the necessary shift from vertical to horizontal. Organizations are having to move from centrally controlled, multilayered pyramids to flatter, devolved structures. That's matched by transformation of business systems: the sequential, departmental, vertical division of work is yielding to the concept of the business system – constructed of horizontal processes that cut across traditional divisions.

Without true commitment from the top, however, the system won't change enough: the process must be total. You dare not, if you want the best results, pour new wine into old bottles, whether the bottle is an information technology system, a customer service department, an assembly line, or a whole corporation. Of course, you mustn't take seven days over a process that only requires 90 minutes, but that always has been management's responsibility. The difference today is that the responsibility has to be exercised within a 'total process' – which can only mean the entire business. Half-measures won't produce even half-results.

The *défi* of Digital Europe

In early 1995, life was looking up for Digital Europe. The ambitions of Vincenzo Damiani, who had arrived as president of European Operations a year before, seemed on the point of being realized. A veteran of 29 years with IBM, ending as general manager of Marketing and Services for Europe, he had instantly drawn up 'The Damiani Agenda' for his new company, a succinct one-pager which stated baldly that:

- The overall goal is satisfied customers.
- The focus is on leadership and management actions.

• Three Objectives and Ten Action Points form the nucleus.

To 'create sustainable growth' (Objective 1), Digital would focus on small- to medium-sized customers; team up with partners and develop alliances; optimize new opportunities for services and consulting; develop specific industry and product markets; improve distribution capability and market coverage; and increase marketing and selling competence.

To 'increase efficiency' (Objective 2), the actions would achieve optimum sizing of organization and reduce organizational structures; and consolidate support activities.

Finally, to 'optimize customer-focused management systems and processes' (Objective 3), Digital would focus on processes and process ownership; and 'show leadership, communicate more, and more efficiently'.

As those last seven words exemplify, Damiani believed that his leadership depended on carrying with him, not just the senior management, but the entire European workforce – and its customers. European business has been infused with the need to become 'customer-driven', and Digital was no exception. Damiani believed that growth was based on giving the customer competitive advantage. Hence the introduction of 'customer-driven processes' as part of his reforms – inverting the previous order of priorities, which put production first.

The Agenda has the ring of command. It speaks of a management clear about its ends and its means – and master of its destiny. Yet 18 months later, Digital Europe, now under different leadership, had been buffeted by fate – not because there was anything wrong with the Damiani Agenda *per se*, but because it was only a subset of a US master strategy which had partly unravelled. Europe had a role, but a subordinate one, in Digital's sixfold global mission, designed by chief executive Robert Palmer to recover from the group's near-total disaster:

One, protect the base. Two, marry the organization and management to market realities. Three, avoid competition with key partners (meaning mostly the indirect suppliers of PCs). Four, build on key strengths. Five, supply superior and differentiating service and support. The sixth mission element was 'make money'. Digital aimed to make profits by the end of its 1994 financial year (which it did), and to stay in profit thereafter, which became harder and harder – even though the overall strategy worked well in some respects.

In very short order, Digital worldwide compensated for the collapse of revenues from the VAX line of minicomputers by strong sales of systems based on the Alpha microprocessor; its historic strength in networking helped expand its position in business computing; and it staked a large claim on the Internet – where its Alta-Vista swiftly became the leading search engine. But in personal computing, a decisive move from vending bought-in PCs to full-line manufacture of its own designs proved too much too late.

With too small a foothold and no worthwhile branding, Digital first had to withdraw, licking its wounds, from the home PC market. Then came a far deeper humiliation: trapped into excessive and over-priced stocks by a combination of mismanagement and fierce price competition, Digital in July 1996 abandoned its head-on battle with Compaq and other leaders in business PCs. Another 7,000 people lost their jobs – following the 65,000 already dismissed since 1989 as Digital struggled for its future. Half the new job losses were in Europe.

The new all-Digital PC range had been intended to improve the European prospect greatly, aided by an historic shift from selling direct to marketing through indirect channels. PC sales were soon doubling every quarter, but Digital was running hard up a steep hill – and found itself losing more in sales to important customers than it gained through sales via third parties. 'Cold light of day replaces false dawn at Digital' read the headline in the *Financial Times*.

'An egregious mistake, frankly,' admitted Palmer, talking of the poor monitoring which left Digital's distributors with a disastrous 15 weeks' supply instead of the usual six. The shift to distributive channels had been taken too far: newly hired sales people had to be thrown into the breach to retrieve the lost direct business.

As for the organizational structure, there was too much chopping and changing. Then, the highly variegated markets of Europe proved resistant to instituting the preferred solution – pan-European management, which, in Palmer's words, is 'easier to talk about than execute'.

According to Louise Kehoe of the *Financial Times*, he 'acknowledged that senior managers in the US might not have done a good job in guiding the changes in Europe'. That is the nub of the matter. To what extent does a European business that accounts for half the corporate sales require guidance from outside Europe – and from above? The nagging suspicion is that, left more to their own resources, the American satellites could make a far larger contribution to the corporate present and the European future.

Europe really does have a vibrant and viable computer industry, with world-class plants producing state-of-the-art products for eager and fast-growing markets. The great catch is that the products, the plants and the markets largely belong to American corporations like Digital. Whether it's IBM at Greenock or Montpelier, Compaq at Erskine, Apple in Cork, or Digital at Irvine, the US affiliates represent Europe's biggest stake by far in the information technology revolution. But for the most part American parents rule the roost.

The issue, and the challenge for companies like Digital, in Europe and worldwide, is one of the leadership culture: where leadership is located, and what kind of leadership it is. To a very real extent, Digital's false dawn – like the fateful lag in PCs – was an inglorious legacy from the glorious past. The culture was uniquely the creation of a great leader, founder Ken Olsen. His dominating personality forced the company through the brilliant phases that made its mini-computers easily the most successful hardware rivals to IBM.

Yet when markets changed, Digital fatefully missed the moment of industry transformation. Personal computers and open systems alike passed the company by as it remained stuck in the age that had created Olsen's triumphs. His successors did move the technology and the product range firmly into the new era. The question remained whether the leadership culture was still too deeply embedded in the bad old days and ways.

Leaders of leaders

In the corporate Europe of the late nineties, different cultures of leadership are competing for the future. They divide broadly between the conventional and the modern. If the leadership for which the Damiani Agenda called at Digital Europe represents the modern tendency, the school under which Digital grew to world stature stands for the opposite approach – the cult of the supreme commander. That is reaffirmed every time a chief executive appears on the cover of a business magazine, jaw jutting or smile fixed, combined with a caption praising his achievements.

Ken Olsen richly deserved *Fortune's* accolade as 'America's Most Successful Entrepreneur' for his building of Digital. The longer supreme commanders last, however, the more difficult it becomes to eradicate their cult – and the more pernicious the latter may become. Strong personalities who have ridden the tide of previous success are especially susceptible to 'chief executive disease' ('founder's disease' in Olsen's case). The illness has profound cultural impact. As *Business Week* recounts, stricken bosses:

1 Can do no wrong.

2 Refuse to concede any mistake.

3 Spend excessive time away from the company.

4 Are surrounded by yes-men.

5 Make every decision – often in ignorance.

6 Fuss about their incomes, comforts and perks.

7 Seek personal publicity.

8 Hang on to power – often undermining potential successors.

In fairness, Olsen was not prone to all these symptoms. It was the first that nearly proved fatal for Digital – combined with the eighth: succession. It is a commonplace that succession provides the critical test for the Great Man culture. At Digital, once Olsen finally and reluctantly gave way, the baton was passed to an insider, Robert Palmer, to general approval. But the findings of Nitin Nohria and Rakesh Khurana, both of Harvard Business School, throw doubt on whether the appointment was theoretically correct. Studying 'The Effects of CEO Turnover on Large Industrial Corporations',[5] they concluded from 222 CEO successions from 1978 to 1994 that 'Having an insider take the reins from a retiring CEO . . . had little effect on performance'.

That kind of promotion does achieve 'slightly better than average performance' when the predecessor is fired (and Olsen was certainly put under pressure to go). For above-average results, however, the incumbent not only had to be sacked, but the replacement had to be an outsider. The crisis that causes the replacement gives the outsider carte blanche to sweep away bad managers, poor practices, loss-making businesses, superfluous assets and people – and all the other legacies of corporate ineptitude.

Rightly or wrongly (usually the latter), an insider like Palmer will be more expected to preserve the *status quo*, with which everybody is comfortable, even if the predecessor has been sacked in crisis. The research also found that, if the new boss comes from inside, but replaces a predecessor who was retired rather than fired, 'company performance will show little effect'. But if it's an outsider who arrives after the last man's comfortable retirement, the outcome tends to be less dynamic still. His arrival in a settled situation sends out mixed and possibly unsettling signals.

Whatever the succession, though, performance will surely be enhanced if replacement CEOs and their leadership culture can pass an eight-point health check:

1 Is there clear and firm direction from the top?

2 Is everything and anything subject to challenge and replacement or improvement?

3 Are decisions taken quickly and surely?

4 And actions?

5 Are communications clear, continuous and consistent?

6 Do actions support words – and specifically sustain a change agenda?

7 Are the basics continuously revised and improved?

8 Is there a shared, reviewed and renewed vision of the future?

On these eight counts, Robert Palmer's performance at Digital can best be called patchy – especially on the issues of quickness and sureness. That could support Nohria and Khurana's theories about promoted insiders – and Digital also fits their answer to what they describe as an irksome question. 'Why didn't the actions of the CEOs have more of an impact on company performance?' Their evidence suggests, remember, that only an emergency appointment made in an emergency achieves any results that differ significantly from the average.

That's because 'in reality, CEOs are limited in what they can do by the very nature of their post. Their constraints are many: company values and procedures, pre-existing lines of business, currently accepted management practices, and bureaucracy.' In other words, the leadership culture is rigid, institutionalized and (especially if chief executive disease is rampant) designed to remove responsibility from nearly everybody but the boss. Palmer saw the results clearly at Digital: 'What was sorely lacking . . . was a sense of accountability. When things went well, there would be a number of people willing to take credit. But when things went wrong, it was impossible to fix responsibility on anyone.'

That didn't prevent an astonishing degree of executive turnover. In 1996 only four people had survived from the 40 top executives of 1992 – and that includes Palmer. The hire-and-fire routine is a hangover from old-style leadership cultures. Its only usefulness in the new climate is to clear the decks. That may be necessary, for the new leadership is very demanding, and many managers cannot meet its demands. At one British factory which went over to total quality, half the executives were unable to join the journey. The change agents discovered, to quote the factory director at the time, that 'Leaders were not used to talking to their people'.

In other words, they were not actually leading in the modern sense. In fact, that director continued, 'a number of managers were administrators – they had forgotten leadership'. Quite possibly, they didn't have much to remember. Within a traditional corporate hierarchy, rules, ranks, precedence and precedents determine what's done, by whom, and how. The need for leadership and direction is passed up the line to the top, which (see above) is constrained in its ability to respond.

The task facing European management is to reverse that upward flow. That requires a many-centred leadership culture – and many kinds of leader at all levels. At first sight, there seem to be as many styles as there are bosses. But one study, *Maximum Leadership* by Charles M. Farkas and Philippe de Backer,[6] boils down the welter of different ways and people to only five distinct styles or approaches: (1) strategic, (2) human assets, (3) expertise, (4) 'box', and (5) change. The authors work for Bain & Co, which took two years to interview 161 executives on six continents. Their five models are:

1 A futures person, concentrating systematically on where the organization needs to go, and how it's going to get there.

2 A people person, who believes and acts on the principle that success flows from the effective management of human resources.

3 An expert, who concentrates on achieving the best possible technical performance and technological strength in the organization's key areas.

4 An 'organization man', in the 'box', who sets up 'rules, systems, boundaries and values' to ensure effective control.

5 A change agent, who loves innovation and prefers enterprise and initiative to control.

Ask a group of managers (or yourself) which category best fits them, and you get a valuable guide to the prevailing mind-set. At one electrical engineering conglomerate, the divisional managing directors opted overwhelmingly for the fifth category. Undoubtedly, the management of change must have high priority in a world of fluctuating markets, rapid technological developments and challenging competition. Significantly, this group was famed for its culture of tight control – so the vote was an encouraging sign of cultural progress.

But anybody in a management position who aspires to be more than an administrator (no. 4) can't function along only one of these dimensions. You may be predominantly a people person – indeed, leadership hinges on personal relationships. But if leaders, however able at managing and developing their human resources, take their eyes off the future, they will fail. Anyway, how can you develop people unless you know what future you're developing them to face?

Similarly, a leader who hasn't mastered the technology or mentally seized the technological opportunities will fail the organization. So will somebody who doesn't ensure that the ship is tightly run – that is, the organization's procedures, processes and controls are simple and flexible, but highly effective. As for change, any organization that isn't continuously mutating will never match the demands of a changing environment – or function well on the other four counts.

The many-faceted nature of leadership applies at all levels and is indispensable to the effective operation of true teams: and a team leadership culture in turn is indispensable in meeting today's challenges.

Meredith Belbin's classification of team roles has stood the test of time – a long time. It includes seven roles, not one of which is clearly that of leader. They are coordinator, critic, ideas person, implementer, external contact, inspector and team-builder. The leader has to play each of these roles at different times, some in combination. Also, leaders must ensure that no role is unfilled. Each function must be somebody's responsibility – the team will not achieve peak performance if any of these roles is neglected or missing altogether.

It remains true that the quality and performance of the ultimate leader will have a disproportionate impact on any team and any organization. But so will the conduct of corporate leadership. Major European offshoots like Digital are easily infected by a corporate version of chief executive disease: parent company disease. The results are the same: power gravitates to, and is monopolized by, the centre.

Parent company disease has five key symptoms. The infected top management:

1 Can do no wrong.

2 Refuses to concede any mistake.

3 Makes every decision – often in ignorance.

4 Seeks personal publicity.

5 Monopolizes power – often undermining overseas managers.

All five behaviours are inimical to successful leadership of talented management. The best leaders now act as a dynamic, but not omnipotent, part of a brilliant, decisive, interlocking group of people – at home or abroad. It's obvious that no chief executive can truly cope single-handed with the increasing complexity, not just of products and processes, but of management itself. The difficulties of pan-European management cited by Digital's Robert Palmer are an example.

Digital is far from alone in removing responsibilities from national companies and seeking to enjoy the benefits of operating on a pan-European scale. At Pilkington, for example, the European headquarters was established in Brussels, while operational control of businesses like automotive glass and building products was centred at the respective main plants. The aim is to enjoy the benefits of both centralization and decentralization – without which it is impossible to make business sense of the new Europe.

By taking pan-European decisions like Pilkington's, and then leaving the responsible leaders to lead, head office justifes its existence and adds optimum value to its subsidiaries. In many companies, however, the progress of parent company disease steadily reduces the central contribution to breakeven point (where the dominant management isn't subtracting any value, but isn't adding any, either) and then to negative. In fact, there's no sensible alternative to devolving decision-making to local levels and allowing managers at those levels more freedom. The principles that should then guide the liberated managers are perfectly clear:

1 Satisfy the customers.

2 Focus on leadership.

3 Create sustainable growth.

4 Increase efficiency.

5 Optimize management systems and processes.

6 Communicate more, and more efficiently.

By no coincidence, that is the essence of Vincenzo Damiani's Agenda for Digital Europe. It bears no resemblance at all to Digital's previous conduct. Take the first point. As Palmer says, it 'failed to anticipate' the sweeping changes in the IT market. 'Then, once we saw the changes, we failed to adapt to them. Instead we gave our customers a lecture, told them what they said they wanted to buy wasn't appropriate.' The internal order-and-obey leadership culture was translated into the external market – and the customers voted with their feet.

The faults could not have survived exposure to those who were close to the market changes and to the customers, and who knew full well that the strategy had become wildly inappropriate. In the standard leadership culture, a one-way Iron Curtain separates HQ from the front line – allowing orders to descend, but letting nothing come back up. The ability to crash through the barrier depends on (1) encouraging teamwork, (2) building subordinate leaders and (3) practising genuine empowerment.

Those are three key features of the human assets approach, which the Bain authors, Farkas and de Backer, found to be the most popular style of leadership: 'Roughly 30 percent of the CEOs use it. It means designing powerful training systems and coherent programmes for measuring performance. It means monitoring relationships between people. It means explicitly teaching employees desired values and behaviours.' In this style of leadership culture, people are empowered to act as this ideal CEO would act himself; then they are rewarded for the results.

That ideal is far removed from the symptoms of chief executive and parent company disease, and equally remote from the principles of the traditional hierarchical pyramid. Today's urgent cultural necessity is to slice the sharp peak off the organization and transform the static pyramid into a dynamic source of productive change – led by commanders who see their cultural role, not as sustaining supremacy, but as leader of many leaders.

The division at Daimler

At almost any time in the last four decades, the idea of Daimler-Benz reporting a loss, let alone the largest in German history, would have been laughable, unthinkable. But in 1995 the unthinkable had to be thought. Daimler lost $3·84 billion and, for the first time in 45 years, paid no dividend. No other event could have dramatized more strikingly the way in which Europe's business world has changed – or shown more starkly how far its great companies must travel to catch up with the management revolution.

No company symbolizes the enduring industrial might of Germany more than Daimler-Benz. Twice in recent years the giant has embarked on radical programmes designed to break with an enormously successful but narrowly-based past, and to forge a corporation that could strike out boldly into the new century. The radical strategies were not mutually exclusive, but pointed in different directions: the first towards diverse conglomeration, the second towards intensified exploitation of the core market – the car.

The debate was settled by Daimler's diversified disasters. They included the destruction of AEG, dissolved in early 1995 after a futile attempt to restore the 112-year-old electrical company to prosperity. The collapse of its investment in Fokker compounded the traumas of Daimler's own DASA aviation subsidiary, ordered to slash its workforce by 56,000 in four years. The grand, high-flying strategy of becoming an 'integrated technology concern' departed, along with its architect, chief executive Edzard Reuter. The truck business was losing money in 1996, too – and only the Mercedes cars reflected the once-shining image.

That image sustained the company's ability to charge near-exorbitant prices for cars bought by the well-heeled executive motorist. This marketing stance has brought rich prestige to the Mercedes marque and rich profits to its parent. But all that is about to be put at hazard. The gamble is without precedent in the motor industry, perhaps in any industry. The car world's great specialist is to become a broadly-based manufacturer, competing in every segment, from top to bottom.

Here the marque faces a double and enormous challenge: first, in marketing. The marketers can take comfort from the earlier remarkable achievement with the C Class cars. These took the brand down-market and down-price into BMW's heartland. Many observers doubted that Mercedes could transfer its image without tarnishing the glow. They were wrong. In 1995, Mercedes sold 314,000 C Class cars, against 200,000 of the E Class (its former staple) and only 63,000 of the exclusive S Class. The new marketing challenge, however, far outstrips the old.

By the year 2000, on present plans, two-fifths of output will consist of brand-new roadsters, minivans, city cars, sport utilities and SMART minis (made with help from the Swatch watch company). The plans take the Mercedes brand into new areas of mass marketing and into zones where the competition, far from consisting of only a handful of rivals, takes in every car company in the world. That raises the second and even more onerous part of the challenge – for some of those rivals, the Japanese, are far more efficient producers.

The German company achieves its high standards of quality and engineering at greater cost than its Japanese rivals. It operates with one hand tied behind its back, because the ideas and ideals of collaborative working have penetrated Stuttgart so belatedly. Older-fashioned working and management methods have been cushioned by that ability to charge super-premium prices. And while the marketing logic of broadening the range is clear ('We want to appeal to a lot of people who don't drive a Mercedes now,' says a director), the production logic is also inescapable.

These new people won't overpay for the Mercedes cachet. The consequent need to reduce costs means that design for manufacture, production speeds, productivity and built-in quality must go far beyond present standards. That can't be achieved without updating methods and manufacturing philosophy. To broaden successfully into a full-line manufacturer, the car division requires a revolutionary management that will break with the worst of the old days and embrace the best of the new.

None of this necessity, of course, is lost on Jürgen Schrempp, the man chosen by Deutsche Bank (which holds 24 percent of Daimler) to succeed Reuter and clear up the group's financial problems. Schrempp's campaign to reform Daimler has included the fusion of top management with that of Mercedes, forced through at a price: the loss of the car company's chief executive, Helmut Werner. The fusion was logical, given the end of diversification, but the old-fashioned power struggle between the two men raised unhappy questions. Could Mercedes' grand strategy succeed without its prime architect?

The larger question, though, is whether a new Mercedes will emerge to carry the strategy to fruition. The new man, Schrempp, plainly appreciated that the old way no longer sufficed. While claiming that the company 'was making good headway' on its journey from record losses to respectable profitability, he promised 'further tough decisions' and affirmed that organizational and cultural change would continue. The 'tough decisions' include closures or disposals – with the aero-engine and regional aircraft businesses seen as prime candidates for the chop. But what about those 'cultural changes'?

The idea of Daimler-Benz even speculating about a need to change its culture, let alone trying to do so, would once have been as unthinkable as its losses. To change that culture radically and successfully, though, requires decisions much tougher than exiting from Dornier's regional aeroplanes. The need for radical cultural change, moreover, isn't only a question for Daimler, but for Germany as a whole. After all, three key German industries were involved in the group's 1995 debâcle – automotive, aerospace and electrical engineering.

Germany's industrial establishment has found it difficult to emulate the kind of corporate transformation that has been shown to be perfectly feasible elsewhere in Europe – and to a greater extent in the US. Yet in the world at large, far more managements have marched down the road to cultural change than have reached their destination. Daimler-Benz has an immense challenge and opportunity. What happens at Stuttgart will be a decisive engagement in the war for world markets.

From leanness to prowess

The call for cultural change is resounding among the bastions of big European business. But what kind of change? What kind of culture?

Companies like Daimler-Benz evolved a culture brilliantly suited to circumstances, common to most companies until the 1960s, that will never be seen again. Market shares used to vary little over time; competition was domestic and played largely by the rules. You made money by maximizing production runs to get the longest possible service from capital equipment and design expenditure. This meant extending product life spans and production technology to the limit.

Marketing was seen primarily as an exercise in distribution and selling – the latter to shift the product of those unceasing production lines, the former to move the products out of the plants, and turn them into cash, as rapidly as possible. Economies of scale, rather than economies of method, were the target of top managements. To obtain those economies, centralized control was essential. Individual businesses and brands existed mostly in name. The corporation itself was the real business, and it created a whole caste of managers who served only management itself.

In today's conditions, all that sounds like a remote dream, an improbable fantasy. The modern business, of any kind, has to cope with the following scenario:

1 Market shares are highly volatile: even when overall shares move slowly, segments within markets are now more important, and may fluctuate wildly.

2 Competition has become global, and may come from sources inside or outside the industry or the country – and from new players who break all the old rules.

3 Variety has totally altered the manufacturing game, replacing long runs and homogenous products with short runs, marked differentiation and briefer life cycles.

4 The technology of both product and process is changing rapidly and generating sudden and decisive shifts in competitive advantage.

5 Distribution has become a crucial component in the ultimate price to customers, whose changing demands are dominating production and altering the nature of selling.

6 Economies of method and exploitation of powerful 'brands' (for which read 'market recognition') are the joint keys to superior profitability.

Europe's boards of directors have been through some painful trial and error in their efforts to adjust their behaviour and their cultures to these six developments. Like many of its peers, Daimler-Benz has discovered the latest supposed magic: 'shareholder value', the financial talisman of the nineties. The received way to raise shareholder (i.e., stock market) value is to cut back on unprofitable and superfluous businesses and people and to insist on higher financial performance. Thus, Jürgen Schrempp began on the road to reform at Daimler-Benz by cutting down the business units from 35 to 25, demanding a 12 percent return on capital from each – and removing 40,000 jobs in 20 months.

But focusing on shareholder value is not a strategy and begs more questions than it answers. The approach is just another phase in a process which Richard T. Pascale calls the 'ebbs, flows and residual impact of business fads'. The ebbs and flows have been more like a tidal wave from the mid-seventies to the present day. Pascale has counted two dozen 'fads' in this period, ranging from diversification to downsizing. The former has now gone into reverse as companies (see Daimler) concentrate on 'core businesses' and sell off their diversified interests.

Downsizing – the drive to become 'leaner and fitter' – has also come into heavy question, especially in the US. Critics point out that leanness takes precedence in the pairing: surplus factories are shut, blue-collar and white-collar employees are dismissed, businesses are sold, and products are delisted. After the initial heavy costs of 'rationalization' have been absorbed, however, fitness is supposed to follow automatically. Even if the company is only producing the same output, fewer assets and people are being employed. Productivity and profitability should soar accordingly.

So, in theory, should shareholder value. But reality and theory diverge. Many downsizing managements call to mind the old-time physicians who drew blood from their patients, thus weakening their resistance, observed the deterioration and prescribed more of the same – until the patient died. In the car industry, as Alex Taylor III pointed out in *Fortune*, 'while *productivity* – the number of cars produced per worker – will improve, *efficiency* – the number of worker hours required per car – will not.'

In other words, companies tackle the symptom (low productivity), but not the cause of their problems, which is inferior competitive prowess. Turning relative weakness into competitive superiority cannot be achieved by the downsizing cutbacks which still disfigure the strategies of Europe's corporate leaders. As Michael Hammer, Dr Re-engineering himself, has admitted, 'The real point is longer-term growth on the revenue side. It's not so much getting rid of people. It's getting more out of people.'

You can't enhance the performance of axed employees. Hammer told the *Wall Street Journal* that, 'reflecting my engineering background', he had been 'insufficiently appreciative of the human dimension. I've learned that's critical.' How could anyone, even an engineer, ever have thought otherwise? Progressive deployment of people, from managers to shop-floor and counter, to optimize the present and build for the future is the only route to sustained organic growth.

The human dimension demands, as at Daimler-Benz, a radically renewed company. Top managers mostly accept the need for renewal. They are understandably frustrated by the difficulties and disappointments of getting individuals lower down to behave in the ways demanded by the organizational purposes. But the obstacles too often stem from top management's own failures to act.

The questions below are a pertinent test. They come from a checklist of the best practices of 121 winning companies, compiled by Britain's Department of Trade and Industry. The longest list of items referred to unlocking the potential of the human dimension through 'creating a culture in which employees are genuinely empowered and focused on the customer; investing in people through good communications, learning and training (the Holy Trinity again); and flattening and inverting the organizational pyramid.' That raises key questions like . . .

1 Do you empower all employees by creating individual ownership and focus on customers?

2 Do you simplify internal systems wherever possible?

3 Do you clearly communicate company performance?

4 Do you encourage a team approach?

5 Do you train at all levels?

You can ask the right questions, but getting the right answers is quite another matter. Ingersoll Engineers quizzed senior executives of 325 major British firms in 1996 to discover how they rated their own performance.[7] They thought themselves most effective on distribution, financial management and manufacturing processes, notably less effective at sales and marketing, worse and worse at everything else. Manufacturing technology was an area of particularly serious self-confessed lag. But equally lagging, and contributing to all the other defects, were training and people development.

Where the human dimension is mismanaged, nobody can be surprised to find disenchantment running right through the company. Ask middle managers to rate their companies and themselves on criteria like integrity or teambuilding and – in my experience – they almost always score themselves higher than the organization. It's not that these managers have conceited views of their own performance. They always agree that they have room for improvement on the criteria that measure personal effectiveness.

Their lower rating for the organization, however, plainly indicates that the culture is getting in the way of the very performance which top management wants to encourage. Before downsizing came along, the four leading 'fads', as identified by Pascale, were all concerned with the human dimension:

1 Continuous improvement/learning organization.
2 Empowerment.
3 'Workout'.
4 Visioning.

But are these truly 'fads'? Since every operation and function can always be profitably improved, and people enjoy being involved in the improvement, doing so continuously must surely be part of any progressive culture. Equally, since people know more about their work than anybody else, and since only they can show initiative, their empowerment to take decisions and actions on their own is wholly logical. 'Workout' refers to a practice, instituted at General Electric in the US, in which co-workers gather to discuss, jointly, ways of improving their joint performance. Visioning only means the formation of corporate objectives which can be simply expressed and widely shared. Think of the alternatives, which are to have no objectives, or aims which are unclear and unshared, and the importance of visioning is obvious.

The four approaches provide key ingredients for the learning organization – or what a former Royal Dutch-Shell executive, Arie de Geus,[8] calls a 'living company'. He lists its priorities as follows:

1 *Sensitivity to the environment* – is the company able to learn and adapt?

2 *Cohesion and identity* – is the company innately able to build a community and a persona for itself?

3 *Tolerance and decentralization* – can the company build constructive relationships with other entities, within and outside itself?

4 *Conservative financing* – can the company govern its own growth and evolution effectively?

According to de Geus, these are the four key cultural characteristics that best describe the company which can 'survive for very long periods in a changing world, because its managers [are] good at the management of change'. That is not an optional extra. The thrust of Pascale's teaching is that 'the better you are at your game, the more vulnerable you are to abrupt change', but the more likely 'the organization' is to resist that change. The people who have 'muscle' (none more muscular than a German top management) are those most likely to be stuck in the past.

Writing in the *Business Strategy Review*,[9] Thomas S. Robertson notes that firms get locked into the mind-sets of their previous success. If this results in pursuing inappropriate strategies, or implementing appropriate ones badly, defeat must follow. Edzard Reuter's enormously expensive ventures in aerospace and electrical engineering amply demonstrated this painful truth at Daimler. No miracles had been accomplished by organizational or cultural change; but even if they had, fiascos like the Fokker bankruptcy would have pulled Daimler's figures down – and with them the morale of the workforce and the management.

That morale is the acid test of a corporate culture. Many companies are spending money and time to develop managers in the cause of making (or trying to make) the individual and organizational hearts beat as one. But most of those well-intentioned managements are wasting the time and the money. They want to create a people-based culture. They cannot do so while the top-down and middle-up views are not just incompatible, but inimical.

Probe beneath the divergences, and the cultural causes prove to be significant. On integrity, for example, managers at lower levels are made cynical by the organization's pressure for sales to be clinched at all costs. Their cynicism is intensified by the further pressure to boost quarterly results – especially for the last three months of the year. When you see unmade profits being stuffed into the accounts in the lead-up to Christmas, you are certainly witnessing a cultural phenomenon: but you are not over-impressed by the scrupulous honesty of the system.

I was fascinated to hear one senior executive say that 'what we need in this company are twelve Decembers a year'. He worked for a mighty multinational. Presumably his counterparts all over the world were busily engaged in the same creation of phantom profits: taking credit for licensing agreements that had been signed, but had not actually begun to operate, or getting suppliers to defer invoices, and so on.

Executives who dislike this disingenuous fiddling have a real point. Spurious short-term activity diverts attention from the sources of true profit and flies in the face of their own evident conviction that honesty is genuinely the best policy. Excellent management of the human dimension eliminates the negative and accentuates the positive. The twelve-Decembers culture does the reverse. The gulf between words and actions explains why miracles of cultural change happen rarely – and why, in many companies, nothing happens at all.

A company's problems can be divided into two varieties: the things that were not done (at Daimler, matching the best in Japan) and those that were (the awful diversifying). The first set spring from lack of creative responsiveness, the second from imperfect mechanisms for making decisions. Mercedes needed both genres of error to persist in entrusting quality to inspectors, rather than to high-quality processes. It allegedly used more people to inspect than Toyota needed to make its Mercedes rival, the Lexus. The discrepancy was widely known inside the company – but for years nothing was done.

At another large firm, confronted with evidence of equally glaring problems, the answer from long-service executives was that 'we've heard all that before'. To that, there was only one possible reply. If that was so, why did the problems still persist? The grandmother of all cultural problems is to spur the organization into the actions it knows to be right: and which its people know to be right. Bright and creative people abound in most companies: they are seldom allowed to contribute their intelligence and creativity wherever it can be useful – which includes deciding where and how the business should be moving.

The awareness of culture's power as a lever to achieve superior prowess came across strongly from a series of 'Lessons from the CEO' which Price Waterhouse Management Consulting presented to the World Economic Forum at Davos in January 1997. Percy Barnevik, chairman of the electrical and engineering conglomerate ABB, said that 'you can build a lasting competitive edge through the excellence of your organizational structure', which he described as 'the most difficult competitive advantage to copy'.

From the other side of the Atlantic, Michael Dell talked of the management flexibility that enabled Dell Corporation to change strategies 'when things were not going right' in its PC business and of 'leadership that was strong enough to change things quickly'. He added an organizational lesson: 'Companies that learn to manage change are in the best position to continue to take the risks needed to stay out in front.' At Sky Chefs, Michael Z. Kay's 'core message' has the same combination of operational efficiency and culture:

1 Change culture and employee conduct by introducing new values plus high-stretch financial goals.
2 Create SWAT teams that are accountable for analysing and reconfiguring operations to yield dramatic transformations and economies.
3 Propagate the new values relentlessly and incorporate them into the accountability structure.

The management of culture looms as the radical challenge for Europe's businesses: in the words of Melvin R. Goode of Warner-Lambert, culture is 'a living thing that should animate the hearts and minds of workers . . . and give them a more productive and rational environment'. Developing cultural prowess does not happen overnight, though. Barnevik says that ABB 'is far from fully exploiting the advantages of its organizational structure' – and that is after nine years' hard work.

If the road is long, it is wise to start the journey at once. The risks run by cultural laggards are far too heavy. As de Geus says, 'in today's increasingly volatile business environment', most managers 'will find that their companies do not have the habits to accomplish what they hope to achieve'. Changing old habits comes hard to those who are wedded to their pride in the past and its structures. Rigid areas of control, internal veto powers, and squabbles over jurisdiction are inimical to New Century Management. Yet cultural change has long been resisted by the corporate psychologies of Europe. They are probably more dangerous to European business than the Japanese competition which they have done so much to encourage.

FOUR

Dividing to Rule

The boom of the breakaways

As the twentieth century closes, the magnetism of capitalism rich and triumphant has never been stronger. Allied with a restless search for achievement, the lure has generated an unprecedented and productive migration of people between companies. What, for example, do the following firms have in common, apart from some weird and wonderful names?

Tangram, Digital Equipment, GRiD Systems Corporation, Adobe Systems, Cauzin Systems, Apple, Metaphor Computer Systems, 3-Com Corporation, Acorn Computer, Data Point Corporation, Microsoft, SAP.

The easy guess for the common factor is information technology. But there's an odd man out. All save one of these companies are the 1988 American business residences of men who created the personal computer inside the Xerox Corporation. Most of this incomparable team left Xerox after it turned down their wonderful invention, maybe the most wonderful of the entire century. The oddball is SAP – German and nothing to do with Xerox: it broke away from IBM.

When their world-famous employer decided to transfer their project away from Stuttgart, a quartet of engineers quit to pursue their dream independently. They ended up in 1996 with the world's fifth largest software company, thanks to single-minded pursuit of what's become known as enterprise-wide computing. Using their expensive software, a company can bind together its key administrative and accounting functions on a common platform. SAP not only confronted US leaders like Oracle: it wrested market supremacy from their grasp.

The quartet – Dietmar Hopp, Hasson Plattner, Klaus Tschira and Hans-Werner Hector – acted no differently from the mostly American men behind the other high-tech names. Several of these aces also co-founded their own companies. In fast-moving technologies, breakaways led by brilliant people seeking to exploit their brilliance under their own control are hardly surprising. Europe thus has plenty of other high-flying names in software, like Black Sun Interactive, Business Objects, MAID, Oxford Molecular and Baan (a rising competitor to SAP). But they don't add up to a European Silicon Valley.

That phenomenon was described by one venture capitalist as 'a technology crucible. Every engineer in the valley has at the back of his mind that if he comes up with an interesting product, he can start a company.' His remark was quoted in a *Financial Times* article by Geoffrey Owen and Louise Kehoe, which observed that 'the hyper-competitive atmosphere of Silicon Valley, with its adaptable giants, cheeky spin-offs and ambitious start-ups, is an American asset which no other country has yet been able to match'.

With every further advance in the technology of the electronic age, the asset gap has become more significant. This is an economic race that Europe has lost in hardware – for ever. In specialized software, Europe is still in with a chance. Riding on its phenomenal success in America, SAP saw its market capitalization rise to nearly $8 billion in 1996 – turning all four founders into paper billionaires – as its R/3 software established clear market leadership. That market value, bizarrely enough, exceeded the capitalizations of Lufthansa and Volkswagen.

With enterprise-wide computing, the SAP quartet had followed the advice of one Xerox genius who ended up with Apple, Alan Kay. He once uttered an immortal line: 'The only way to predict the future is to invent it.' With rare exceptions like SAP, Europe has largely followed the pack, neither inventing the future nor predicting it. Insularity ruled. Electronics leaders like Philips and Siemens lagged in recruiting top technologists and managers from outside. Nor did they forge timely alliances with the American powers – rather than constantly reinvent the electronic wheel.

While there have been European breakaways from the giants *à la* SAP, very few were in mainstream hardware. The European opportunists sought rather to develop the best use of expensive new computers, tapping the new stream of income provided by customers wanting workable systems to run on the hardware. Even here, though, no European has rivalled H. Ross Perot's Electronic Data Systems in size, spread, sheer growth and wealth. Companies like Logica in Britain and Cap-Gemini in France have grown wonderfully well, but without emulating SAP's full transition to global corporation.

That took plenty of time. It was two decades before R/3 software, designed for client-servers rather than mainframes, produced an electrifying surge in revenues – from $532 million in 1992 to an estimated $2.7 billion for 1996. As the shares soared in step, every quarterly financial report was watched intently by Wall Street analysts looking for signs that this breakaway boom was losing momentum. The shares consequently became highly volatile. But the boom of Europe's biggest breakaway has continued in the place where it counts most: the market. In 1995, for example, turnover jumped by 47 percent, and profits rose in step.

In software, SAP counted among the established giants: it remains small compared to the American leaders who dominate the highways of computing in hardware and software. But the multiplying byways of computing still hold out the prospect of fast capital gains like SAP's. As *Business Week* noted, software start-ups can draw on Europe's scientific and mathematical skills and on an improved supply of money for investment. Above all, 'the emergence of networked computing and the rise of the Internet have caused a profound shift in the kinds of software that business customers demand and in the way these products are distributed'.

The four disgruntled software engineers who formed SAP will have many imitators. Europe's misfortune – or mistake – is that the breakaway boom in IT was immeasurably larger and more successful in the US. Yet there are other technologies and other businesses outside the heartlands of the electronics revolution: and here, too, the breakaways are booming. Many are flourishing by management methods that large, rigid corporations are trying hard, and with too much difficulty, to imitate.

Once again, the Americans have exploited the new technology of management more vigorously. But that technology is freely available to all. Europe contains plenty of examples to show that the breakaway triumph of SAP can be repeated by those with the wit and the will to succeed. Breakaways on their own, however, won't provide enough firepower for European retaliation in the high-tech wars. The great companies of Europe, with their deep reservoirs of technology, have a crucial role. They could yet be a richer source of new, internal enterprise than their American counterparts – if they can prove better at nurturing and nourishing breakaway cultures in-house.

Formula for freedom

The big corporation has the money and muscle to accomplish tasks that lie beyond the scope even of medium-sized firms. To that extent, the book of the breakaways is an indictment of the big company managements that failed to exploit the genius within their own empires. Probably every high-tech company in Europe has to some degree emulated the inventive success and commercial failure of the electronic era's mainspring of inspiration, the Palo Alto Research Center.

PARC was not a breakaway, nor a start-up in a garage, but a richly financed operation of a mighty multinational, Xerox Corp. No large established electronics manufacturer matched Xerox's serendipitous assembly of the multifold talents whose work underpinned all future development of the personal computer: and no start-up could have done so either. In a sense, Xerox did what European prime companies need to do: it mimicked the garage breakaways – creating a new lab in a research field where nobody had a presence.

Established companies mostly create their scientific and technological establishments round the needs of established product lines, rather than by invention of brave new worlds. Because it was doing something 'wrong' – investing billions in a blue-sky effort unrelated to existing business – Xerox did everything right, including the choice of Palo Alto, where West Coast mores nurtured an unbuttoned, unencumbered, loose management style.

The research, however, was focused tightly and with uncanny accuracy. In March 1970 (over a decade before the personal computer age started to realize the dream), Xerox CEO Peter McColough had unveiled a truly amazing vision before an audience of security analysts:[1]

> The basic purpose of Xerox Corporation is to find the best means to bring greater order and discipline to information . . . even a casual examination of Xerox reveals that we already have most of the raw materials of advanced architecture of information technology: computers, copiers, duplicators, microfilm, communications devices, education techniques, display and transmission systems, graphic and optic capabilities, heavy research and global scope.

Tragically, PARC's work on the advanced architecture of IT didn't create a business for Xerox, whose rigidly controlled businesses showed no interest in exploiting the lab's masterpieces of free-form invention.

Europe possessed all the same raw materials as Xerox. It failed even to form a compelling vision of what marvellous advances could be achieved by combining those ingredients – let alone make the advances. The vision isn't even half the battle. It's the visionary focus on clearly determined objectives that produces the decisive action.

A fascinating study by five McKinsey authors of 'fast-growth tigers'[2] rubs in this truth. It found 41 publicly listed companies (after screening 9,450) which, by 'focusing on one major line of business' had grown revenues and operating income by 20 percent annually, creating over 300,000 jobs and adding $110 million in market value. These tigers had followed 'new game' policies, providing radically different products and services, and reshaping the markets in which they operated. Such companies 'create new markets with few if any rivals, and are able to preserve their competitive advantages for long periods'.

New Century Management needs a guiding light, an understanding of the environment, a determination to stretch the bounds of the possible, always with practical intent and within practical boundaries. The vision must be brought down to earth, must be turned into a new reality. One of the McKinsey fast-growth examples was First Direct, the Midland Bank subsidiary. Its vision was to launch telephone banking in the UK, and the pioneers set about their task with enormous determination and down-to-earth, practical commitment. The marketing impact was so powerful that one direct mail campaign achieved a 25 percent response rate, against a typical 1 or 2 percent.

The McKinsey mavericks have all created contrarian cultures. For example, they don't prioritize: they do 'all the right things right'. The conventional wisdom holds that you should concentrate on 'key success factors'. That would be fine in a stable, linear system. But business systems are composed of unstable 'feedback loops': malfunction in any one factor will adversely affect all others.

The McKinsey authors express this concept well: 'Trying to beat a competitor that exploits four growth accelerators by focusing on two will probably produce not half the results, but none at all.' To innovate, managers thus need a climate free of the corpocratic constraints which dampen endeavour. Emulate the breakaway spirit within the corporate culture, and you can have your cake and eat it, too – high creativity coupled with driving commercialism; low-cost and defect-free manufacture combined with rapid spawning of new products; freedom of action with disciplined pursuit of objectives.

More, the successes show that the *combination* of these contrasts is the crucial factor. The contrasts may sound paradoxical, but that's no weakness. The accountancy giant Price Waterhouse conducted interviews with 200 executives, seeking to discover 'how high-performance companies manage chaos, complexity and contradiction to achieve superior results'.[3] The research found no fewer than five 'key paradoxes':

- Positive change requires significant stability.
- To build an enterprise, focus on the individual.
- Focus directly on culture, indirectly.
- True empowerment requires forceful leadership.
- To build, you must tear down.

The weight of theory is leaning towards this mode of management and away from the bureaucratic paradise of the culture of control. Elements of the paradoxical culture are creeping into many companies. Few, however, would go so far as an organization called St Luke's:

1 Everybody, from the managing director to the receptionist, is an equal owner of the business.
2 Juniors are encouraged to criticize their seniors openly.
3 Upward appraisal and downward appraisal co-exist.
4 People partly determine their own rewards.
5 Nobody has an office to themselves.
6 The business is organized by customer, rather than by function or department.

Managers in more orthodox companies have usually discounted the relevance of the 'unbuttoned, unencumbered, loose management style' referred to above and commonly found in Silicon Valley. It is is perfectly acceptable in people who are hired for their creativity: St Luke's is a London advertising agency, a 45-strong breakaway from the huge Omnicom. Indeed, its set-up can be seen as a brilliant piece of branding: the agency's original parent, the New York advertisers Chiat/Day, used similar approaches (wacky office design, no personal offices and a fashionable emphasis on 'virtuality') as a means of differentiation.

It is true that no major corporation has all six of the St Luke's features. But there are no personal offices at Honda in Japan, either. The admirable John Lewis department stores in Britain have been owned by an employee partnership for decades. Upward appraisal is spreading, too, even in Europe, even among corporations that were once infamous for their bureaucracy. While few employees influence their own pay directly, linking rewards to results has become widespread at all levels of the firm.

The most striking conversion of the giants, though, is the move towards organizing round the customer. This represents a logical progression from the old-fashioned functional organization via today's dominant mode of organizing by product. As conventional a company as IBM has rebuilt its marketing structure round customer groups. The flatness of the St Luke's structure is being ever more widely adopted – and old corpocratic rules of thumb, like 'never have more than seven people reporting to one manager', were thrown out of the window long ago.

The culture of loose control can be wondrously effective. But can it be applied by Europeans in the way that won the commanding electronic heights for the US? The answer must surely be yes. Silicon Valley is not destined to be the only fount of technology and enterprise. What has been described as its 'rich infrastructure of electronics engineers, subcontractors, venture capitalists, public relations advisers, headhunters and lawyers' can be imitated anywhere – along with its emphasis on 'fun'.

Today, even sober-sided businesses are advised to make it 'fun' to work for them. The fun formula fits neatly with the St Luke's culture and Price Waterhouse's five key paradoxes. Above all, it is a Formula for Freedom:

1 *Celebrate success*. Use regular and irregular small parties, plus the occasional big bash, to boost morale, create acquaintances, and breed community and communication.

2 *Encourage individual initiative*. Everybody is potentially creative. Their potential can't be exploited if ideas must struggle through bureaucratic processes, internal memoranda and repeated meetings. Talented people working independently are strengths, not nuisances, if their talent is allowed expression.

3 *Apply a firm hand with a light touch*. This balancing act is the hardest part of the formula: staying very close, but keeping your distance. One dominant figure in a software house did that literally. He moved his base from Britain to the Bahamas, applying the firm hand electronically from thousands of miles away.

4 *Create a unique and powerful corporate culture*. That provides the essential environment for points 2 and 3. Individuals aim themselves in the direction encouraged by the culture. The cultural norms

provide a means of control without whips. And the celebrations (point 1) help strengthen and develop the culture.

5 *Achieve real, continuous two-way communication.* Meetings of all employees are one effective method, but each culture develops its own ways of achieving mutual understanding. Every piece of paper is a potential means of communication. The Franco-Italian-British SGS-THOMSON neatly gives everybody the same desk diary, with a suitable message on every page.

6 *Manage for the long term.* An innovative company has to understand that success doesn't always come overnight, and that the passage of some new product ideas to market takes years, not months.

7 *Accept the permanence of impermanence.* This paradox is based on the hard fact that staff, product strengths and markets alike can vanish overnight. Even if a high-tech venture has come to dominate its sector, some new entrant may break through.

In a world of burgeoning, vital technologies and ideas, monopoly of thought can never be achieved. The newcomers keep on coming – and coming on strong. The large corporation's overall stability offers a real advantage in such an unstable environment: but only if it can master the power of the Formula for Freedom. Judging by the past record, it is hard to have unbounded faith in Europe's ability to make the formula work: too few high-tech opportunities have been taken – or taken far enough.

It is easier to see the warning signs of further deterioration: 'slower employment growth, a decline in venture capital financing, slowing growth in pre-competitive research and development spending and a shortage of skilled workers'.

These 'warning signs' were reported by Louise Kehoe in the *Financial Times* in 1992. They referred, though, not to Europe (where they currently exist), but to Silicon Valley. The Stanford Research Institute survey she was quoting has proved far too gloomy. But if the Valley must from time to time look to its laurels, Europe by comparison has too few to view. Its major economies lack, in the report's words, 'a dynamic community that supports technology enterprises and retains value-added manufacturing, employment and wealth'.

So long as a cluster of like-minded firms gets together within easy reach of a first-rate academic campus, the Technopolis can expand and flourish. Indeed, when Apple wanted to locate a new plant in Europe, a consultant wisely advised his clients to follow this prescription. The company instead expanded at the existing site in Cork, close neither to other high-tech businesses nor to academics. The choice was much the cheaper, but similar decisions by indigenous Europeans explain why Europe's Technopolis has failed to compete with the Valley.

That is not the end of the story. The Global Technopolis is developing fast. Though America's valleys (of which there are several) will remain its heartland, they won't be all-American territory in any sense. The Japanese and other Asians have moved into the valleys in force, and have spread into Europe's. The American electronics companies have migrated too. The technology is global, and can't be kept exclusive.

The management style of the electronic pioneers – their receptiveness to new ideas, jaunty conviction that brains beat size, hatred of hierarchy and formality, and reliance on the independent spirit of man – can also be copied. But its imitations outside the US valleys are too few, too far between and too underpowered. That's a serious error. In any business, in any sector, today's opportunities are greatest for managements and managers who accept that the breakaway culture, just like a PC or even a microprocessor, can be cloned; and who, knowing that, dare apply the Formula for Freedom to their own corporations.

The Adidas mind-set

Powerful obstacles – literally powerful – lie in the way of creating a breakaway culture and applying the Formula for Freedom in Europe's major corporations (and in many middling and minor ones). The most common cause of failure to achieve genuine, long-lasting, total organizational change is the issue of power. The overlords, even though they promote change for others, won't change their own domineering behaviour, the overbearing ways in which they work, the self-made agendas on which their minds are set, and the culture which they love to dominate.

After all, such behaviour is only what is expected of the corporate leader. Consider the case of Adidas. Two years ago, Robert Louis-Dreyfus became the sporting goods' company's chairman and chief executive after lack of leadership had led to 'serious financial difficulties'. The *Financial Times* went on to say that by 'shifting its focus from manufacturing to marketing, he has enabled Adidas . . . to compete once again . . .' After an early decision to move manufacturing out of Germany, Louis-Dreyfus slashed fixed costs 'to the bone' and freed management to concentrate on repositioning the brand.

Although Louis-Dreyfus 'tries to play down his own role' ('There were a lot of good people in the company in the wrong positions'), that cuts no ice with the paper. It is his 'medicine' that 'has put Adidas on a solid financial footing after several years of losses'. The emphasis on the chief executive's all-powerful contribution is just as apparent in the same paper's account of Georges Blum in his role as chief executive of Swiss Bank Corporation.

He came armed with a reputation as 'the tough guy that SBC sent in to extricate it from difficult lending situations'. By the end of 1963 Blum had 'restructured SBC's top management'. He also established 'clear lines of responsibility' for the business, saying that 'The trouble with matrix structures is that too many people take credit for successes, but no one takes the blame for failure.' The whiff of autocracy is not misleading. While 'he graciously acknowledged' criticisms, Blum simply 'carried on with his programme to improve SBC'.

Both cases are highly typical of an expected and prevailing management mode. The nature of this Adidas mind-set can be understood from these questions. Answer Agree or Disagree:

1 Strong personal leadership from the top is essential.
2 The way 'we do things round here' is superior to that of other companies.
3 'Downsizing' – reducing the labour force and other costs decisively – is a regrettable but necessary top management task.
4 The role of subordinate managers, and all those beneath them, is to execute the policies decided by the leadership.
5 Reward should be related to individual status, with the highest rewards going to the highest positions.

Broadly described, a set of Agree answers marks out managers as rightist candidates rather than social democrats. The mind-set is marked by traditionalism, authoritarianism and faith in one-person leadership. The Adidas and SBC cases enshrine a belief that in business *successful* dictatorship is by definition benevolent: that the end generally justifies the means. The obvious difficulty is that dictatorship cannot coexist with the genuinely devolved and democratic corporate culture which is the modern, 'leftist' management ideal.

Yet praise for the 25 'best managers' picked out by *Business Week* for its first issue of 1996 also reflects the rightist mind-set. The non-Americans include Bernd Pischetsrieder, 'who drove BMW into the big leagues as a

million-unit-a-year producer'; Tadasgi Sekizawa of Fujitsu, who 'restructured ingrown business practices and dumped nationalistic policies';
SKB's Jan Leschly, who 'spent 1995 digesting $5 billion' of buys in man-
aged care and non-prescription drugs; and Thomson Multimedia's Alain
Prestat, who 'provided the amazing $599 12-inch dish and set-top box
that made direct satellite broadcast one of the biggest hits of 1995'.

Note the assumption that these leaders were the prime, if not the
sole authors of the corporate achievements. They 'drove', they 'restructured', they 'provided'. But every manager knows that, even in autocratic
corporations, big business reality doesn't fit this theory. Fujitsu's Japan
is the temple of consensus management; in BMW's Germany leaders are
first among equals. Anywhere, any success has many authors. If these
men hadn't filled their chairs, somebody else would have occupied the
seats. Perhaps the alternatives would have done worse, perhaps better;
quite possibly, their strategies and implementations would have been
much the same.

Chief executives are inevitably affected by their own publicity, however they actually manage their companies and colleagues (maybe in a
more open and collegiate style than the quotations suggest). Their actions
often reflect the assumption behind the Adidas mind-set: that the individual, single-handed, dynamic leader dictates the course and consequences of the business plan. While the presumed Adidas saviour
specifically denies this, his words ('There were a lot of good people in
the company') are the hero's standard form of self-deprecation.

The rightist mind-set inevitably has rightist outcomes. For example,
the controlling shareholder and chairman of a big American services
company owned a small German subsidiary. For three years an able
managing director struggled to make it viable on a shoestring, with little
assistance from head office. The man was brought back to head office to
fill an important post. His number two was persuaded to accept the
Frankfurt job, although he would be left with fewer staff and no cover
for the many essential roles uniquely filled by his predecessor. It was
made clear that, for him and the business, it was a matter of sink or
swim. But the treatment of the German subsidiary betrayed no awareness
that the head office, in particular the chief executive, had any responsibility for the success or failure of the man out on that European limb. He
was not part of the head office team, nor they of his. If he succeeded,
on criteria which they laid down, he would join the heroic ranks. If he
failed, so would the subsidiary and those who worked for it.

That's the law of the rightist jungle: however hard and well individual managers work, their work may be vitiated, and their jobs ripped away, for reasons wholly outside their control. The leftist devolution which is the key to wide mobilization of talent revolves round the sharing of power. Today's managements are easily powerful enough to corrupt the competitive ability of their corporations. They also have enough power to strip away their own monopoly of authority. They can use that power, if they choose, to build a new kind of company with a different mind-set.

Taking it from the top

The rightist Adidas mind-set has a total contrast. 'Over the past fifteen years, as organizations have grown more interested in encouraging high-quality teamwork, many . . . are making a significant shift at their most senior levels . . . these organizations are moving away from the "great individual" model of leadership, and moving toward being led by a team of executives instead . . . Even when an executive team is not formalized . . . it is less frequent that the individual sitting at the top of the pyramid is the sole leader.'[4]

The author, Charles Kiefer of Innovation Associates in Framingham, Massachusetts, writes that executive team leadership by a group of people differs hugely from the rightist pattern, featuring:

1 Shared responsibilities and clear accountabilities.

2 Formation of strategy in concert.

3 Decision-making by consensus.

4 Collective assumption of the roles performed by the chief operating officer.

5 Seeking ways of 'realizing all the talent and intelligence of the most senior people.'

These are clearly leftist ideas. Instead of the authoritarian, traditional, hero-worshipping pattern, leftists believe that a group sharing many minds is intrinsically superior to one-person leadership, not least because the collective mind will be more open to changes that overturn the established ways of operation. Kiefer correctly observes that 'Leaders and managers, reconceiving their own job as setting forth broad visions and strategies, now grant subordinates much more power to plan and implement.' But that still leaves the leaders as prime movers: 'In any organization led by influence, people are moved and convinced when they see a group of people at the top truly sharing a vision and strategy and modelling it in their behaviour.' When people don't see this collectivism in action, 'their confidence and commitment will be less'.

Logic and experience alike suggest that (a) the lower the confidence and commitment levels, the worse the results; and (b) the largest, most bureaucratic companies find it hardest to achieve collectivism in action. The figures reported by the world's largest 500 companies, as listed by *Fortune* in 1995, confirm these expectations. All are huge businesses; but the highest returns on revenues and assets are recorded by companies whose average position is significantly below the midpoint of the size league.

The leaders in financial effectiveness, moreover, include companies like Intel, Marks & Spencer, Johnson & Johnson, Volvo and Hewlett-Packard which are all known for their management openness as much as their muscle. The liberal, democratic, open management theory of the 'learning organization', which deliberately evolves, mutates and improves, is based on two key practical propositions: that the whole is greater than its parts, and that an excellent team, as it evolves and learns, raises the performance, capabilities and contribution of its members.

Division into teams, many of them temporary, is a matter of logical necessity in modern business. 'Tough' business leaders are adopting the practice for thoroughly practical reasons – not because it simply works better, but because, without it, the company may not work at all. Teams cannot work effectively, however, without eradicating the old rightist culture. For that purpose, a new style of corporate leadership may well be needed – a team style, even a collective chief executive. The Swiss presidency provides a model: just as that rotates between the cantons, so the leadership of the executive group can rotate.

The object is to achieve real synergy and total understanding between corporate components whose interactions are becoming more and more decisive. The top-down culture of control has to be inverted. Managers of the new school have invented a graphic representation of the change. They draw the organizational pyramids upside down. In the new order (an ideal, it has to be said, rather than a reality), the customers are on top, and the inverted pyramid of customer-focused levels balances on senior management – the servant rather than the master.

The ideal is becoming real in one key respect. In this supporting role as servants of the organization, managers can no longer, as they love to do, 'defend their turf' and operate only on that patch of ground. They represent their special concerns, of course, but they also look across the boundaries to seek the best results for the totality of the business. Value statements act as the cement for this style – if, that is, top management genuinely does have 'respect for individuals', is really 'dedicated to helping customers', and truly adheres to 'the highest standards of integrity, innovation, and teamwork'.

Such fine words are typical of the genre: the generally brief value statements produced, often after prolonged gestation worthy of a three-volume novel, by companies all over the world. But the vision will not be shared throughout the organization unless the fine words are turned into good deeds – and rapidly. As one senior executive observes, 'Much of the world saw the problems that have afflicted some . . . big companies for as long as 15 years.' The managers of those companies didn't see – and this blindness is the greatest danger of the Adidas mind-set.

Rightist managements equate the exercise of leadership with preserving the *status quo*, and are therefore blind to anything that threatens the old order. That applies to organizational change, where the adverse consequences of conservative obstruction may be suspected, but are hard to prove. In technology, however, the results of *status quo* management are not only invariably disastrous, but easy to identify – and very common.

For example, other tyre companies resisted beyond the point of no return the new radial technology introduced by Michelin – one of Europe's few great post-war innovations. The abject surrender of Fort Dunlop, once a power centre of European industry, to the Japanese group Sumitomo was only one result of this resistance. A large part of the case for leftist collectivism is that leftists will readily embrace new ideas. Their instinct is to oppose the powerful forces inside companies which resist new technology as they resist anything which threatens to upset the old order.

What are those 'forces'? They are human beings, professional managers. They have plenty of options – nothing, not even their genes, compels them to resist new ideas. Yet as a class, these professionals find managing innovation particularly difficult. That is because innovation manifestly requires leftist approaches, which puts the typical rightist organization in real difficulties.

Rightists do have an innovatory role. Subjecting technology to market disciplines, and to managerial expertise, is indispensable. A prime role of management is to finance, enable and ensure technological leadership: to see that, wherever the company chooses to compete, its products and processes equal or surpass the competition, both in satisfying the market and in timeliness. The rightists use their power and know-how to provide a disciplined framework within which the leftist innovators and iconoclasts can give freely of their brilliance.

The sustained success of these disrespectful people, however, may well depend on the way in which they are encouraged and allowed to turn dissent into constructive proposals and actions. Giving genius its head is a profound management test – as ICI discovered with Sir James Black. When his management would not finance research into inhibitors of stomach acid, that brilliant British pharmacologist left for the company that became SmithKline Beecham. There he proceeded to discover the anti-ulcer Tagamet, the first billion-dollar drug.

At all times, though, the strong leadership beloved by the rightists will be required to maintain the innovatory momentum. Black's new American management, once it became convinced that Tagamet was a potential big winner, poured in resources at high speed and considerable risk to drive the product to early success. This leadership role may seem to raise a paradox, but in fact it highlights a key principle of devolved and democratic management. Left-right synergy, rather than conflict, is the key to success.

Take the Adidas and Swiss Bank Corporation cases discussed in the previous section. If Robert Louis-Dreyfus hadn't stepped in, would anybody else have initiated action to reduce the cost base, concentrate Adidas on delivering 'the best sports brand for athletes', raise the technology and widen the global market reach? Similarly, only somebody in Georges Blum's pole position at SBC could have insisted that a loosely connected bunch of divisional barons be brought together into a coherent and competitive organization. In both cases the same question arises: will the rightist initiative have a leftist follow-through?

The third case makes the same point negatively. The position of that German subsidiary was certain to remain lonely and lowly unless the group chief executive decided to reshape its future within a properly conceived global strategy. That was another essential which awaited the starting push that can only come from the top. From that point on, however, results had to depend on how far the subsidiary management had the freedom, authority and resources to pursue its own destiny.

You can see the results of oppressive rightist control within European car companies. The talent lay ready, for certain, to reduce model development costs and lead-times to the Japanese standard. *Status quo* management accepted the four-to-six-year norm as conventional wisdom. There was no technical or economic justification – except that, on outdated accounting principles, the longer basic models and engines ran, the more money you seemed to make. The fact that competitive power was steadily eroded carried no weight. It literally wasn't taken into account.

Who is to blame? The technologists don't call these shots. That privilege is reserved for top management. 'Strategy' is determined by the corporate strategists, which doesn't mean the staff experts (a now diminished breed) who do the strategic analysis and present the cases. The strategy that ultimately controls the pyramidic layers of management is that of the senior group. Only their strategy is free from checks and balances, whether or not it seems successful.

Failure is often allowed to run for an unconscionable time: Fort Dunlop didn't fall overnight. The common cause of major management calamities, in firms of any size, is the rightist concentration of strategic and operational power at the top in the hands of individuals who lack the will or ability to think leftwards and manage leftists. In seeking today's and tomorrow's managers, these questions will rapidly sort out the rightist goats:

1 Have you kept abreast of the relevant technologies, and do you understand them well enough to give technologists effective support and guidance?

2 Do you have experience and a current knowledge base in strategy?

3 Do you maintain high personal visibility inside the business and outside – where the customers are?

4 Have you devoted all the time required to refresh and expand your management knowledge?

5 Do you shun and suppress internal politics?

6 Do all your external involvements genuinely serve the vital business of the company?

7 Do your rewards reflect only achievement that relates directly to your efforts?

Armed with a sevenfold kit of Yes answers, those at the corporate centre can contribute a number of non-operational, but priceless elements to their devolved colleagues. The first is to set the overall 'strategy', intelligent and communicated, which covers broadly the choice of destination and the means of getting there. Within that general framework, the centre has specific roles:

1 It sets minimum and high standards.

2 It represents investors in seeing that each business is earning excellent returns on their money – and will continue to do so into the foreseeable future.

3 It facilitates ambitious plans with money, advice and connections (including interconnections with other group businesses).

4 It appoints excellent top managers, and insists that they recruit excellently.

5 It looks after relations with outside agencies, including governments and other corporations, which need handling centrally.

The list could go on. It's demanding enough to provide plenty of occupation for men at the top – for which read 'the topless top'. Once top people build their management merely on giving orders to their appointees, the game is over. The bureaucratic silt builds up again. The best people quit in hope of finding a better environment, and the personal initiative on which devolved corporate success depends dries up. That won't happen if the authority which rightists love is used to establish a leftist working philosophy.

The unprecedented volatility of today's markets demands freer-form, fluid management. That leftist requirement can be reconciled with the need for rightist discipline and concentration on achieving excellent business results. Established corporations with rigid traditions and set procedures are not, however, about to change their habits easily. MIT's Peter Senge[5] warns that you have to fight the entrenched, rightist forces 'preserving the *status quo*', and that when the enemy 'begins to espouse all the same goals, objectives, and ideals . . . it is easy for people to think that the work is over. In fact, it may just be beginning.' It's crucial to start, but equally vital never to stop.

The zip at Zeneca

A variety of the old maxim *de minimis non curat lex* (the law doesn't care about little matters) applies in huge companies. Corporations tend to lose interest in little businesses. The trouble is that a little business in corporate terms may be large by normal standards – like the American company Grow Group, for which ICI offered $290 million in May 1995. That was a mere 3 percent of the giant's market value. Yet the buy has high relevance – not to mention a certain piquancy.

Grow's business is in speciality chemicals (architectural paints and coatings) and is American. Such purchases in ICI's recent past have 'only created new management problems'. Those problems were invited by an acquisitions policy which 'increased the complexity of an already complicated and hard-to-manage portfolio of businesses'. The words are those of Geoffrey Owen and Trevor Harrison, explaining in the *Harvard Business Review*[6] why top management opted for demerger to lift these self-created burdens off its shoulders.

The consequent separation of ICI's mostly older, duller businesses from pharmaceuticals and the other, mostly sexier operations placed into Zeneca was an evident stock market success. Zeneca soared away to a market capitalization over double that of its erstwhile parent. Combined, the two halves have far outperformed any share rise that might have been expected from an intact ICI.

That raises some fascinating questions about mighty corporations. Sir Denys Henderson stepped down as chairman laden with plaudits for abandoning the task of making ICI worth as much as its parts. Demerger, to quote the *Harvard Business Review* article, results in (relatively speaking) 'simpler organization, narrower focus and more homogeneity'. But that's precisely what today's guru-blessed management is supposed to accomplish within an undivided mammoth.

Apart from offering investors the more glamorous business of drugs (and therefore attracting a price-earnings ratio twice that of ICI's), what did the demerged Zeneca accomplish that couldn't have been done inside the ICI whale? There was no excuse for the fact that in 1992 ICI's speciality chemical businesses, later to form part of Zeneca, earned a midget 2.8 percent on sales of £930 million. True, the market was in recession. But management consultants Kalchas, reported the *Sunday Telegraph*, asked some pertinent questions. In the words of partner Michael de Kare Silver:

> We asked them, is the market as a whole suffering, or is your performance particularly bad? We asked them whether they were right to sit and think: oh, well, there is nothing we can do, the market is down – or whether they were losing their way against competitors. We found out how competitors responded to challenges and what were their performance benchmarks and best practices.

The response of chief executive Rodney Brown was positive. With the consultants' help, costs, jobs and assets were cut across the division;

profits duly doubled. As Brown said, 'If you are spending 2X and your competitors are spending X on the same activities, you know you are going wrong somewhere.' The Kalchas benchmarks left 'no room for manoeuvre'. Not only could managers determine what they had to achieve, but their bosses could make very sure that it was achieved – Brown ended up with an organization that 'was not only cost-competitive, but still a market leader in various sectors'.

But, of course, it should always have been a cost-competitive leader. Look back at those pertinent questions asked by Kare Silver. Why weren't they posed before the old owners, ICI, left the field? What misfired?

Disproportion was a factor: the speciality chemicals business, with 'only' £930 million of sales, is heavily outweighed (five to one) even in Zeneca, where pharmaceuticals are heavily dominant. But that wasn't the real problem. These businesses could still have been better run.

Another fundamental factor was that, instead of the corporate system helping, it positively hindered. The parent's size, centralization, and control mechanisms got in the way. Owen and Harrison praise the much better 'parenting' that ICI's component businesses now receive from the split command: more value is being added to them than in the past.

Yet ICI's celebrated near-revolution of the 1980s, led by Sir John Harvey-Jones, was an exemplar of the leaner and fitter movement. Were its multitudinous small buys (many in speciality chemicals, and designed to strengthen the portfolio) bound to weaken its management? If so, why was the demerged ICI at it again with Grow?

Plus ça change, plus c'est la même chose. The world's great companies aggrandize themselves by acquisition and diversification in pursuit of lofty strategic ambitions – in this case, to lead the global paints industry. If the companies are harder to manage in consequence, that's because managers haven't yet solved the problems that they and their predecessors have created.

ICI is hardly alone. Many boards have presided over complex, wasteful, counterproductive and top-heavy establishments – for no good reason. Rather than just cheer Royal Dutch-Shell for its central reforms of the mid-nineties, for example, ask why Shell's contraction followed so long after Exxon's (1986) – and, better still, why bloating occurred at all. The explanation is always the same. Numbers and complexities increase with efforts to manage the unmanageable. What's really needed is reduction of the unmanageable to manageable proportions. And that should be feasible without demerger.

The issue isn't only the heavy cost of a centralizing head office, but the heavy hand it lays on the too many layers below. As noted earlier, there seems to be an inverse correlation between size and performance in most industries. That is no surprise. In manufacturing, the largest company seldom leads its sector on any financial criterion. Long-term total returns to shareholders are likely to be greater lower down the corporate leagues: the last is far more likely to be first than the largest.

Do these results testify to the evils of gigantism – or to the underperformance of giant managements? You might conclude from the chemical industry's history that gigantism itself is to blame. After a Nazi-tainted IG Farben was forcibly chopped in three by the Allies post-war, each amputated limb (BASF, Bayer and Hoechst) grew to individual sizes greater than the old, undivided ICI – and to collective mass that Farben would never have achieved. Much the same tale followed the enforced break-up of Rockefeller's Standard Oil Trust: Exxon, Mobil, Socal and so on sprang from the trustbust loins.

More recently, the figuring is that the trustbusting of AT&T enormously enriched the shareholders – not only via the Baby Bells so created, but through the growth of AT&T itself. Over the period 1982-92, the combined telephone wealth rose threefold: this $132·4 billion accretion of loot was six times the equivalent figure for the unbroken IBM, saved from trustbusting by the Reaganites.

That seems to place the onus on those who are not divided. Divide and prosper *à la* ICI-Zeneca seems to be the message. In fact, directors down the ages have commonly complained that the market's overall pricing undervalues their wonderful separate businesses. Yet it has usually required a threat – trustbusting in AT&T's case, the menacing presence of Hanson in ICI's – to stimulate the urge to demerge.

That motivation may now be on the rise. In the US, the ur-conglomerate ITT has sub-divided, while AT&T is breaking up again, this time voluntarily. In Europe, Thorn-EMI and Hanson itself, the arch-predator, have joined the trend. As some demergers have shown, moreover, there's no case for stopping the process with division by two. Why not three (Farben)? Or four, five, six (viz AT&T)?

The management test is not whether the parts add up to less than the whole in the stock market. It is whether the components are optimizing their performance under the reigning leadership. The rough rule that Bigness Is Bad for You has plenty of exceptions in well-led businesses which nobody could call homogenous. Undoubtedly the highly assorted technologies of a chemical colossus like ICI are more challenging than Shell's relative homogeneity. For all that, the champions have simply proved more adept at pressing the right control buttons of the right management processes at the right times.

Demerger set the Zeneca management free to use abilities which had been bottled up inside ICI. But demerger in itself doesn't achieve such necessary improvement, and surely shouldn't be the only method of unbottling corporate talents. There has to be a better way – and there is.

Parents and children

Time after time, companies bought out from large parents proceed to outperform, not only the parent, but their own previous best achievements – often by several miles. These cases raise basic issues of organization. The mighty fathers and mothers tend to talk of subsidiaries as quasi-independent business units, the building blocks of decentralization. The difference between these units and the buy-outs, however, is that there's nothing halfway, nothing 'quasi', about the latter's independence.

That independence is the enabling virtue. As a wholly owned and controlled business unit, the future buy-out may enjoy everything from a factory that's state of the art to a customer franchise that leads its sector: everything, that is, except the ability to escape from an imposed problem, which is, as one consultant puts it, 'that the parent is busy and neglects the kids'. The malign influence is more than cultural. The subsidiary must help bear the huge overhead costs of a large organization. That weighs it down as it struggles to compete effectively in turbulent waters.

The key word here is *parent*: 'the parent is busy and neglects the kids'. The parental analogy is used very effectively by Andrew Campbell, Michael Goold and Marcus Alexander as the governing metaphor for the book *Corporate-Level Strategy*,[7] their investigation of how multibusiness companies seek 'parenting advantage'. As they note, the parent (the corporate centre or holding company) makes choices no different from a small shopkeeper's: what lines to stock, push, and drop.

So might parents decide which children to keep in the family business, which to promote, which to send forth into the outside world. In the multibusiness company, that translates into which businesses to keep, to back, or to sell. As the authors stress, though, the parental role is not passive. How well or badly the parenting is done affects the outcome. Bad parenting can easily spoil a perfectly good child that might profitably have stayed at home.

The pharmaceutical and other specialized businesses of ICI had mostly been at least equal in technology to the competition; but parenting problems could handicap them in the marketplace. In Europe, for example, wise vendors used concentrated sales forces to sell specialized products like plastic film for information technology applications. These competitors had obvious advantages over ICI, where, under the old central insistence, European salesmen represented a range of products.

In setting free the Zeneca units, ICI resolved the problem of its parenting by ceasing to be the parent. The bigger-is-better school lost out to the middle view: that, beyond a certain point, disadvantages of size can outweigh its advantages. The small-is-beautiful extremists, however, would always pitch that point very low – thinking in hundreds of employees where the rival school thinks in thousands, or hundreds of thousands. But is there any intrinsic reason why small can't be beautiful within the embrace of a large but benevolent parent?

Believers in this possibility have a recipe for universal success. Break down the organization, any organization, into discrete components; place each component under a single manager; hold said manager entirely responsible for the success or failure of this devolved enterprise; reward or remove leaders accordingly. Railtrack, set up to run Britain's privatized rail infrastructure, is an example of the philosophy. Ten zonal managers, to quote the *Financial Times*, were 'given a high degree of devolved power to run their businesses', aiming at quarterly targets set by HQ, 'with financial rewards geared to the degree of success'.

The idea has flourished before. In the sixties it was called giving a man 'a business like his own'. Success was scant, largely because very few boards delegated true authority or chose the appropriate businesses. The question is really one of business economics. Sometimes the economics will favour decentralization, sometimes not. Fragmentation is simply one form of parenting, which can be either good or bad under any organizational form.

How far can the parent analogy be taken? For a start, good parents are always loving and tolerant, at times reasonably firm and justly critical. In terms of parental strategy, they:

1 Encourage offspring to aim for achievably high standards, helping to develop strengths and eliminate weaknesses.

2 Use connections both within the family and outside to improve the offspring's prospects and performance.

3 Make their own knowledge, know-how, experience, resources and abilities available to the offspring.

4 Release the apron-strings as soon as children are ready to leave home.

These parental behaviours equate with four main influences which, say Campbell, Goold and Alexander, parents may use to create value in business units:

1 Influencing stand-alone performance.
2 Forming linkages.
3 Supplying functions and services.
4 Changing the portfolio.

The authors show brilliantly how parents have vacillated around these four variables since 1960, when diversification became a driving strategic force. Probably one company in two diversified, most into 'related' businesses – though the relationships were sometimes bizarrely stretched: gas-maker BOC even owned King Harry Pizza, reasoning that gasses froze the pizzas.

Not surprisingly, by the seventies many diversifiers 'were beginning to encounter performance problems'. The top managements didn't blame the problems on their own parenting. Instead, they placed the onus on their offspring and turned to 'portfolio planning'. The Boston Consulting Group devised its simplified matrix methodology, based on growth rates and market share. It showed parents which children were 'stars', which 'question-marks', which 'cash-cows', and which 'dogs' (to be done away with).

The matrix system helped tidy up many a mess. It did nothing to improve the parental, and thus the corporate, performance. The predators of the eighties, selling off and reorganizing businesses, did plenty along these lines, and not only by ousting failed parents. They stimulated other, frightened managements into 'restructuring'. Cash-cow or star, question-mark or dog, all were grist to the restructuring mills. What happened in Europe mirrored events in America: between 1974 and 1987, diversifiers fell from 63 percent of the *Fortune* 500 to 41 percent.

Reporting that fact, Constantinos Markides of the London Business School concluded, alas, that 'companies that restructured to reduce diversity were . . . characterized by [relatively] poor performance'.[8] Hence, in the latest phase, the parent (like ICI with its paints) concentrates on 'core businesses' (those left after restructuring), or 'core competencies', and relies on 'sharing activities and transferring skills' (in Harvard professor

Michael Porter's words) – the object being to achieve profitable synergies and better performance.

In 1997, ICI even took the extreme step of changing much of its core – swapping its low-return basic chemicals for the speciality chemicals owned by Unilever, which was engaged in a similar strategic refit.

As *Corporate-Level Strategy* points out, this goes right back to ideas originated by Igor Ansoff, who wrote the path-finding *Corporate Strategy9* in the conglomerating sixties. The wheel has turned full circle, but the vehicle still doesn't move fast enough: witness the old, undivided ICI. The parent has two tough tests to consider. First, does the business perform better under its parent's care than it would independently? The three authors think this test doesn't go nearly far enough. You must also prove, second, that the business does better in your ownership than *any other parent* could achieve.

While that test may sound hypothetical, it certainly places corporate parents on the spot. They must decide how to achieve the authors' 'parenting advantage'. What insights can they contribute to improve the value of their businesses? How do they behave as parents, and what businesses fit this behaviour? What is their 'heartland' – the business or businesses where they feel most comfortable?

The logic of these questions points towards fragmentation. Monoliths are well-advised to evolve into sets of stand-alone businesses, simply because most markets have fragmented into separate segments. The idea is to gain the advantages of specialized, concentrated companies without losing the large companies' assets: advantages of economy of scale and breadth of market. But whatever the pressures and arguments in favour of decentralization, demerger and other forms of fragmentation, top managements have always found aggrandizement much more attractive.

The history of strategic fashions reviewed earlier can easily be understood as a series of justifications for central managements – for parents. The post-war wave of mergers and acquisitions, each adding power and riches to a parental organization, has continued remorselessly. The fact that so many mergers disappoint is now taken for granted. It shouldn't be. If the acquired company had been properly assessed for its strategic and financial value, if the proper parenting mechanisms had been installed, and if the opportunities for synergistic savings had been taken, the acquisition would most likely have succeeded.

Bad buys must have sprung from bad management. Buyers are notoriously prone to stumble over a fundamental issue spotlighted by Campbell, Goold and Alexander: diversity versus concentration. Totally homogenous, one-product companies are theoretically vulnerable: ergo, strategic diversification. However, Royal Dutch-Shell provides a cautionary result. It has parented its homogenous oil businesses with conspicuous, consistent excellence; but in the early nineties its chemical business fell, not for the first time, into the soup. Oil companies have generally misfired in the chemical industry. Managing outside petroleum simply isn't an oilman's parenting skill.

Managing diversity is a skill in itself, but that art, too, has limits to its powers. The scale of diversified conglomerates, however large, offers few economies. They enjoy no managerial congruence akin to oil's, or even ICI's, and lack any coherence; their basic principle is fragmentation. The break-up of ITT in the nineties can stand as the tombstone for the illusion that, despite these disadvantages, the management expertise of the diversified conglomerate would be all-conquering.

In fact, the managing formula is identical to today's favoured style of parenting. Each conglomerate unit was supposed to have the 'high degree of devolved power to run their businesses' sought by Railtrack. The latter's quarterly targets set by HQ, too, are the method with which Harold Geneen created ITT's conglomerate legend in the sixties. Railtrack's 'financial rewards geared to the degree of success' are another beloved conglomerate ingredient.

Together, the ingredients sound as if they should make parental supervision a breeze, almost superfluous. But there's no halfway house. Full independence requires full powers. If a subsidiary doesn't control its marketing or pricing or investment strategy, for example, the heart is ripped out of the business – so the half-separation will not work. The corpocracy will take charge and the parent's largeness, centralization, and culture of control will gravely impede the subsidiary's drive for sales and profits. Yet centralization of vital functions is the essence of big company parenting. How can the conflict be resolved?

The answer lies in the admirable, inevitable parenting exemplified by the joint ventures now being formed by companies all over the world. Since no parent has total powers, and none interferes with management on a day-to-day basis, the ventures can develop their own cultures, combining their own evolving characteristics with attributes drawn at will from the partners. Throw in different nationalities as well, and the mix could be most appetizing – and it's a mixture that Europe is especially well placed to provide.

Joint venture managers and other staff are not insulated from the marketplace and its realities by central bureaucracies. They can accept the highly educative challenge of independence while benefiting from the established parents' financial and other strengths. The role of the parents is limited and simple: recruit excellent people for the joint venture, motivate them intelligently, and get out of their way. That differs not at all from the fundamental formula for good parenting of any business, jointly or wholly owned.

Bad parents never apply that simple recipe, never appreciate that real and deep difference in performance can only be achieved by more effective parental behaviour. To repeat, the control of subordinate businesses rests on four parental imperatives: Encourage, Network, Reinforce and Release. The test of excellence in applying these principles is the test of any parenthood: a happy, healthy offspring who is a source of rightful pride.

FIVE

Exploiting the Organization

The new power at Unilever

Should management hearts rejoice or mourn over Niall Fitzgerald's promotion to the Unilever summit in 1996? He is labelled as the man who gave you Power – the off-colour detergent that handed the arch-enemy, Procter & Gamble, a sudden opportunity to savage its rival and gain market share. Unilever's denials and contorted efforts to defend the ill-fated product merely compounded the original error. That was to ignore technical risks that the Power formula might in some circumstances damage the wash.

The fiasco – for which a weighty price had to be paid in foregone profits, extra marketing spend and lost market share – was Unilever's equivalent of the New Coke disaster, perhaps the grandest error in the history of fast-moving consumer boobs. The parallels go further. The authors of Coke's débâcle, which saw the new formula spurned by the market, forcing the return of the old, were neither disgraced nor dismissed. Since Roberto C. Goizueta and Don Keogh were already the top twain, they couldn't, like Fitzgerald, be promoted. But the board awarded the duo handsome bonuses for their initiative – despite its flop.

In failing, Unilever and Coke pursued remarkably similar strategies. Locked in interminable vendettas with Pepsi and Procter & Gamble respectively, both seized on technological advance to vault – they hoped – clear of the competition. The lofty ambitions not only gave birth to the plan, but obliterated any counterarguments. This is the Arnhem complex. Confronted with photographs of Panzers in the drop-zone, the manager, like Monty's staff officers, ignores them or asserts that they aren't real tanks, and even if they are, they haven't any petrol or ammunition.

Once Power had gathered momentum, nothing could stop it – except, alas, the external enemy. Like Arnhem or New Coke, this wasn't risk-taking: if the tanks could fight, if one new formula harmed clothing, or the other dismayed drinkers, failure wasn't a risk, but a certainty. In pardoning their appointees, the boardroom overlords presumably felt that the culprits had learnt that particular lesson (i.e., listen to Cassandra – she may well be right): they were allowed an error, however gargantuan, in the cause of progress.

The Unilever expectation was that, like Goizueta at Coke – under whose aegis the company's market value soared by an Olympian $140 billion – Fitzgerald would force through major change, attacking bureaucratic and constipated processes and encouraging the enterprising spirit that, in the case of the Power detergent, went several bridges too far. It's none too soon. The arch-enemy, Procter & Gamble, started much earlier along this by now well-travelled road to replace authoritarian hierarchy with self-managing, team-working brotherhood and sisterhood.

In most cases, including Procter & Gamble's, the crusade has been neither easy nor altogether succesful. The key to ease and success, though, may lie in Fitzgerald's elevation. There is one excellent reason to applaud that appointment. Allowing people to take initiatives without fear of failure or its consequences is a Great Leap Forward in management terms. Large companies far too readily develop and sustain a 'blame culture', in which the establishment seeks scapegoats whenever anything goes wrong.

The 'blame culture' discourages venture and encourages groupthink, where nobody dares oppose the prevailing policy. On the other hand, the blame-free culture, which encourages venture at the price of possible failure, runs another risk: that of developing a management which neither admits nor analyses error and never exacts extreme penalties from managers who fail. A narrow tightrope has to be walked between the two cultures.

The way to avoid falling off the tightrope is plain. For any job, back whoever you believe to be the right apppointee and only intervene (and then decisively) as soon as it's clear that you were wrong. A single flop is no evidence – on that score, the overlords at Coke and Unilever were plainly right. Forgiving Fitzgerald, however, will only be successful to the extent that the new Hercules clears up this horrendous mess:

> Overlapping managements for countries, regions and product
> categories are a source of confusion and frustration throughout
> the group.

That's how the *Financial Times* neatly expressed the general insider view of Unilever's famed matrix system.

Unilever has been through *three* major upheavals since the late eighties. First, authority was removed from country managers and trans-ferred to executives in charge of product categories and regions – a now standard response to the proven inadequacies of matrix organization. Then manufacturing was reformed, at a cost of £305 million in excep-tional charges. This programme, going under the code-name 'Beethoven', made no music: it 'delivered next to no improvement in profits'. And then came 'Encore', which generated another £490 million in restructur-ing costs. Two years on, 'the first meagre fruits' of Encore were 'trickling through to the bottom line'.

Understandably, an anonymous senior executive observed that: 'There's been a lot of hallway talk in recent years – "Should we do it this way? Should we do it that way?" – and we've changed bits and pieces in European foods and detergents. But we need thorough change.' What sort of change? 'It can't be a terribly simple structure because we are a very complicated business, but it can be much clearer.'

That statement underestimates what can be achieved, even in a 'very complicated' business, by determined leadership. Did the reshuffle of senior management, announced in March 1996, mark such a decisive step? To be effective, responsible managers must have direct control over decisions and their execution. The clearcut means to this end is to define a business closely – so that you can 'put your arms round it'; then you place a manager, preferably the right one, in charge with enough rope to run the show – or sometimes to hang him or herself.

At first sight, by breaking itself into 14 business groups, Unilever did precisely that. At second sight, though, you see that one 'president' runs Foods & Beverages Europe, another Foods & Beverages North America, another the whole of the vast subcontinent of Latin America, with all its multifarious businesses. And above these 14 important plenipotentiaries sits a seven-man executive committee that is supposed to 'target markets and businesses to develop and allocate resources to them'. In other words, Unilever has merely substituted an improved top-heavy structure for another.

How many of the 400 senior managers who heard about the reorganization at the annual conference in Rotterdam were genuinely pleased? Since this was the so-called 'Oh Be Joyful' meeting (referring to the psalm 'Oh Be Joyful in the Lord All Ye Lands), nobody dissented. But every Unilever insider knows that efforts to reform the group are hindered by a dual Anglo-Dutch structure which contributes nothing but complexity, cumbersome committees and delay.

As one outside commentator observes, the fact that Unilever has only just recognized the need for reform, years after its competitors, 'speaks volumes about its culture'. It isn't just a Unilever culture. All over Europe, multinational managements, established to cope with stable markets in which the giants held strongly fortified positions, have been attempting to cope with instability and increasingly fragile franchises by old methods.

The future will be even more challenging. Meeting that challenge doesn't rest on the 21 people now placed in Unilever's key positions, or even the 400 who met so joyfully at Rotterdam. It lies with the younger men and women in middle management who have – or should have – the power to launch new businesses, new ideas, new processes and new growth. The job of the centre, and the way for Fitzgerald to justify his promotion, is to enable this dynamism to flow through.

How management adds value

How do you know if top management is mismanaging? Look out for repeated, systemic errors – for persistent gaps between effort and achievement. For instance, research and development is widely believed to be the powerhouse of corporate growth. Yet the biggest R&D spenders do not generate the greatest innovative power. General Motors, IBM and Siemens each spent annually above the $5 billion mark, three times as much as Hewlett-Packard, in the early nineties. Yet HP has a far better recent record in the profitable exploitation of new technology.

The ten biggest R&D spenders in the early nineties outside the US included, in addition to Siemens, Philips and Fiat, both then deep in the corporate doldrums. Philips outspent Canon three-to-one, but in 1992 the Japanese company earned the same profits on half the sales. Large R&D budgets are evidently a function of size; but size, equally, threatens to make the spending relatively ineffective. Unilever, after all, spent some £200 million on Power, which was the child of highly ambitious R&D.

Contemplating these European giants prompts a variant on the famous question: if you're so clever, why aren't you rich? If you're spending so much on R&D, why aren't you more successful? As noted, a consistent pattern of shortfalls is one sign of ineffectiveness at the top. Then, repeated U-turns or aborted initiatives in policy show that the appointees don't know what they are doing: one Power or New Coke can be an accident; two such disasters are more than a coincidence.

Above all, promised results that never materialize are a bad sign (witness Unilever's Beethoven and Encore flops) and deeply counterproductive. The longer you take to implement a change process, the more likely it is to be overtaken by events. Speed of thought and action is one of the principles by which a chief executive succeeds. What are the others – and do these principles apply to all managerial work, right down the organization?

The ingredients of success plainly have terrific power, and the issue of R&D results provides important clues to their nature. The values adopted by R&D winners apply widely. To emulate the best achievers:

1 *Concentrate* on areas where you are already strong.
2 *Work concurrently* by bringing all affected interests together at the earliest possible stage.
3 *Decentralize* the task to the business units.
4 *Go truly multinational* by bringing different nationals together.
5 *Go cross-cultural* by using leaders from foreign cultures.
6 *Plan up-front*, and thoroughly, before starting any projects.
7 *Forget protocol* – encourage good 'unauthorized' projects.
8 *Invest in success* by backing good projects to the hilt, but . . .
9 *Identify the weak projects* early on – and put them out of their misery.
10 *Remove barriers*, so that good ideas aren't blocked by vested (or dumb) interests.

The ten principles have immediate relevance to big company success or failure – and Unilever should be well-placed to exploit them. For a start, as an Anglo-Dutch company, its management is *cross-cultural* by definition. The ethos has always been *decentralized*, explaining the enthusiasm for matrix management, which sought to devolve authority without losing control. As Unilever has now concluded, devolution must be taken further and tackled differently if it is to succeed.

The top management also accepts the need to *concentrate* more than in the past. Among Unilever's huge portfolio of businesses some have already failed to survive scrutiny. But what criteria should be applied? New boss Niall Fitzgerald can do no better than copy Coke's Robert Goizueta. Initially, he concentrated Coke by applying Rules 7 and 8 in the highly planned up-front way recommended in Rule 6:

You make a chart. Across the top you put your businesses . . .
Then you put the financial characteristics on the other axis:

margins, returns, cash flow reliability, capital requirements.
[Some] like concentrates will emerge as superior businesses.
Others, like wine, look lousy.

The latter, naturally, you sell. Goizueta followed up this simple
approach with another. All the remaining operations would be judged
by their 'economic profit' or EVA (Economic Value Added) – that is,
operating profit after, not only tax, but also a charge for capital employed.

Unilever hasn't gone the whole way along the EVA route, but its
new yardstick for corporate performance, 'trading contribution', does
have a similar flavour. Managers will be judged on after-tax profits
(adjusted for working capital inflation and replacement cost depreciation),
less a capital charge of 1 percent above Unilever's cost of equity. The
group's conversion will doubtless persuade other firms to adopt a concept
that has one supreme virtue: elemental simplicity. Its elementary proposition is that a business must earn more than the cost of its capital.

That's obvious in the case of debt, although many companies, often
unwittingly, commit the cardinal sin of earning less on their debt than
it costs (quite a feat, considering that debt interest attracts tax relief).
But even companies that appear to be handsomely clearing their interest
costs may truly be consuming their capital. A company which never
borrows, but finances itself on equity capital, probably never bothers its
head about the 'cost of capital'. But equity has to be serviced, too.

At first sight, it seems like very cheap capital, and if you look simply
at the cost of the dividend, so it is. But EVA advocates argue that the
cost of equity is much higher than that of debt. The money entrusted to
your care by shareholders could have been invested elsewhere, and will
be if your returns become less attractive. 'Returns' means not only dividends, but also capital gains. Lumping both together, shareholders expect
to better long-term government bonds by several percentage points.

The average 'cost' of US equity at end-1993, for example, was over
12 percent (the cost is higher for volatile stocks, and lower for stable
ones). The weighted average cost of equity and debt is the true cost of
capital. If that number exceeds profitability, the company is eating its
own flesh. But insisting on clearing the capital cost has other virtues.
Basing strategy on the cost of equity will do more than impose realism
on the financing. It will force managers to concentrate on keeping down
capital employed by managing inventories and costs intelligently.

These two considerations are basic. First, the key financial statistic
isn't the gross margin on sales, but what it helps to achieve: the margin

between the cost of capital and its return. Second, managers who aren't held responsible for their use of capital won't use it to the best advantage of the business. The two fundamentals apply to any company – the reasons for large-scale corporate downfalls in Europe certainly include the damaging propensities identified by the EVA measure.

Reliance on the traditional Return on Capital Employed figure is open to two grave criticisms. The accounting definition of capital may grossly understate the funds actually being employed, and thus overstate the rate of return (even if – a big 'if' – profits are stated accurately). Second, comparing ROCE with the cost of capital will be invalid and misleading unless all capital costs are taken into account, which (see above) must mean equity as well as debt.

But there's more to the EVA figuring: what's the capital?

Under EVA, capital includes not only fixed assets and plant and equipment, but also 'revenue investment': that is, expenditure on essentials like R&D, training and even marketing (of which more later). How you account for revenue investment seems a fuzzy area. But that makes no difference to the power of the EVA concept, which is both strategic and operational.

Strategically, it demonstrates to top management whether the positioning of a business is viable or not. If EVA is negative – that is, after-tax operating profits don't cover the cost of capital – the business is ultimately doomed, even if a company is still showing profits at the operating level. When capital is being savagely eroded, small wonder that investors prefer to put their money somewhere else. Small wonder, either, that high EVA and high stock market performance show a close correlation, and vice versa: low correlates with low.

Operationally, the concept has two virtues. It gives top management a way of measuring the value of individual operations, and the achievements of their managers, while still, as bosses, keeping their proper distance from the operators. At the same time, it directs operational managers towards the right actions and away from the wrong. Also, it enforces a close look at the organization to ensure that capital is properly allocated to those who use the money. That sweeps away the confusion which in many businesses makes proper measurement and direction impossible.

Very complicated businesses like Unilever can be broken down into sub-units, each with its own capital, instead of keeping all capital accounting at the centre. An individual unit can then work out its own EVA by deducting cost of capital from after-tax operating profit. If the result is negative, the call to action is immediate and compelling. At the strategic level, the response may be negative, too: close or sell the offending operation. But operational managers can also respond positively and profitably to save their business's bacon – and their own jobs.

Cutting back on total capital employed is the most effective way of raising EVA in an unrestructured business. But restructuring to eliminate negative operations and reinvest in highly positive ones is also miraculous. That's an excellent example of how a well-directed chief executive adds value. I've no hesitation in urging extreme attention to the EVA performance – not because it's a management panacea (there is no such thing), but because it uses one clear financial ratio to focus attention on the realities of the business.

Worries arise about lumping in revenue investment with capital costs. The thrust of EVA is to minimize the latter; but managers should be encouraged to invest in innovation, training, and marketing – not discouraged. The marketing investment on which Unilever so heavily depends is a case very much in point. In theory, marketing expenditure should be treated as an investment, because (like R&D) it purchases a future benefit. Nobody questions that a brand is a capital asset. It's illogical to recognize this capital value, but to treat the marketing money which created the asset as a lost expense.

Market-leading companies in businesses like cosmetics and ice-cream (where Unilever is the world's largest) tend to outspend their competitors. That's how they end up with and defend their dominant market shares. Is this a chicken-and-egg issue? Companies commonly allocate marketing expenditure as a percentage of sales revenue. So a firm whose sales are soaring above the competition will automatically outgrow them in marketing spend.

That doesn't weaken the argument. Rather, it stresses the essential truth: that present marketing investment creates future sales and profits. Cutbacks, equally, jeopardize the future, a point which managers ignore at peril. I was once asked by an advertising agency to meet one of its clients, a brewer who (to the agency's understandable distress) had challenged the value of a multi-million-pound spend. His profits from beer were far lower than those made by the owned premises which (among other catering services) sold the brew. Didn't it make sense to divert his marketing millions to improving the outlets?

If the premises had accounted for all his beer sales, that strategy might have been more reasonable, but the brands sold nationally in many other outlets. It proved unnecessary to argue about the effectiveness of advertising to dissuade the brewer. Who, I asked, had the largest market share? And was this leader's proportion of beer advertising greater or lesser than that share? The answer was 'greater', which promptly ended the argument. Two *Harvard Business Review* authors deserve the final word, though.[1] They write that: 'Considering the time and effort needed to get customers from awareness to loyal usage, when companies wilfully disrupt a message or fail to reinforce it consistently, they shoot themselves in the foot.'

Building a brand or building sales (ultimately one and the same thing) is a long-term investment which should not be jeopardized by short-term decisions. During recessions and restructurings, however, that's precisely what most managements do. That only gives more astute companies the opportunity to increase their 'share of voice' and ultimately their share of market. The question for managers is not what percentage of sales is appropriate for the marketing effort, but rather, what spending is required to meet the marketing objectives – those that will pay off in a high and rising EVA.

What would the brewer have found from analysing his EVA? Did his beer truly offer a worse return on capital than his outlets? Probably not. Both EVA and the concept of marketing as revenue investment stress the crucial importance of looking at the business anew and making it come to fuller and richer life by applying the results of that different viewpoint. If you're using the wrong map, don't expect to reach the right destination.

It doesn't have to be a purely financial map. The importance of financial numbers is obvious, but their management value is currently under attack for many reasons. For a start, the most-used financial measures look objective, but are only approximations of reality. Second, accounts can measure the results of past management, but that doesn't add up to 'helping managers to manage' – the telling Japanese phrase for 'management accounting'. Third, the financial figures are an outcome, the result of decisions and actions that are inherently non-financial.

Hence the newish concept of the 'balanced scorecard', in which financial performance is only one of the elements. The scorecard might concentrate on the customer, innovation and learning, internal business factors, and financial results. To illustrate their nature, 'customer' would include the customer satisfaction index; innovation and learning would take in the staff attitude survey; while 'internal business' would mean aspects like levels of rework – taking rejects back and rectifying the defects.

Like total quality (with which it is sometimes combined), the balanced scorecard starts with a 'vision' or 'mission'. Writing in the *Harvard Business Review*, Robert S. Kaplan and David P. Norton describe a process that has four stages:[2]

1 What is my vision of the future?
2 If my vision succeeds, how will I differ
   (a) to my shareholders
   (b) to my customers
   (c) in my internal management processes
   (d) in my ability to innovate and grow?
3 What are the critical success factors (on each of the four above counts)?
4 What are the critical measurements (again on the four counts)?

The fourth question gives you the balanced scorecard. Advocates claim that it links measurements to strategy. A common cause of failure in revamps like Unilever's three failed or semi-failed efforts is that measurements are inconsistent with the new strategy. So managers go on managing in the same old unwanted way. That's another argument against relying solely on monetary measures, especially the familiar, established ones. They are rigid, unchanging in concept, and narrowly focused.

The scorecard's principles are plainly superior. But the process won't of itself stop top managers from mismanaging. Rather, it runs the danger of persuading managers that, by going through more elegant motions, they are playing a better game. The damaging gaps between effort and performance will persist. By the same token, it wasn't the intellectual power of EVA which created Coke's megawealth, but the managerial power with which Goizueta and Keogh ensured that the principles would be applied.

Successful top managers insist on having clear responsibility, and giving it to others: they pick the best complementary partners to work with them, and they share power; they choose powerful, accurate, quick performance measures that they, their colleagues and the corporation can live by. In all that, they use action-oriented philosophies (like those embodied in the Ten Rules of R&D) to add value for all parties. And they do so within the shortest possible time-frames. That's the way you make a great company in the first place – and keep it great in the second.

The fumbling of Philips

In March 1996, the Philips management precipitated an 11 percent fall in the price of the company's shares with a shock warning that first-quarter profits would be markedly lower. To long-term watchers of the Dutch electronics empire, though, the decline was entirely predictable. Time after time, Philips has promised a bright future but collapsed into a dismal present.

True to form, 1995 had encouraged the *Wall Street Journal* to observe that Philips seemed 'to be recovering from a prolonged slump': then came the profits warning. One specific reason for renewed gloom was the sharp reversal in the empire's business in semiconductors. That made the bad first-quarter figures a double blow for the retiring chief executive, Jan Timmer.

The archetype of toughness, in burly, militaristic looks as well as action, Timmer had refused to include semiconductors in his hit list on taking over in 1990. The group had just lost £1.7 billion, but Timmer saw a brilliant semiconductor future – and brilliant profits seemed to bear him out. By August 1995, semiconductors were accounting for 60 percent of operating profits, and Philips was planning $650 million of investment per year to expand semiconductor output to the end of the decade.

So strong was the demand for chips for PCs and other electronic gadgets that the workforce, slashed by Timmer from 300,000 to 244,000 in only two years, had recovered to 265,000 by 1996. But then PC sales and chip prices foundered – leaving Philips still stuck with the low profitability (under 4 percent of sales) that had bedevilled it before and after Timmer's arrival.

A far larger percentage (nearly 7 percent) was piled into R&D, true. But the technological genius of Philips had somehow never created the array of world-leading products that Sony could boast – even though Philips started from a much stronger base. Those veteran Philips watchers knew that this gap between promise and performance had its causes in a culture that rooted the company in constipated ways.

The company remained deeply conservative, for all Timmer's progressive adventures into multimedia. Its technologists were 'working on everything', reported *Business Week*, 'from set-top boxes for interactive TV to personal computer-compatible compact music disks with advanced video features.' The latter miracle is related to the Compact Disk-Interactive (CD-i), which Philips launched in the US in 1991 as 'The Imagination Machine'. In five years, it sold a scant 200,000 copies (a fifth of one year's Sony PlayStation sales) and lost an estimated $1 billion.

To quote the *Wall Street Journal*, 'Not only did Philips invest its hopes too heavily in a technology that became obsolete even as it rolled off the assembly lines, but its Dutch management pushed that technology into a market it didn't understand.' At Philips, investment in management technology has received nothing like the same enthusiastic attention as high-tech development – even though, as with CD-i, mismanagement can wipe out all the benefits of technical advances.

The new management modes hold out the promise of lower costs and higher productivity; yet Philips is not alone in missing these managerial benefits. Europe's hereditary defects have never been more clearly epitomized than in an interview which Lindsay Halstead, then head of Ford of Europe, gave in 1992. Motivated by his division's money-losing performance (where once Europe had been the mainstay of Ford's worldwide profits), Halstead made the following discoveries:

1 'An investigation' showed that 40 percent of the 21,000 white-collar workers were 'indirect' staff, mainly clerical, legal and adminstrative.

2 The corporate structure of seven management layers was too weighty, time-consuming and bureaucratic and had become out of sync with assembly lines slimmed down to improve efficiency and output.

3 Reaction times were too lengthy: 'We are too slow to report and we just have to find a better way to respond.'

4 Senior executives, including Halstead himself, were asked to confirm decisions, about which they had little or no specialist knowledge, by subordinates unable to act on their own initiative.

5 The new Escort, which ran into severe criticism and poor market reception, was probably 'over-researched' by some of these seven management layers: decisions on styling should have been left to the designers and engineers.

Halstead now wanted to remove two layers of the bureaucracy that was gumming up his works as part of a review likely to require (like Timmer's turnround at Philips) two years of voluntary job-losses.

Philips and Ford shared the same disease. The European vice is to employ too many costly indirect workers within over-large bureaucracies, to have too many management layers, to concentrate on productivity in the plants, while ignoring that in the office processes, and to slow down decision-taking through hierarchical discussions. These faults breed over-long reaction times, too much reference upwards, and too much chewing over proposals and plans – what the Americans long ago named 'paralysis by analysis'. Three questions leap out from these cases.

First, why doesn't a basic manpower issue like the oversupply of white-collar indirects become the subject of continuous analysis and control? It certainly shouldn't require special investigation to discover the awful truths about overstaffing. Second, everybody knew about the paper-pushing bureaucracy at Philips. Why are such defects only recognized as suitable cases for treatment under the pressure of poor results? Third, why do Europe's corporate reforms take so long?

One thing is certain: any reform undertaken over a protracted period will confront a different situation at the end than at the beginning. The reorganization runs the risk of applying the right solution to what has become the wrong problem. Timmer's investment in semiconductors was thus threatened by slowing growth in PC sales to corporate customers: in 1996 they appeared to conclude that temporarily they had enough PCs – and enough powerful ones – to delay purchase of still more potent equipment.

If Philips had moved decisively into this market before Timmer took the helm, it wouldn't occupy a mere eleventh place among the world's semiconductor suppliers. Its hopes, moreover, would be running higher than the current ambition: to achieve a still mediocre seventh place by the millennium. Doing the right thing at the wrong time is part of the Philips Syndrome. It also embraces doing the right thing in the wrong place.

A consultant working for Philips noticed with some awe that work on reforming its processes concentrated on those areas where results were poor: for instance, in some of the Latin American businesses. These, however, accounted for only a trivial part of the whole. In contrast, the vast businesses like lamp bulbs, cash cows which were still churning out large profits, were left untouched – even though the leverage to be obtained by applying effective reform to gigantic turnovers must be far greater.

This ill-directed attention helps to explain why Timmer's reign showed a sadly regressive tendency. When he took over, noted the *Guardian*, 'the group was overmanned and without a clear sense of direction'. The 30 percent rise in sales per employee is Timmer's most visible legacy, but it had taken five years to achieve; his reign ended with the new strategy under threat, and another 6,000 people losing their jobs. Now his successor, Cor Boonstra, is yet another hero expected to recharge

Philips' batteries, refuel its engines, and achieve a new burst of performance. Why is it taking the Dutch so long to break through – and break
clear?

Fixing the framework

The obvious question, when corporate silt builds up (or refuses to wash
away), is what top managers were doing, and where they were looking.
Probably, the top men were doing the very things which Ford's ex-
European boss Lindsay Halstead highlighted – pushing paper, taking
decisions on inadequate knowledge and second-guessing people who
were paid and qualified to eliminate the guessing and get it right first
time.

Sir Derek Birkin, the RTZ mining group chairman, has expounded a
far better approach:[3] 'even if we wanted to intrude in the management
of operations in the field, which we do not, we could not do so to any
significant extent. We maintain short chains of command to give us an
ability to act quickly ... Once we have agreed strategic and financial
guidelines with our chief operating units, they are left to manage themselves ... Accountability at all times matches the autonomy, but we do
not have massive volumes of data flowing back and forth between Head
Office and the operating units...'

At Europe's behemoths, the stultification begins in head office itself,
where management levels multiply, and operational interference reigns,
under the board's nose – and with the directors joining in. Across the
world Philips was and is an impressive apparatus for designing, building
and distributing often complex pieces of equipment that generally work
well and reliably. The management machine, though, sputtered, stalled
and sometimes misfired completely.

By firing tens of thousands of employees to cut payroll costs, cutting
other costs ruthlessly, and closing plants and businesses, Philips con-
formed to the conventionally wise pattern of heroic management. There
was an excuse: the urgency of the crisis, the need for sheer survival,
made the retrenchment appear inevitable, whatever the consequences –
even secondary problems, to use a medical metaphor.

The discovery that the secondary effects can nullify the primary objectives is among the major contributions to management understanding
made by MIT's Peter M. Senge. 'Shifting the burden' is his phrase for
treating the symptom rather than the underlying disease, and thus

making the latter worse. That's probably the most common infringement of Senge's Fifth Discipline. The necessary discipline is that of thinking about the whole system, not just the primary problem that immediately confronts you. Senge propounds eleven disciplinary Laws:[4]

1 *Today's problems come from yesterday's solutions*: witness Philips' belated arrival in force in the semiconductor market.

2 *The harder you push, the harder the system pushes back*: the more output a company tries to squeeze from inadequate capacity, the higher costs rise.

3 *Behaviour grows better before it gets worse*: misguided policies will show good initial results.

4 *The easy way out usually leads back in*: if the first round of job cuts doesn't work (which happens more often than not), try another.

5 *The cure can be worse than the disease*: the very success of the semiconductor venture made Philips peculiarly vulnerable to falls in that sector.

6 *Faster is slower*: why do so many high-growth start-ups run into high-octane trouble?

7 *Cause and effect are not closely related in time and space*: manufacturing problems may not arise in the plant at all – but in design, marketing or somewhere else.

8 *Small changes can produce big results – but the areas of highest leverage are often the least obvious*: changes in reporting systems can radically improve management performance.

9 *You can have your cake and eat it, too – but not at once*: low cost and high quality aren't incompatible, but eventually go hand-in-hand.

10 *Dividing an elephant in half does not produce two elephants*: artificial boundaries between functions and departments cause all parties to underperform.

11 *There is no blame*: outside factors such as specific or general recession (like that which 'caused' Philips's setback in the mid-nineties) are not what damaged you and your organization – you did it to yourself.

The Laws help greatly to explain the ultimate failure of radical changes designed to achieve the opposite result. In these cases, the fact that the symptoms haven't responded to treatment must mean that the disease, far from improving, has probably become worse. This would be no surprise to Senge, whose stimulating book, *The Fifth Discipline*,[5] provides acute analysis of why managements get into trouble – and how they can avoid it. Every company, he points out, works in a 'limits to growth' structure: when growth halts, or goes into reverse, you know that the limits have been reached.

So far, so very obvious. What's less clear, and demands extra careful analysis, is the question, What are the true limits?

If the company has been stimulating demand by progressive price cuts and discounts, management will tend to stimulate sales by more of the same. This may have a short-run effect. But if the explanation is different – if the company's service and product range are at fault, say – the new price cuts will have no impact on the underlying adverse situation. Similarly, if excessive costs arise from poor processes, cutting worker numbers will reduce the wage bill, but overall costs will remain stubbornly and disappointingly high. Worse still, the sloppiness may increase; the excessive numbers are often needed to make inefficient processes work at all. Mass cutbacks in staff, moreover, are seldom selective and often deeply counterproductive: the best employees, who will most easily find new and better jobs, are the quickest to seize their money and run. That will intensify any service and sales problems, especially since morale is inevitably damaged by the redundancies.

The 'limits to growth' are sometimes all too clear. But sometimes they are hidden in apparently worthy aims. For example, the common strategy of at least 'growing with the industry' is understandable. Loss of market share is hard for any management to tolerate. But unless the causes of lost share are properly understood, intelligent responses cannot be devised. Senge quotes an industry-leading manufacturer of industrial goods which found the right answer, thanks to an MIT team of 'system dynamics' experts. They used computer models to uncover the truth:

> Because it cost so much to store its bulky, expensive products, production managers held inventories as low as possible and aggressively cut back production whenever orders turned down. The result was unreliable and slow delivery, even when production capacity was adequate.

The 'unreliable and slow delivery' readily explained the decline in market share. In fact, the computer predicted that the delivery problems would actually worsen if demand turned down in a market slump. In the recession of 1970, the firm took MIT's advice, maintained output, improved delivery performance, and won back market share from satisfied customers. But 'during the ensuing business recovery, the managers stopped worrying about delivery service': when the next recession came, they returned to the old policy of 'dramatic production cutbacks'.

Rather than mocking their stupidity, it's important to note that this reversion to type is common among companies. Senge blames the 'mental models' held in this firm: 'Every production manager knew in his heart that there was no more surefire way to destroy his career than to be held responsible for stockpiling unsold goods in warehouses.'

This same 'inertia of deeply entrenched mental models' applies widely in Europe. That's why car companies have been slower than their best rivals to adopt 'platform teams' for simultaneous engineering of new models. But forming teams, or even dividing the whole corporation into self-contained businesses subject to less central control, isn't enough. As Senge emphasizes, without changing mental models, little will be achieved.

In a culture that's intolerant of mistakes, for example, managers will cover their backs by referring decisions upwards. If that's ruled out, they will put off the evil day by procrastination. The delay is likely to produce grave secondary effects in an age when markets are increasingly intolerant of slow reactions. But faced with a choice between external requirements and internal anxiety, fearful managers will opt for their own perceived interests every time and leave the customers (and thus ultimately the company) to look after themselves.

The problems faced by European giants like Philips all look amenable to specific action. Tackling them one by one, though, will merely lead to further problems down the line. Only general reform of the entire corporate system will remove the difficulties.

The set of management misdemeanours listed below are failings to which all organizations are prone.

1 'Filtering' of instructions and intentions from on high, so that they never penetrate to lower levels of management, or do so in diluted form.

2 Plenty of good excuses for bad results (Field Marshal Montgomery memorably defined this process as 'inventing poor reasons for not doing what one has been told to do').

3 An internal perception of quality as excellent which is not echoed by the customers.

4 Too many meetings at all levels of management.

5 Too little urgency and too much 'waiting to be told what to do'.

6 Low priority given to issues of operational performance.

7 Lack of focus on each distinct business.

8 Toleration of low performance and low performers.

9 Excessive numbers of people in key areas.

Are these failings symptoms, or systemic? Evidently, none of the faults represents a self-contained system. All are symptoms of what must be much wider breakdown. The holistic defects of the system will always be exposed by external events, such as the recessions of which Philips complained. Booms can also strip the defects bare. If reaching the limits to growth is the systemic problem, dramatic loss of market share, in Senge's language, will act as a 'balancing process', bringing the company's sales into line with its true ability to serve the market.

In such circumstances, shifting to a totally different system is essential. The route to that system doesn't lie through reshuffling the organization (though that may be a necessary adjunct). The true road runs back from the customers to rethink the way the company serves them within the industry structure – whatever form that structure takes. The rules of rethinking are as follows:

1 Always look for the underlying cause of any problem, and make sure that you treat both the manifestation and the systemic cause.

2 In choosing and monitoring treatments, check all Senge's Laws to make sure that you're not about to prove them right.

3 The 'just-around-the-corner syndrome', in which promised renaissance is continually postponed, is a sure sign that Senge's Laws are at work.

4 Watch the long-term trends when analysing short-term problems, and when short-term trends surprise you, realize that something more than the reporting system is seriously wrong.

5 Always ask, what are the limits to growth? And concentrate on extending those bounds, without exceeding them.

6 If at first you do succeed, reinforce success: never reinforce, or return to, failed policies.

7 Find out (you may need outside help) what 'mental models' govern organizational behaviour. If those models don't match what the market wants, change them: don't just change the organization.

In rethinking the organization, as part of the total business system, some of the principles are proven and widely applied. One is simply physical: keep head office small both in numbers and dimension, for this will stop the otherwise inexorable process of expansion. The second essential is to keep lines of communication short, with no 'relays' who pass on instructions and information without adding anything (except possibly confusion).

The third necessity is to ensure that jobholders (from the chief executive downwards) know how and where they can add value. The corollary is that the company needs to adopt a culture (for which read 'set of mental models') that will assist in the achievement of that value. That presents an immediate problem. John Kotter of Harvard Business School writes perceptively about cultural transformation and large companies. In *Fortune's* words, he concludes 'that corporate insiders . . . can seldom transform an organization beset by inertia'.

Backsliding is the giveaway. Ford knew all about the way to break inertia from its own experience in breaking across organizational lines. Briton Alex Trotman, the chief executive wrestling with Ford's problems in the mid-nineties, was the same man who as an executive vice-president in 1990 started to attack the departmental barriers by forming a single product development team of fifty line executives representing all the Ford functions.

He also put 20 young designers, engineers and product planners together as a 'skunk-works' team to speed up development of the product, the new Mustang, aiming, wrote *Fortune*, 'to cut costs by speeding communication and reducing confusion'. The vaunted success of the Taurus, the car which vaulted Ford's profits ahead of General Motors', was also ascribed to multidisciplinary team-working. Yet Ford's deteriorating performance was attracting deserved criticism in 1996. Change had not gone far enough: partial change inevitably achieves partial results.

Senior managers are fully aware of such truths – in conversation. Confront top managements with the tough realities of their situation at a strategy session or a presentation, and the chief executive is likely to say something like, 'You've done exactly what I wanted today.' However critical the judgement, it's what they nearly always say. But the overriding issue is what they *do* to change the system – no matter what the cost to themselves, their privileges and their authority.

There's the rub, and there lie the roots of failure. Fumbling can rarely be corrected by the arch-fumblers themselves. Their ability to react and achieve will be obstructed by the organizational and cultural framework.

That must be changed – not partially, but right across the board, from top to bottom. Unfumble the system, and the fumbling has to stop.

The culture changers of Europe

Europe has usually followed slavishly in the footsteps of American management teachers. The position hasn't been much improved by the rising prestige of management schools such as Insead (France), IMD (Switzerland) or the London Business School. Several of their professors have built lucrative careers as consultants and speakers. But the European management bestsellers, and the main speakers on the business circuit, tend to emanate from America.

Theory is one thing, however, and practice quite another.

The strongest all-European contribution to management thought in action is coming from the consultants, several of them featured in this book. Nobody outside Europe has spread the gospel of customer service more effectively than Jacques Horovitz, or put across the principles of employee motivation more powerfully than Klaus Møller of TMI, or presented the cause of Total Quality Management with more thoroughness than PA Management Consultants. Marketing by the big American consultants has generated breakthroughs with concepts like Business Process Reengineering, but their European rivals have major presence in the most important market of all – Making Things Happen. They have to happen, and fast, for Europe to sustain, let alone improve, its position.

The business requirements of the eighties are vanishing before those of the nineties: focus on shipments is giving way to customer focus; manufacturing efficiency to the critical factor of value added; identification of the supply chain to its integration; regional business to global; data gathering to information access. That's the paradigm shift identified by Baan, a Dutch software company whose startling rise, in sharp competition with SAP, itself signals the changes underfoot in European management.

Jan Baan only founded the company in 1979, and only developed the software side after his brother Paul joined in 1981. The business revolves round the core of software for manufacturing, but has evolved into 'enterprise resource planning', or ERP. The resources which Baan's software coordinates include purchasing, inventories, production and distribution; the tasks undertaken for clients like Philips, ABB and Boeing are thus basic to the success of the enterprise and affect everything the corporation does.

Like Baan, Europe's best consultants are building and broadening their businesses by seizing hold of the change from a stable world to a turbulent one in which (to give one example) a personal computer launch must achieve full global distribution within two weeks – or fail. That can't be achieved without advanced information technology, and here the Europeans neither fear American competition, nor want for American applause.

Following SAP's lead, Baan was launched triumphantly on American stock markets. Between May 1995 and the following February, the shares rose by 160 percent as sales growth outpaced SAP's to hit $216.2 million. The two ERP rivals are spectacular examples of a significant trend towards indigenous European IT services companies with global spread. Sema Group is another, a combination of British and French elements ('the pragmatic with the conceptual', says a senior executive, in all serious-ness). Turnover is a huge $677 million worldwide, thanks to clients such as Adidas, Zeneca and IBM.

Like other European consultancies, Sema has built its practice on carefully considered and well-articulated principles. The focus is on what the client business is trying to achieve, and what policies offer the best promise of reaching those objectives. Sema lists 'key competitive factors' which translate into five powerful questions:

1 How do we achieve superior customer relationships?

2 What are we really good at, and how can we obtain the utmost mileage from that excellence?

3 How can we share the rewards among those who created the achievement?

4 How can we respond flexibly to the political, economic, sociological and technological environment?

5 How can we best use external 'expert partners' (a phrase which obviously includes the culture-changers of Europe themselves)?

The first question is central. The discovery of the customer, and the effort to build business systems around giving customers what they want, where they want and how they want it, has transformed European business-speak: and it is beginning to affect real-life management. Man-agers are trying to live up to words like Swissair's 'service promise', which swears to provide customers with 'Total safety – Dynamic adaptation to market needs – A modern fleet – Impeccable service in line with the Swiss hospitality tradition'. The words were written under the influence of Jacques Horovitz, founder of the MSR group, whose full title (Management of Strategic Resources) exemplifies the European viewpoint: that customer service is integral to strategic success.

Living the theory isn't easy. As Horovitz says, 'The biggest issue is the logic of the firm as opposed to the logic of the customer. How to protect the company from customers is the logic of the firm.'[6]

Correcting such illogical logic is the keynote of the European culture-changers. The best practitioners seek to alter behaviour decisively for the better, rightly seeing this behavioural transformation as the key to changing and improving the culture of the firm. The emphasis is wholly pragmatic. Europe does have a few high-flown business philosophers. However, the single-idea academic or consultant, author of the bestselling one-solution tome, is far more commonly an American.

Some of the tomes sell well in Europe; as for the US consultancies, they have sold marvellously. But the history and practice of European companies are antipathetic to single-issue solutions and more sympathetic to the holistic approach – looking at the organization as a whole. It's no accident that Baan and SAP have seized the lead in enterprise-wide work: the European thinkers have taken naturally to the concept of the enterprise as indivisible.

That must be right. Against what Sema calls an 'old world/new world' shift, companies 'need to recognize and plan for a continually evolving set of integrated resources'.[7] These resources are people, processes, money, information, technology and time: all six revolve round the core of strategy. Claus Møller expresses the same holistic approach, in a core TMI diagram, with a series of three interlocking circles: the trio are Productivity, Relations and Quality.

The holistic approach is intrinsic to Total Quality Management, which, after a dreadfully late start, has brought substantial business to many of Europe's indigenous management advisors, including PA Consulting Group. The consultants aim to guide clients along the road to global competitiveness. The journey has four stages:

1 Quality awareness (a few champions trying something).

2 Quality promotion (almost everyone trying to do things better).

3 Quality management (all improvements aiming in the same direction).

4 Quality empowerment (everyone involved in planned and/or voluntary self-sustaining improvement activity).

On that journey, the destination is global and never final. The aims get higher, renewal is required at regular intervals, and the better behaviours have to be repeated over years, not months, before they become embedded in the culture. As for globalism, even being best in Europe is not enough. Not only are world standards essential if you want to compete in world markets, but domestic markets in Europe are increasingly vulnerable to world-class competitors from outside.

The native gurus – more to be found in consultancy than in the academic world – are fully aware that the European imperative is global. They have spread out widely from their domestic bases (PA, for instance, has offices in 14 countries) and they have evolved world-class methodologies that have found global customers. Those mentioned here form only a fraction of an army of pragmatic, holistic, largely unsung missionaries and (in the best sense of the word) mercenaries.

That army is fully capable of supporting a pan-European response to the global challenge. The culture-changers are working steadily away to underpin and make good the structures of European business. They have built global success and riches for themselves in the process. Inevitably, their clients also will be pulled towards the light of New Century Management.

Progress through processes

Whatever route they follow, European thinkers end up as exponents of what I've called 'the management consensus'. The gurus of the consensus (meaning virtually every guru) believe you should:

1 Involve employees at all levels in making decisions.
2 Adopt 'best practice' ideas and methods from within and without the organization.
3 Attack every process and procedure in the company with the aim of simplifying, compressing, economizing and improving.

The initiatives at many European companies reflect every part of this triple prescription. In project after project, in manufacturing and services alike, total tangles have been turned into orderly patterns, with major gains in productivity, by employees using their own intelligent efforts. It's a very powerful, basic tool. Much the same technique can redesign entire 'business systems'. After finding out where cost and time are most spent and most wasted, you can design detailed plans for reducing or eliminating both cost and time.

Workshops can be used to uncover specific proposals for improvement from large numbers of people. At British Airways, for instance, company-wide seminars have been held at which, writes the *Guardian*, 'staff are invited to contribute their own views on how BA can improve its service to the customer and its position in the market'. In one £750,000 event, no less than 4,500 seniors and juniors were assembled in the Concorde hangar at Heathrow to participate in detailed discussions of the airline's plans – including the latest proposed innovations.

If you ask people's opinions, or involve them in projects, you must react positively. The boss must decide swiftly whether to agree or disagree, and, if it's the latter, must explain why, fully and frankly. There may be a need for more information before the Yes/No decision is taken, in which case a team should be appointed to deliver the data by an agreed date. The psychological pressure should be to agree rather than reject. That doesn't, however, remove the equal need to win results that are demonstrably worth having.

Such workshops are a teaching and learning process, which has high value in itself. Teaching and learning are the foundation of management's new world, and of organizational change. The body of individual collections of knowledge, passed on like some great library from one employee generation to the next, constitutes much of what is known as corporate culture. In a changing culture, however, words mean less than actions: if more effective actions producing much better results are not flowing, the culture has not been changed in any meaningful way.

Words, however, do have an important role. In *The Super Chiefs*[8] I remarked on the long-term performance of twenty companies that were committed verbally to 'values'. They had outperformed the economy tremendously, thus providing the proof of the pudding.

Cultural change that doesn't give rise to large and real results is valueless. Much nonsense is written and talked about 'culture' – largely because quite different concepts are thrown into the same pot. The problem starts with the word itself. 'Culture' in the sense of 'the organizational norms of a business' is a very recent meaning; the word used to refer to 'improvement or refining by education and training', coupled with 'the intellectual side of civilization'.

Education, training and broad intellectual awareness are the foundations of managerial excellence. But every company also has a distinctive nature, a set of traditions, often dating back deep into its past, which can only be broken by a radical change in circumstances. These traditions are only harmful if they become embedded in obsolete or inefficient systems. Physical structures (organizations, factories and offices no less than cities and landscape) also influence how people behave.

Behaviour is what gives an organization's culture its aspect. You may talk about your devotion to the customer, how much you respect and value the individuals inside the company, and how dedicated everybody is to quality, but these are meaningless concepts unless translated into, and proved by, behaviour. It is the processes that enshrine culture in this respect. Inevitably, changing the former for the better changes the culture – for the better.

Look at the ten rules for R&D winners (see page 110), and you see example after example of process change. Look at the companies that excel at serving their customers. What does 'high attention to the customer' mean? Process. All the following processes have a profound effect on service levels:

1 *Commission systems*. (These always distort the pattern of effort: for example, if you want to ensure that small customers are treated with as much consideration as large, don't pay commissions at all.)

2 *Profit-sharing*. (If all employees share in profits, it will markedly improve their attitudes.)

3 *Training*. (The best means of providing people, not only with the tools of their trades, but with the motivation to perform better.)

4 *Customer research*. (Don't rely on number-crunching alone if you want to ensure that purchasers are indeed satisfied – speak to individual customers and listen to what they tell you.)

5 *Employment*. (If you want people to see the business as their career, you must give them genuine careers.)

6 *Remuneration*. (Companies that seek above-average performance must provide above-average pay which is clearly and fairly linked to that performance.)

7 *Share ownership*. (Enabling people to obtain shares in the company, right down the line, is more than motivational – it's fair.)

8 *Recruitment*. (This is where everything starts and where the true potential of the company ends.)

9 *Pricing*. (A key part of the service equation, which revolves round value for money.)

10 *Top-level involvement.* (If the chief executive doesn't spend, say, a quarter of his time where the customers are, and allocate another substantial chunk of time to relating to employees, the service and the business will suffer.)

In most respects, large companies would on the whole espouse these cultural principles – most managements will pay lip service to training, meticulous recruitment, and having employees as shareholders. The difficulty lies in removing the lip from the lip service and substituting the deed.

The no-commission rule, for instance, stands in total contradiction to practice in the big, sales-driven company, where the sovereign dominance of commissions has been a well-known obstacle to change. But commissions, if a salesman is greedy, can work against customer satisfaction – another good end to which virtually all companies pay at least lip service. Many managers now understand that 'satisfaction' is not good enough: that only when customers are 'very satisfied' by 'excellent' service will customer retention rates rise to the 90 percent-plus levels which spell premium profits. According to an expert from Bain & Co, 'Raising customer retention rates by five percentage points increases the value of an average customer by 25 percent to 100 percent.'

Those companies whose processes link executive pay to customer satisfaction don't usually employ retention rates as their yardstick. They use what one consultant calls 'the Big Brother customer survey' – and they don't make the vital distinction between 'good' and 'excellent'. Moreover, their measures aren't reliable: as a professor of accounting at Wharton, David Larcker, rightly says, 'Customer satisfaction is too complicated to measure by means of an unsatisfactory sample giving you a knee-jerk rating on a scale of one to five.'

Certain crude conclusions can be drawn from this imperfect number, however. Statistics suggest that, unless your numbers are over 75 percent satisfaction, you have no competitive advantage. Second, ratings vary markedly between industries – far more than between companies. It follows that, in addition to customer retention, companies must look at satisfaction relative to the competition. In an industry where customers are prone to unhappiness, a greater possibility exists of achieving competitive breakthroughs by a better customer satisfaction strategy.

But you won't discover the correct strategy from an index. Different processes – anecdotal, qualitative surveys – are essential to unearth, for example, the reasons why banks are held in relatively low regard, and supermarkets respected less than the manufacturers whose brands they stock. When you know the negatives and positives, you can eliminate the former and accentuate the latter.

Once the specifics of dissatisfaction are laid out clearly, it is very hard to ignore the evidence and to avoid the necessity of improving. The effort will certainly pay off. And the pay-off may well come in an absolute financial figure: the share price. Larcker discovered that in one six-month period the share prices of companies which were the ten top satisfiers in the most satisfying industries rose at six times the overall market advance.

So satisfaction processes appear to work brilliantly. The crucial questions are:

1 What is our present rating on customer satisfaction and retention?
2 What operational improvements can be made to increase satisfaction and retention while reducing costs?
3 What people policies must be introduced to generate these improvements?
4 How will we share the financial rewards from improvement on the first three counts in order to recognize success and stimulate further progress?

The fourth question helps to answer itself – for, if the share price does respond to customer satisfaction levels, share ownership schemes will provide warming rewards at all levels of the company. Whether or not this powerful way of linking rewards to results is available, profits equally supply a strong potential link between pay and performance – because companies whose customer satisfaction ranks high tend to have returns on capital comfortably in excess of their capital cost. After all, if a supplier offers better quality and service than its competitors, its customers are highly likely to stay and to pay a premium for the privilege.

But these measures to raise customer satisfaction can't make enough difference without another vital ingredient: 'atmosphere'. In the right atmosphere, people are bound to the company by love of their jobs and loyalty to a culture which genuinely puts them first. The people priority is inescapable, because nothing can be executed save through people. 'Right-sizing', for example, will be far better done if the employees are involved, not as a final thought, but as a first. At SGS-THOMSON, job cuts were approached culturally, as a total quality exercise. The object (brilliantly met) was to ensure that only dispensable posts went; that all necessary strengths were left intact; and that everybody agreed with the decisions and their implementation.

Processes of this nature build the idea that making and accepting practical suggestions is part of the way the company manages. The best way to make sure that this idea penetrates people's consciousness (and thus the corporate culture), is not by exhortation, but by example. The best example, of course, is that of the 'best practice', another vital part of the vitalizing kit: select the companies whose performance is superior, look at their best practice, and exchange management ideas.

The approach is so simple that its neglect is amazing. Other companies offer important lessons from which you can benefit. Not Invented Here should be a recommendation, not a cause for rejection. Winners take ideas from anywhere as they concentrate on process – *how* you manage – rather than on function – *what* you do. But how long will the borrowings and the concentration take to change the culture decisively and brilliantly?

Decisive and brilliant change won't happen overnight. Some wise heads believe that 10 years are needed to alter an established hierarchical culture into a horizontally organized grouping of participative, successful people to whom change is a natural order, in which the role of managers is to facilitate rather than command and control. In other words, a company starting on the journey of reform in the mid-nineties must persist until long after the millennium.

Ten years? Are cultures truly that resistant? The ideal of the management consensus is that the culture should become self-generating and self-regenerating. That must take years – maybe ten. It takes no time at all, however, for somebody, or some group of people, to determine that 'we're going to change'. It takes little more time to start the process – by vigorously changing the processes – and then the new world is on the way to being won.

SIX

Keeping the Competitive Edge

The Europeans from Japan

Ever since the German economic miracle faded, the pace in management kudos has been set by the Americans, and most recently by the Japanese. Europe's management contribution hasn't been widely famed in either manufacturing or services. So it is quite daring of three authors, Helen Bloom, Roland Calori and Philippe de Woot,[1] to have produced a book which describes its title subject, 'Euromanagement', as 'a new style for the global market'.

The authors argue that Europeans can counter the Japanese (and the Americans) by exploiting an alleged lead in four key areas: managing international diversity, social responsibility, 'internal negotiation', and orientation towards people. But the authors acknowledge a downside. Management is still more production-led than customer-orientated. And Europe's management systems are looser – a vice which the book presents, however, as leading to a considerable virtue.

This managerial laxity, the authors argue, necessitates the development of 'internal negotiation', explained as 'a mixture of top-down and bottom-up communication between different levels of management and employees, and between headquarters and business units'. As a top Robert Bosch executive explained, 'The European director is more forced to cooperate ... We have learned to work *with* our employees.' The conventional view – that cooperative working is a Japanese speciality – is thus turned on its head.

A well-placed Japanese, however, claims that Japan still rules in cooperation, although that leads to the disadvantage, not the advantage, of Japan. Kageo Nakano, managing director of NTT Europe, says that in his home country the top man 'confides and shares all his secrets and details with his subordinates (notably the heads of the departments), and then simply signs his name'. In Europe, top management is no rubber-stamp; 'by contrast, the president and his executives show great involvement, initiative and leadership ... To me they seem very active and dynamic, and I admire that very much.'

Is Europe working towards a synthesis between top-down and bottom-up, between the Western command-and-control mode and the Japanese model of delegation? In fact, the contrast between the mode and the model is false. For example, Sony's history, under the partnership of Akio Morita and Masaru Ibuka, laying down principles sustained by their successor managements, is a superb demonstration of dynamic 'involvement, initiative and leadership', with delegated contributions at every level.

It's history is one of responsive adaptation to the environment. In the spring of 1994 Sony announced that it was reorganizing itself to improve the speed and quality of its corporate decisions. Management layers were being cut. Seventy divisions and departments were disappearing, a 20 percent reduction. Eight new internal companies, focused on their specific markets, were being formed under individual bosses whose enhanced powers would include design, manufacturing and marketing. But why had Sony, possibly the most brilliant success of the entire national economic miracle, been pressured into reorganization?

This vigorous internal reaction to Japan's challenges of the mid-nineties isn't confined to Sony. Matsushita, whose successful product strategy used to consist of following the leader (meaning Sony as often as not), got there first on reorganization. It reduced administrative staff by 30 percent in December 1993 in a basically similar slash. Did these two mighty upheavals in the mightiest of Japanese electronic powers imply that the country had caught the Western disease of overmanning and underperformance?

In fact, the explanation is an old, old story. Success locks companies into established ways – and the principle of lifetime employment has helped to litter Japanese executive structures with surplus bodies. The West's acceptance of the hire-and-fire philosophy has left it no better off, merely in the same position. Yet its companies do have an advantage in coping with the need for change. As *Euromanagement* argues, the Single Market's own diversity, creating a new style of diverse, truly multi-national management, promises to be highly effective. But the Japanese aren't mere bystanders at this feast.

NTT's Nakano is living proof that Japanese management is part of Europe: indeed, I was once politely but publicly rebuked by the chief executive of Citizen Watch Europe for calling it a Japanese company. They regard themselves, he said, as a *European* firm. The lines between

East and West are truly becoming blurred. Witness the way in which (for only one example) Toyota *doubled* non-Japanese output in a mere two years. Japan is moving West just as fast as the West is learning Eastern management lessons.

So devout fans of both Eastern and Western management should have been distressed by a *Financial Times* report. It noted that 'Just-in-time, the Japanese tool so widely admired and imitated around the world, appears to be failing in its country of origin . . . Just-in-time, it seems, has become just too much . . . for the first time some Japanese groups are beginning to take action to break down the system.' JIT, remember, was once the West's prime totem of Japanese management and its superiority.

That's not all. Another pillar of Japanese supremacy is speed-to-market. After years of rubbing the noses of Western car rivals in the dirt for their sluggishness, though, Japan's car makers decided in the early nineties to slow down the pace. The faster the new model programme, they concluded, the less time available for originality and creativity: sameness creeps in, which weakens the customer impact of new models – and that impact is vital to offset the lower profitability of shorter product life spans.

None of this is any surprise to Professor Manfred Perlitz of Mannheim University. He has been warning Western managers for some time that, by imitating yesterday's Japanese model, they are missing today's challenge. Product quality, for instance, is reaching a point of no competitive return. As one Western car executive points out, nobody produces 'dogs' any more: by the millennium, quality and reliability should be uniform across all makes, if only because any laggards will have left the unequal competition.

The same phenomenon applies to inventory control. Once you have achieved a sensible balance of just-in-time arrivals, you can be sure of two things: opponents will catch up, and no further competitive gains are possible on that dimension. The JIT backlash has arisen because the balance hasn't always been sensible. The customer has simply transferred his inventory problem and costs to the supplier, rather than cooperating with the latter to ensure the most economic and effective flow throughout the combined business system.

Maximizing mutual benefits by mutual action, via what is known as 'strategic alliance', is one of the ways forward that doesn't bear an exclusive Japanese trademark. It is the distinctive feature of what two previously cited Western experts, William H. Davidow and Michael S. Malone, have called 'the virtual corporation': 'a single-source, vertically integrated organization' that is 'really . . . made of strategic partners with complementing core competencies,' as one company proudly described itself.

Fans of Japan will retort that its manufacturers have long operated more or less in this mould. But sceptics should consider one fact. Two years after the reorganization described above, Sony's 1996 results showed that, despite the strength of the yen and the intensity of competition, profits had trebled the figure of two years before on a 23 percent increase in turnover. This reflected its success in simultaneously cutting costs and launching brilliant new products. That is the Japanese reality – and that's the challenge which Europe still has to surmount.

'Euromanagement' may be evolving in the best Western firms. But vigorous European implants will simultaneously provide Japan with a working laboratory for developing its own new-style management. Nothing in the amazing national record suggests that the lab won't be intensively used by the Japanese. Europeans have access to the same experiences. They had better learn all they can – as fast as they can.

Management East-West style

After long and damaging resistance, most Western management preachers and practitioners have accepted the obvious: Japanese practice offers examples and methods which the West can only ignore at its peril. The obvious response is to imitate whatever is valuable. Westerners are no longer in denial. They have swallowed their pride and the Japanese pills: many of the new approaches now being urged on Western managers are old hat in Japan. From total quality to time-based competition, the West is following in Japanese footsteps.

To build a new kind of Western company and management requires more than imitation, however. The task is one of liberating the voluntary energies of individuals and guiding them towards a common end. There are Western traditions on which to build – such as the old foundations of Douglas McGregor's permissive, collaborative Theory Y. The idea of 'a free association of like-minded men and women', a phrase used by Sir John Harvey-Jones when reforming the culture and performance of ICI, is very attractive to democratic Western minds.

The basic assumptions that led McGregor to savage Theory X (that people only work when forced to) in favour of the Y alternative[2] are equally attractive:

1 Work is as natural as play.

2 Self-discipline is as effective as external disciplining (and by implication more so).

3 The psychological rewards of achievement motivate people towards attaining corporate objectives.

4 The average human being learns, under proper conditions, not only to accept but to seek responsibility.

5 Imagination, ingenuity and creativity are widely, not narrowly, distributed among people in organizations.

6 Most companies don't utilize the full potential of the people employed.

The cynic might describe efforts to turn Theory Y into practice as doing with difficulty what comes naturally to the Japanese. There, excellent managers apply principles of behaviour which translate perfectly into Western language – and which have long been echoed in the progressive areas of the West. Yet you still encounter the old ostrich attitudes that caused Western companies so much damage in the past: for instance, the argument that to emulate Japan is impossible because of its peculiar culture.

But the famous national enthusiasm for good business and effective management isn't simply a product of Japan's culture. After all, sloppy Western habits, like investing too little in productive capacity, new products, training, quality and marketing are hardly cultural – not unless bad business economics are built into the Western mentality. What are the true lessons that remain to be learnt from Japan?

One is the necessity for thinking beyond the short term. For instance, recessions are generally shorter than new product development cycles. So cutting back on development in recession guarantees that innovations will miss the first and very probably the second year of upturn. Culture comes into the equation in only one way: if everybody else is doing likewise, no competitive disadvantage will result. But in a global economy, that breathing-space has disappeared. The better opponents are playing by different, more dynamic rules.

For Western competitors, the Japanese economy outside Japan is a basic threat. Its managers – both transplants and adopted Westerners – have shown repeatedly that Japan's domestic methods can produce equal or better productivity and market penetration in foreign cultures. These methods are no more culturally determined than the technology of the internal combustion engine. Just as McGregor's principles make sense in any language, so do those of productivity.

Despite years of benchmarking, Europeans (and Americans) still tend to employ so many more indirect or overhead workers than the Japanese that they massively offset what may even be superior productivity on the line. I'm often tempted to believe that the most important rule in business economics, and thus in management, is the simplest: *KEEP DOWN THE OVERHEADS*. You can be sure that, in their expansion across the world, now concentrating more on Europe than America, the Japanese are following this precept and many others of like simplicity and power.

That helps explain how Nissan, assembling cars at Sunderland in Britain, produced over three times Rover's cars per employee. Rover, however, is not an assembly operation but a full-scale manufacturer. A fairer comparison was with General Motors, whose Vauxhall employees assembled 40 percent fewer cars apiece than Nissan. The latter have been outshone by Toyota's performance in Derbyshire, where it produced 35 percent more cars per employee than Nissan – and over twice as many as the GM plant.

Toyota's performance greatly shocked union leaders, who calculated that Rover, the last British-owned competitor until it fell to BMW in 1994, would need only two-fifths of its labour force if Toyota's methods were adopted. What is this magic methodology? It includes:

1 Complete flexibility between crafts.

2 Daily and changing production targets.

3 Stopping production if faults appear.

4 Insistence on achieving the day's production targets even if the assembly line has had to stop.

5 Longer working hours – 39 against 37.

Toyota's use of these methods to crack the German monopoly of the luxury executive market with its Lexus models set the seal on the eighties as the era of Japan. In this age, Western management reputations, and some managements, were swept away by the tide of Japanese success. But did the seeds of its own decay begin to sprout within that success? Japan's rocky experience in the nineties seemed to confirm the fears (or hopes) of its critics.

Even the European ventures had problems. In 1996, the KPMG accountancy group reported that 'Japanese companies are generally disappointed with the profitability of their investments in Britain', which totalled £19·4 billion. According to the *Financial Times*, none of the 70 industrial companies surveyed 'thought their profits were high, whereas 40 percent said they were average, and 53 percent said they faced low profits or losses'. Although the prime reason for the poor results was the disappointing economic performance of the Single Market, the figures don't speak well for Japanese management.

There was the additional excuse that greenfield projects (the typical Japanese investment) can't pay off rapidly. All the same, nearly 70 percent of the companies admitted to competitive shortcomings: accounting, marketing focus and after-sales service all needed improvement, while organization structures were duplicating administrative support and preventing local managers from taking quick decisions without a clumsy and time-consuming process of referring back to Japan. That's no mean indictment – delivered by the Japanese themselves.

Criticism of their weaknesses by Europeans has swollen to loud accusations that, stripped of benefits like cheap raw materials and underpriced money, Japan's managers are no more effective than anybody else's. When Nissan was riding high (on the way to losing billions of yen later on), nobody bothered about its excess of components (86 different steering wheels, 173 different steering columns, etc.) or models: 29 in all.

Those unbothered by Nissan's proliferation included not only its management, but outside observers. The failures of Japanese carmakers were hidden by successes on very obvious and important points such as manufacturing costs, product quality, delivery performance and market share. What you look at is what you see. What you don't look at goes unobserved and without criticism.

The Japanese policy of lifetime employment, for instance, was universally admired. In hindsight, it's obvious that, combined with vigorous competition for graduates, it must result in steady bloating of the executive ranks. Many aspects of Japanese management, including the large number of minds brought to bear on debating and deciding issues, reflect this body-count inflation. But who cared, so long as sales and profits were advancing?

The proliferation of models and components arose because Japanese car firms matched their product strategies to the peculiar conditions of their domestic market. Its booming growth allowed too many manufacturers to compete across the board. They prided themselves on the manufacturing genius which enabled factories to spew out an excess of models at remarkable speed. But as soon as domestic demand reverted closer to the worldwide norm, the strength became a weakness.

Piling up product upon product seems to be a national addiction. One Japanese food manufacturer, cited in the *Financial Times*, was reducing its lines to 2,500: that looks even weirder when you learn that two-fifths of its products provided only 3 percent of sales. One major difference between East and West, though, is that, on finding failure, most Japanese react swiftly to achieve success. That's the best reason for supposing that Japan's idols may return to the pedestals from which they fell.

In any event, the Japanese remain tough, resourceful competitors, even if their edge is being eroded. In the US car market, for example, domestic and Japanese quality are now, in many cases, on a par. Emulating the Land-Rover Discovery in Britain, Chrysler has succeeded in launching a new sports model (admittedly, on a short production run) within a Japanese timeframe. In other words, the occasional best of Westerners matches the fairly standard practice of Japan.

So far, in many respects, the nineties can still be seen as Japan's era, in management and competitive terms. Exported competition, far more than exported goods, is what has galvanized the more alert Western competitors into learning new lessons. In cars and electronics alone, key components companies all over Europe are wholly or partly Japanese-owned. The mistake for Western managers would be to identify the troubles of Japan's overall economy with its potential at the level of the globally competitive firm.

Japanese managerial prowess didn't follow the plunge (very prolonged) of the Tokyo stock market. Their prowess, true, may have been exaggerated. Like high-riding companies, soaring national economies encourage misplaced belief in superior quality of management. While the rise of Japan's overseas operations appears to endorse that quality, so did that of America's European affiliates in their time. Set up shop on a brand new, 'greenfield' site, back good, new local management with all the parent's resources in money, technology and expertise, and if you don't win, you should be ashamed.

Nobody, however, is more shamed by bad performance than a good Japanese manager. The reaction – outdo yourself – is admirably demonstrated every time the virus of a soaring yen triggers an epidemic of bluechip blues. The typical Japanese management picks itself up from the floor and demonstrates its celebrated resilience all over again. Any time lost while the Japanese are bandaging their wounds is time most grievously wasted.

Even if Japanese competition makes no further thrusts forward, the penetration already achieved in world markets makes Japanese managers the team to beat – and that includes the broadly defined computer industry. Japan's share of this wondrous market looks puny on the surface. But below the surface, Japanese suppliers have built massive market shares and profitability. For example, billions are being lavished on new semiconductor plants, some making products, like NEC memory chips, with fantastic performance: one gigabit, 15 times today's most advanced product.

In the poor market conditions of the mid-nineties, Western chipmakers (including Siemens) were starting to cut back expansion while the Japanese were moving in the opposite direction. Economic modelling has convinced the Asians that maintaining investment through booms and recessions alike optimizes profits and market share. Europe won't match such powerful competition without applying the same techniques, or finding new and improved approaches, to the vital business of achieving more with less: more output, more on every attribute of importance to the customer, but with less cost, fewer man-hours and less error.

Japanese management methods are mostly founded on Western insights and precepts, but most executives in the US and Europe persist with puzzling reluctance to practise what is preached in Western sermons. For instance, Total Quality Management is a largely Western concept, developed by the Japanese, and imported back into the West, only to be bad-mouthed in the end by local managers.

In total quality, which is about creating and maintaining far better managed businesses, Japan still leads. Dr Michael Cross wrote to the *Financial Times* in December 1993 to report on a long search for world-class manufacturing operations. Europe was heavily and embarrassingly outnumbered. Out of 1,039, classified on the criteria used for the Malcolm Baldrige Quality Award, no fewer than 675 were Japanese. North Americans owned 221 operations in the world class, but only 113 were in North America. Nearly five times as many of Japan's world-class plants (510) were in Japan.

In other words, Japan's relative strength is greatest where its manufacturers lack the innate advantage of greenfield plants and imported technology. They simply have the advantage of superior management. Five to one is a formidable gap. But Westerners with world-class willpower have one large, bright, hope. Japan's management technology is no secret. It can be begged, borrowed, bought; and even – with perfect impunity – stolen.

The clues to Club Med

At first glance, Club Méditerranée is another spoiled child of the sixties – an innovative, wonderfully enterprising foundation that created its own market and exploited that niche with undoubted brilliance. In the nineties, however, Club Med has struggled, suffering losses at its worst and recording only low profitability at other times. The original formula appeals less to the younger generation than to their parents. The latter may still take a Club Med holiday, but they've grown older and staid: and so, despite its $1.8 billion of worldwide sales, has the company.

One element of the earlier years, though, is as vibrant as ever. Simply, Club Med is one of the very best service providers in the world. This wasn't always so. Jacques Horovitz, now Professor of Service Management at IMD in Lausanne, developed his ideas and techniques through long-term work with the company. His appointment sprang from a disturbing discovery: Club Med holiday-makers, expensively won by advertising, were 'coming back unhappy' – and then not coming back.

Horovitz was introduced to Club Med by Serge Trigano, who has now handed on the task of rebuilding his father Gilbert's legacy to a top recruit from Eurodisney, Phillipe Bourgignon. He will win or lose on whether Club Med continues to epitomize the customer-led business of the gurus' ideal. It does have an advantage lacked by many other companies: living, breathing customer contact, day-in, night-out. The Club philosophy, moreover, integrates customers and staff: the latter are *gentils organisateurs* (GOs), and serve the *gentils membres* (GMs) as equals, to levels of visible excellence.

Horovitz deliberately used this nexus to raise Club Med standards. GOs and GMs met to discuss quality issues and feed back the results. This was part of a large-scale programme of communication and training – at the start, Horovitz's 60 quality staff trained 3,000 people in a mere two months. There were no less than 1,000 standards, derived from defining the promise to the customer in ten short lines. What would Club Med give the GMs? For example, how long would they have to wait for wind-surfing?

The standards, the communication and the education were only a start. Club Med's service quality wasn't attained overnight: nor were a thousand and one nights enough. 'To achieve quality of service takes ten years,' says Horovitz. 'After that it's irreversible. If you don't take ten years, it's reversible.' Club Med has constantly instituted projects to improve service, ranging from the best substitute for butter in sauce hollandaise (in countries where butter can't be found) to transforming unfocused country managers into dedicated service coaches.

You can never leave service alone. What Horovitz calls 'redesign of the service offer' is one way of enhancing customer satisfaction. You base the redesign on analysis of the value provided. Thus, what value did Club Med put on daytime leisure activities? And how did that compare with customer perceptions? Club Med long ago learnt how to measure the effort and cost that goes into each piece of the offer (the legendary lavishness of the food, incidentally, is much less expensive than it appears). That cost knowledge is essential to satisfying the customer.

Part of Club Med's trouble, however, was that overall costs had risen too high. Gilbert Trigano cut employment by 10 percent in his final year; Serge continued the cost-cutting process while dropping his father's forays into airline ownership and apartment rentals. Nor will Club Med be building any more hotel complexes like that in Vienna. It will, however, be adding four new villages a year, bringing the total to 130, with special emphasis on Asian sites that can attract the Japanese – who already supply 80,000 visitors annually. As European business generally must, Club Med has gone truly global.

Further expansion to other seas and oceans will be partly financed by the $180 million of new capital which Club Med has raised from its shareholders, headed by the Fiat-owning Agnellis (with 13 percent). The company must also spend money on refurbishing the more time-worn villages while cutting $700 million of debt.

The excellence of the service offer and delivery hasn't saved Club Med from the familiar problems of the entrepreneurial business that outgrows its entrepreneur and its original concept. Whether the latter maintains its validity will depend on whether the tried and trusted formula of sun, sea and sex can be extended over a much wider age span, attracting disproportionately greater numbers of clients to fill capacity (because average stays have shortened), and making decent profits from price-conscious customers in a highly competitive leisure market. Does Club Med still have a Unique Selling Proposition to offer?

Trigano naturally thinks so. 'I've lived through periods of people saying the concept is dead,' he says, 'but then our competitors imitate us. You don't copy a concept that is dead.' He's probably right. But the company's recent history rubs in the salient truth – that superior customer service is not enough. It is only part of a totality, which has to answer many other key questions. Horovitz lists three:

1 Who gives the initiative?

2 Who allocates resources?

3 Who says what you can and cannot do?

These questions, and others like them, weren't answered properly in the twilight years of the founder's reign. The troubles of the nineties would never have descended so thickly if Club Med had got all its answers right. But the pioneering business is now climbing its way back along the correct route. Qualitative research, for example, shows that you can't give too much information to prospective Japanese customers: accordingly, they get detailed maps of the airports used to take them to the resort. Giving the customers what they want, however hard their requests are to believe, must be the foundation of Club Med's future – and everybody else's.

Dancing to the customer's tune

Customer satisfaction surveys are the Alpha and Omega of most total quality programmes: the beginning, in the sense that they establish the company's starting point on the road to perfection, and the end, in the sense of 'objective'. The whole programme is directed towards raising customers' opinion of the firm, its goods and its services. But while most managers rightly see the value of customer surveys, they wrongly trust in survey statistics that are all but valueless.

For a start, Jacques Horovitz warns against relying (as most companies do) on a single overall measure of customer satisfaction. His own consultancy's breakdown gives a total of 40 measured variables, reporting the reactions of anything from 1,000 to 5,000 customers – far more than you need just to measure overall satisfaction. Crude overall measurement is usually reassuring. Invariably, customers' responses to truly detailed enquiry produce a quite different effect.

When the whole truth is revealed, says Horovitz, 'we get a fantastic change of attitude'. Before receiving the facts, there's always a 'perception gap' between management's own (higher) and the customer's (lower) view of the firm's performance. Simple lack of listening skills means that companies are out of touch with the reality of customer perceptions. Managers even argue against perceptions. How can the customers have got it so wrong? Whether the perception is right or wrong in the manager's own eyes is immaterial. A perception is a fact in itself.

Only by recognizing that truth can you find guidance on the most important aspect of all: how to close the gap. This isn't by any means exclusively a matter of customer perceptions. They are vital. But they need to be set against other perceptions of the company and its capabilities in the market. My own consultancy, Strategic Retail Identity, enquires among managers, other employees and suppliers as well as customers – and may well interview other 'constituencies' (for example, competitors), in order to form a picture of the overall perception of the business.

Companies in crisis might well have changed their wrong-headed ways much earlier if top management had measured its own perceptions against the total internal and external view. The perceptions of people inside the company, at all levels, have profound direct and indirect impacts on performance in the market. The perceptions of all those who constitute the market impact even more heavily on success. To optimize performance, the inner-perceived view of top management must be aligned with the realities of the workplace and the marketplace.

Outside perceptions will then be calling the tune. In his book *Relationship Marketing*,[3] Regis McKenna stresses the crucial importance of 'dynamic positioning', which has three aspects, all of them concerned with the outside view:

1 Product positioning. How does your product fit into the competitive marketplace? What is its selling proposition – low cost, high quality, advanced technology? How should you segment your markets? Who are the target customers?

2 Market positioning. How is the company *perceived* by customers and by the 'industry infrastructure': retailers, distributors, suppliers, analysts, journalists and other opinion-makers?

3 Corporate positioning: What do people *think*, not about your products or services, but the company itself?

As the italicized words indicate, perception is central to the positioning – and it is seldom a clear-cut issue. Take product quality, which is especially stressed today. *Perceptions* of quality are influenced by many items: not only performance, reliability and durability, but 'knobs, bells and whistles', aesthetics, status enhancement, availability, service and reputation.

You dare not leave the perception to fate. Management must focus on one or two elements in particular, and the choice must be very deliberately made and implemented and communicated to customers. The object is to persuade them to prefer your product or service. Change of prefer-ence (that is, change in perceptions) is what the astute marketer of fast-moving consumer goods seeks to achieve: it is the most meaningful test of an advertising campaign's success or failure – far more meaningful than spontaneous or prompted 'recall' of the ads.

It may seem ridiculous that mere names can create commercial suc-cess, until you remember the Chinese gooseberry. That was the name of a product, grown in New Zealand, which was all but unsaleable until some genius renamed it the Kiwi fruit. At one time or another it was impossible to market ballpoint pens, Post-It Notes, vacuum cleaners, liquid soap, Vicks VapoRub or Vaseline, not because of any disadvantages in these splendid products, but because vital links in the market chain – like retailers or distributors – had negative perceptions of these future wonders.

One of those links is the company itself. Market leaders tend to the preconception that they excel the competition at every point. The competition tends to believe the same thing, and the smaller their market share, the greater their faith in the leader. That's why industries so often play follow-the-leader. If the biggest fast food company starts building bigger and fancier restaurants, with larger and fancier menus, so do all the others. This flies in the face of the Unique Selling Proposition. If you're not perceived as different, why should anybody buy from you rather than somebody else?

The perception that a competitor's larger share is the decisive advan-tage is likely to be false. Many market leaders by size have small returns. The reasons for their low profitability include inept marketing. One study found, for example, that some 51 percent of a group of low-return leaders shared more than 80 percent of marketing programmes with other lines. That compared with only 39 percent of the leaders with high returns. Leaders may also lag seriously on two of the most important aspects of perception: relative *perceived* quality and relative *perceived* service. High scores on these dimensions can help to substitute for a lower market share.

The essential point is that you can't know too much about your customers, or how they perceive your competitors. If you proceed on your own preconceptions, and not those of customers, you are certain to make mistakes. As noted, the object is to align their perceptions with yours. Many cases show how, when perceptions were changed by aban-doning the entrepreneurs' own false notions, product failures were turned into historic successes. In *Getting It Right the Second Time*,[4] author Michael

Gershman offers a dozen telling Ps for those who want to emulate such triumphs:

1 Pitch it the right way.

2 Look for a Piggyback ride.

3 Have faith in public Perception.

4 Correctly Position the product.

5 Don't overlook the Package.

6 Sell in the right Place.

7 Set the right Price.

8 Consider a Premium.

9 Don't skimp on Promotion.

10 Use the full power of Publicity.

11 Add a Promise to the product.

12 . . . And at all times Persevere.

Gershman's examples for Pitching it the right way include the shift of Kleenex from beauty aid to simple nose-blowing. The Zantac success in anti-ulcer treatment was initiated by a Piggyback: Glaxo first used the much larger Hoffman-La Roche sales force in the US. The change in public Perception achieved with Volkswagen overcame the American prejudice in favour of large cars, and against small ones. The Position switch of Tesco from 'pile it high and sell it cheap' to that of quality supermarket is a classic of marketing.

In pharmaceuticals, which traditionally turns a blind eye to the package, Boots gave the radically different analgesic Nurofen (which contains neither aspirin nor paracetamol) a radically different pack. The Place chosen by Swatch to defeat the Japanese watchmakers was any place where Swiss watches had not traditionally been sold. Zantac's Price (and Promotion) gambit was to raise prices and marketing spend when they had traditionally been cut. Wrigleys' Premium move was not to offer gifts to the customers who chewed its gum, but to give dealers who placed large orders free coffee grinders, cheese cutters, lamps and ladders.

With the aid of Promotion (samples distributed to doctors) both Vaseline and VapoRub got off the ground. The Publicity stratagem used by the legendary Patrick J. Frawley to save Paper Mate's day was obtaining endorsement by the ballpoint pen's severest critics, educators and bankers. The best kind of Promise is the service or product guarantee –

like the long-standing Marks & Spencer promise, now imitated by several other store chains, to replace any product for any reason, or none at all. As for Perseverance, Procter & Gamble stuck with Pampers through production problems, high prices and buyer resistance. The manufacturer finally outdid cloth nappies by using the customer's point of view – the crucial customer turned out to be the baby.

In all these examples, money was involved, but rarely much of it, and never as the crucial factor. The key to changing perceptions, which are other people's thoughts, is the quality of your own thinking.

If you don't think, you won't change anything. But mental rigidity makes it easy to stop thinking altogether. A simple example lies in the fact that many retailers have no idea what proportion of customers intending to buy enter the store, but leave without purchasing. In one case investigated by Jacques Horovitz, it ran as high as 40 percent.

It doesn't take a genius to work out the increase in sales and profit available from reducing that terrible two-fifths. But even genius won't help unless you analyse the overall result. *Why* didn't 40 percent of the customers buy? Was it a poor salesperson? Lack of sales staff? Out of stock? These questions have their equivalents in any business. What proportion of proposals/bids/sales calls and so on fail? Why? And then, what can – and must – be done to raise the success ratio? If any item on any survey shows a fall from acceptable levels of customer satisfaction, treat that defect as a potentially decisive slippage.

You can see the decisive power of consumer perception by looking at the top ten companies in the British and European lists of companies most respected by their peers. The unifying theme is less their high financial performance than the marketplace strength from which the money derives. Note the power of these customer franchises: leading in Britain are Cadbury Schweppes, Tesco, Whitbread, Vodaphone, Sainsbury, Reuters, Unilever, Marks & Spencer, and Shell. The last three, plus Nestlé, BA, BMW, Siemens, and Fiat, are among the top ten in Europe.

The perception that customer power rules, from stores to airlines, oil to phones, low technology to high, is generally shared among all managements. State that 'getting customer service right' is fundamental to success and you will attract enthusiastic support from managers worldwide, including some who haven't satisfied, delighted, considered or possibly even seen a customer for years.

But what does 'getting it right' mean? Without the clear focus that proper enquiry seeks, nobody can judge whether right has been done. And what if you get it wrong? Does everything else collapse? If so, all companies are in deep trouble, for nobody gets it right, not if the definition is 100 percent customer satisfaction. For instance, corporate users of PCs register only 65 percent satisfaction with the service they receive – and 70 percent counts as merely acceptable. Yet these are among the most reliable, best-produced and most productive devices ever made by man.

Along with other high-tech products, mostly Japanese, PCs have raised the whole level of customer expectations. Even relatively low-tech manufactured products like cars have climbed into a new zone. As Mercedes-Benz found in the early nineties, to its considerable pain, today's buyers won't pay a premium for quality alone. In many markets, for consumer and industrial goods alike, quality, however defined, has become a *sine qua non*. The price for poor quality is paid in the costly shape of Rework, Recalls, Replacements and poor customer Retention.

The last of these four Rs is the crux of the issue. As noted, polling customers to learn their opinions can (and usually does) deal a devastating blow to corporate complacency. Those managements prepared to correct the revealed defects by systematic improvement will find that much else inevitably comes right – though far from 'everything'. For total rightness to happen, improvement must take place within the context of an organization rethought from top to bottom. You can't say 'from start to finish', though, because there is no finish: the process of pursuing customer satisfaction is never-ending.

Retention provides the vital indicator. Measuring customer satisfaction will show companies where they stand (or run) on the upward-moving staircase of expectations. But the votes that count are recorded with the feet, or rather the purse. How many businesses know the scale and cause of customer loss, or have ever costed the profit lost through customer turnover? Typically, 90 percent of the gross margin on an existing customer is dissipated in the effort to obtain a new buyer.

Remember, more positively, that as little as a 5 percent rise in customer retention can increase profits by between 20 and 50 percent. The ultimate logic is that all companies should focus on the external, marketplace environment. The ultimate reality, though, is that people inside companies don't only face outwards, and can't. The customer pays the bills, but not the wages: decisions on promotions, powers, positions, perks and punishments are made internally. The practice of internal politics, in most companies, heavily outweighs the theory of putting customers first and foremost.

Merely look at today's endless spate of corporate commotions. Where (if anywhere) did the customer figure in the wave of mighty mergers crashing over Europe? The usual answer won't wash: that if the upheavals result in greater efficiency and lower costs, the customer can only benefit. True, but that's a million miles away from the ideal: the customer-led focus that runs throughout the organization in a never-ending circuit. That demands commitment to constant change as the customers – rarely satisfied for long, endlessly wooed by others, periodically shifting in their requirements – call the corporate tune.

Commitment to customer-led change comes easier in greenfield organizations such as high-tech ventures. What can be done on a virgin battlefield, with an army composed entirely of volunteers, far outranges the immediate possibilities of long-established organizations. Their armies have old lags, conscripts and some soldiers who, perhaps for the highest-minded of reasons, are conscientious objectors. For the established, the problem is that, once they focus on the customer, almost everything the company does looks wrong.

It takes a brave, rare top management to vacate its throne and set about changing everything, with the willing help of all its colleagues, so that the customer can truly be King – and be treated like one. Significantly, those managements that come nearest to the ideal have been at the forefront of the movement to 'empower' employees: to drive decisions down the organization and hand them over to people who are encouraged to use their own initiative.

The customer-first proposition has become a cliché. So be it. The customers and their perceptions really are decisive. To win, deserve and retain their admiration, managers must endure the destruction of their own comfortable illusions. That beginning is bound to be uncomfortable. But it leads to very comforting success.

The alliances of PixTech

Technological and marketing deals now crisscross the electronics world to form a lattice that is impenetrable even to insiders. There's only one word for it: 'COMPLEXITY!!!' The exclamation marks are those of Michael J. Kami, a consultant of great insight who once worked at shaping the strategy of IBM and later quit to perform the same job for Xerox Corp. One of Kami's slides is a map of computer industry alliances that resembles a subway network gone mad. It has four large hubs of which IBM is only one.

Kami's map portrays only a segment of the maze. By mid-1992,

IBM alone had more than 20,000 business alliances worldwide, including almost 400 equity investments and joint ventures. More such deals are being created almost weekly by many companies: and Europe is deeply involved. Its ability to take the lead in such alliances provides its brightest hope of sharing in a stupendous revolution. Microelectronics are infiltrating, even taking over, activities across the entire spectrum of human life and business.

Microelectronics makes many bedfellows. There is one company, for instance, which had Motorola, Texas Instruments, Raytheon and Futuba of Japan as original partners. That drawing power suggests a powerful entity. The company in question, however, was little more than a start-up, the brainchild of Frenchman Jean-Luc Grand-Clement. His company, PixTech, at Montpellier, exists to exploit part of the technological cornucopia spawned by Europe's uncounted research laboratories.

LETI, near Grenoble, was typical of these: government-owned, enormously expert in a particular field – flat-panel displays – and doing little or nothing to exploit its patents commercially. Grand-Clement changed all that by licensing all sixteen patents and rounding up financial backers for his plans to tackle the flat-screen champions. These competitors are all Japanese: liquid crystal displays made by Sharp, Toshiba, NEC and others have crowded even the US out of a global market worth over $11.5 billion.

PixTech's field emission displays (FEDs) offer several technical advantages over LCDs, winning on thinness, simplicity and production cost – in theory. The practical problem, though, is to get the invention to market and then crack the market. Hence the alliances with powerful partners, one of them, Motorola, Grand-Clement's previous employer. As an engineer, he has no illusions about the obvious difficulty in the marketplace: the strength of the technological competition.

It is not only the awesome Japanese who are working on LCD and FED technology: Grand-Clement has maintained his lead over the US companies that are also developing FEDs. That gives some measure of the challenge the European high-tech pioneers face merely to win the technological race. Grand-Clement could claim in the summer of 1995 that, 'We don't have any technological hurdle today. There is nothing more to invent.' But that's only the beginning.

PixTech rests on a most unusual 'flexible alliance', which, if it succeeds, 'could become a model for others that are trying to bring risky and complex technologies quickly to market', according to one commentator. The allies compete with each other, but share all their resources: PixTech, acting as the node, can sublicense one partner's display technology to all the others. It's an extreme example of a general trend.

Once, companies could afford and achieve product exclusivity. A product was made entirely by the producer, from its own technology and designs, in its own plants, with its own components, often on its own equipment – and none of these were available to outside companies. Outsiders were allowed in only as suppliers of those necessities which such omnicompetent companies chose not to manufacture themselves: few outside products reached the final assembly lines.

In Henry Ford's prime, iron ore came in at one end and finished cars went out the other; and as in Dearborn, Michigan, so in Dagenham, Essex. Today Ford and all other car-makers are very substantial consumers of outside components and complete assemblies. The bought-in proportion, once a sign of weakness, is now an indicator of strength. Kami's complexity is evident in all industries. Other networks may crisscross less than those in high technology, but the same forces are at play.

By the early nineties major new alliances had become a way of life. Usually, no financial terms were disclosed. Often, contradictions abounded. A European company, for example, would join a partnership to wrest market share from American manufacturers. Simultaneously, the same company's deal in another technology would be pulling Americans into Europe. The sheer profusion of these crossborder deals is making the old issues of economic sovereignty increasingly academic.

The biggest issue in all alliances is quite simple: whether or not the project will work out, commercially or technologically. High-flying joint ventures have a bad habit of aborting, partly because of internal problems, partly because of unpredictable events in the outside market. But the risks of failure seem much less alarming than those of being left on the outside looking in. In making as many link-ups as possible, companies are seeking to bargain their own technological competencies and marketing reach against an assured position in the future.

Size, strength and status can no longer be preserved by market domination, price leadership, technological supremacy, or any other traditional means. As in the PixTech network, the best of enemies in one area will be the best of friends in another – and alliance skills will be fundamental. Every company is becoming more and more 'virtual', part of a business system composed of strategic partners whose core competencies complement each other.

Partnering sounds simple enough, put that way. Maintaining market strength through an interlocking network of alliances, on the other hand, sounds complex. Whether PixTech can realize Grand-Clement's ambitions depends on his ability to fuse all the elements of financial and development resources to break free from the limited scale which has bedevilled so many bright European hopes: full-scale production is scheduled to start at Unipac in Taiwan – another ally – in early 1998.

A market expected to reach $21.6 billion by the millennium will require that amount of muscle. But Grand-Clement has unquestionably chosen a promising route. Tomorrow's leaders are mastering the direct paths to the centre of the alliance webs. They have no choice.

Partnering for profit

Companies that are still vertically integrated in a vertical industry – the conventional model – are in trouble. The new age is horizontal, in organization, management and markets alike. And that produces some fascinating, unseen results in global business. As companies cease to make everything they need, concentrating instead on their 'core competencies', a new breed of businesses is emerging into the limelight: multinationals with enormous shares of invisible markets, making components, not finished products.

This is Europe's largest opportunity in the new technologies. Philips, for all its difficulties with its own brands, is a dominant supplier of colour TV tubes to its competitors – just as Sony enjoys three-fifths or more of three key component markets. These are world-leading players. But how many people have heard of Murata, Nideq, TDK, Futaba, Mabuchi and Kyocera? Nideq has 85 percent of the world market for spindle motors for Winchester drives; TDK possesses 60 percent of world sales of printer heads; the others all have similar strengths in various key electronic components.

The attraction of their submarkets lies in the power of horizontal strength, which is inherently difficult to dislodge. These component operations lie at the centre of the networks of complexity. Willy-nilly, their competing customers are all in partnership with the same suppliers. The companies in these driving seats possess core technologies. The resulting competencies create parts at the core of other people's products – which, being end-products, are more vulnerable.

The vulnerability lies in the rapidly fluctuating nature of end-product markets. In the early nineties, large PC companies suddenly found themselves losing money, while their suppliers, led by Intel and Microsoft, were coining cash. The partnerships with these horizontal businesses, alliances which had been the key to fabulous growth and profits, were now sources of much irritation. The anger was futile and died down as the PC brand owners realized that, like it or not, they were indissolubly married to the suppliers.

That being so, the secret was to make the best of the job, good or bad, by optimizing what was within the PC makers' control. That included making other, less involuntary unions for purposes like speed-to-market. In markets which are fickle, and change very fast, even fast-moving companies can be too slow. The strategic alliance aims to speed up progress by pooling existing technologies, instantly achieving combined strengths that would otherwise take years to build. When an IBM, say, joins with others to develop vital technology, it is much less a question of saving costs than saving time.

Two heads should be better than one: two foundation users of the technology will create faster acceptance in the market and quicker payback of the investment. It is the same principle as synchronous product development inside the firm: the savings in time are substantial. They are also essential, for research has shown that time overruns are far more damaging to a product's economics than excess development spending.

To Peter Drucker, time is the 'only one true cost' now left. Whatever the starting-point of management theorists and consultants, they all end up urging speed from their different perspectives. It must be true that the less time your processes consume, the lower your true costs, and the more competitive and profitable your business. To Mike Kami, it's an urgent 'or-else' issue: 'Act faster or perish!'

Massive reduction in normal speeds, according to Kami, is a must: a 20 percent gain isn't even worth considering in most cases. Delivery time should be cut by 50–70 percent, development time by 50–60 percent, inventories by 50–80 percent. Available efficiencies on the plus side include a rise in 'first pass yield' by 60–80 percent, and gains in productivity by from 20 percent (if you're very, very good already) to 80 percent. Return on capital employed, again, should rise for the already good leaders by at least a fifth, and by 80 percent for the laggards.

All these demands apply to alliances. But it is hard enough to generate a sense of continuous urgency in a company with a defined culture and history; how can the necessary impetus be achieved in an *ad hoc* partnership, or a joint venture which exists in the no man's land between two companies? Making alliances *per se* isn't the answer: it's the ability of the allies to achieve decisive advantages together that counts.

The greatest gains won't be won from existing processes and strategies. That holds the clue to the first principle of alliance management. The fact that new partnerships travel without luggage facilitates a familiar but revolutionary type of management: greenfielding. Allies and partners can start from scratch, just like a new factory on a greenfield site.

C. K. Prahalad strikes to the heart of the greenfielding philosophy with a simple question. Which of these two situations would you prefer?

A. Low resources and high aspirations.

B. High resources and low aspirations.

It takes a mere smidgen of soul-searching to arrive at the right answer. Every manager would prefer to work in a rich organization. But the poor company has the urgency of its poverty. As Prahalad asks, 'Would you invent Just-in-Time if you were rich?' Of course not: instead of striving for on-time delivery, you would afford and tolerate unnecessary inventory. Innovation is inherent in the firm which, because it has high ambitions, but lacks the means to achieve them by conventional methods, must break the conventions to realize its ambitions at the least possible cost.

That must mean in the fastest possible time. The low-resource company with high aspirations is the better place to be: for those ambitions, if realized, produce towering payoffs. If your aspirations are low, whatever the resources, achievement will match the low aims.

Greenfielding requires the combination of high ambition with tight targets, for both time and cost. The greenfielders' working partnership needs to be geared up in two dimensions:

1 *Internal speed*, quickening all processes and developing a state of readiness which can produce crash programmes at will.

2 *External speed*, generating fast responses (which will include such programmes) to the demands and the changes in the marketplace.

The need to achieve the internal/external combination punch is no different, of course, in an established organization. The difference lies in the greenfielding mentality, which is the opposite of bureaucratic, hierarchical conduct. But corporations are themselves under compulsion to form internal alliances as well as external ones – bringing groups of people together for a specific, clearly defined purpose and disbanding them once that object has been achieved. There's nothing new in this principle where projects are involved, but its use with *processes* is proving revolutionary.

In New Century Management, new process (innovatory, challenging, continuously improved) is the core of the ability to achieve, and team-working is the universally applicable tool. Inside teams – and within well-found partnerships – contributions vary according to time and circumstance. Football provides the analogy. If the outcome of the World Cup semi-final hinges on the last kick of a penalty shoot-out, the kicker, for that brief moment, is the most important person on the team – but only then. The business analogy is the internal or external expert who joins the team for a specific task, kicks the goal, and then leaves the field.

The results can be spectacular. At the giant Swedish food cooperative ICA Handlanars, Andersen Consulting came in to solve a bundle of problems. Three sales regions couldn't share their data. Distribution to the stores was inefficient, and marketing campaigns were sometimes in conflict. Against that backdrop, the co-op couldn't mount an effective response to the challenge of the Single European Market.

Reengineering transformed its powers. After the cure, reported *Business Week*, all 3,350 stores shared the same database. With a third of the warehousing and distribution centres shut, overall costs had halved – thanks only in part to a 30 percent cut in wholesaling labour. Since revenue has risen by over 15 percent, the payoff must have been huge. The prize could not have been won by the use of internal skills and resources alone.

This observation applies powerfully and increasingly to more and more activities. The specialist has a specific range and depth of talents that are applied every day of every week of every month. For a generalist to maintain the same armoury would be absurd.

It follows, however, that a new meaning has been given to Attract, Motivate and Retain. That's the old Holy Trinity of personnel management. To win the competitive wars you need specialist allies. *Attracting* them is superficially no problem: they are hungry for your business. But that's no guarantee of effectiveness. You want to *attract* the best partners, *motivate* them to achieve their best work, and *retain* them for the desired time (which may be indefinite) at that best level of service.

In the old days, the carrot-and-stick brutalities of Theory X applied to these outside relationships. You chose the cheapest outside supplier and motivated his performance by talking loudly and carrying a big stick: shouting at him, and threatening to take away the carrot – the profits on your business. As for retention, who cared?

The common practice was encapsulated by William H. Whyte Jr in

The Organization Man.[5] He wrote of the car company boss who would take new managers to an exclusive business club and ask them a question. They had employed a loyal, efficient supplier for many years. Out of the blue, a rival undercuts the price by 10 percent. What would they do? Some would give the old supplier the chance to match the new quotation. Others would stay loyal to loyalty. The boss dismissed both approaches out of hand: the new bidder gets the work. Either you're a businessman, or you aren't.

That boss would have been totally bemused by the present-day car industry in which customers insist on improving, not only their own productivity and added value, but the suppliers'. Dependence on supplier alliances has become absolute even for companies where internal collaboration is visibly lacking. When one Volkswagen executive was asked how he could bear to depend on a single source of a single vital subassembly, he simply replied: 'You've got to start trusting somewhere'.

Trust and teamwork are the essence of successful partnering. That's the title of a section in *The Virtual Corporation*, by William H. Davidow and Michael S. Malone.[6] Their ideal of a company without frontiers, which forms a continuum with its outside relationships, can't be realized without expertise in managing those relationships. Yet the book devotes no attention to the management issue, which is of paramount importance.

The wave of the future is the collaborative, jointly managed venture, whether it's a consultancy relationship, a supplier nexus, or a joint company. Historically, joint ventures have had a sad record of failure (the result in 70 percent of cases, according to one study). The ratio is almost certainly far better today, because companies have paid much closer attention to the management issues involved. As Harvard's Rosabeth Moss Kanter has pointed out, joint ventures need to dot six very demanding 'i's:

1 The relationship is *Important*, and therefore it gets adequate resources, management attention and time.

2 There is an agreement for longer-term *Investment*.

3 The partners are *Interdependent*.

4 The organizations are *Integrated*.

5 Each partner is *Informed* about the plans and directions of the other.

6 The partnership is *Institutionalized* – bolstered by formal mechanisms which make trust possible.

In *When Giants Learn to Dance*,[7] Kanter quotes a Harvard Business School colleague on this list: 'The rewards of these things must be incredible to justify all the extra short-term costs that go along with them.' Given the exponential increase in partnerships since the late eighties, when the book was published, that's an intimidating thought. 'Incredible rewards' can scarcely be earned from everyday relationships: 'these things' have become requisites for staying in business, not building-blocks for bonanzas.

'Extra short-term costs', moreover, are insupportable at a time when cost disadvantages can be lethal. What's the answer? Look again at Kanter's list: it translates readily into a catechism of teamwork. Team objectives must be *important*: they will not be achieved without supporting *investment* in adequate resources: the *interdependent* roles of the team members are fundamental: their work and disciplines must be *integrated* to achieve the common purpose: everybody must be fully *informed* at all times to fulfil their roles.

Interdependence, integration and information are the standard toolkit of successful teamworkings. Turf wars are abolished, differing agendas are harmonized, unnecessary secrets are no longer hugged to jealous bosoms. Horizontal management based on project and process thus eliminates vices that bedevil established organizations. Exactly the same benefits, without extra cost, are reaped by effective partnerships.

But what about Moss Kanter's sixth principle: institutionalization?

The word has become as ugly in reputation as in sound. The principle, though, can't be gainsaid: unless the institutional set-up of the partnership, as of any team, matches the mission, the latter will fail. The author writes of 'a framework of supporting mechanisms, from legal requirements to social ties to shared values'. What's happening today is the downgrading of mechanisms and legalisms and the upgrading of a seventh 'i': the *informality* which is a social bond, a value in itself, the underpinning of the formal values, and the way to save partnering from extra costs.

For example, Allied Domecq, like most wine and spirit companies, has a long history of successful alliances, including the quarter-of-a-century relationship which culminated in union with its Spanish component, Domecq. 'Managing the relationship with partners is quite embedded in the culture,' says Tony Hales, the chief executive. But, while you must get the legal framework right, then 'you stuff it in a drawer', because 'the relationship is what matters'. 'Drinking a bottle of Ballantine's together once a year' is equally important.

So the password is not 'institutionalized', but 'instituted': that is, 'put in place', preferably by the partnering people themselves, and in a form which, like the workings of the partnership, is flexible and continuously developing. This is not an unnatural requirement. On the contrary – it is the natural way to behave. And the results should be excellent – naturally.

SEVEN

Achieving Constant Renewal

The luxury of Hoffman La Roche

'While it's good for top executives to have equity stakes in their company, they may grow excessively cautious if their stakes become too large.' This research finding flies in the face of the popular view (especially popular among executives, naturally) that the higher the stake of senior executives and directors, the higher their interest in building the business by taking risks.

Peter Wright at Memphis State University suggests further in the *Academy of Management Journal* that the magic number could be 7·5 percent. When insider ownership passes this barrier, the degree of risk-taking falls in step with the rise in the equity stake. My suspicion has long been that the grotesque rewards paid to top managers in the US focus their attention, not on the company's real needs, but on their personal wealth. The corporate needs and executive riches don't necessarily go hand-in-hand.

This phenomenon is confined to hired hands; large proprietorial holdings are neutral in their impact, which should really be good news for the descendants of Fritz Hoffman. They have daily cause to bless the year 1896 when he founded Hoffman La Roche. The drug group's voting shares are still majority-controlled under what chairman Fritz Gerber describes as 'the luxury of family ownership'. Since much of European industry – notably Germany's *Mittelstand* group of powerful medium-sized firms – is privately owned, that should provide Europe with a potential edge.

But companies are not exploiting that advantage. Roche built its marvellous reputation and wealth on the R&D risks that produced products like Valium, which transformed pharmacology. Despite its luxurious ownership, though, Roche has been slipping on important measures. It has dropped down the league table of sheer size: from fifth in global market share in 1993–4 to ninth and falling. Although that largely reflects the merger wave between rival giants, Roche's conservatism has certainly been another factor.

Its financial management is superb – but piling up Alps of cash is the reverse of taking risks. The management has run risks, but outside the labs, in the merger and acquisitions market where its 1997 buy, Boehringer Mannheim, cost a cool $11 billion. Roche is not alone in the odd managerial view that bids and deals are risk-free, but experience tells a different story: Syntex, purchased by Roche for $5.6 billion, and Genentech (a 60 percent stake bought for $2.1 billion) have produced, respectively, inferior yields and no yields at all.

Despite the weak returns, Roche's overall growth in earnings per share (28 percent per annum over five years) has been outstanding. However, expansion in sales, up only 22 percent over the entire five-year period, played only a minor part in the growth of earnings: it was cost-cutting which achieved that. Now the rate of earnings rise is expected to halve. For Roche, as for many Euro-companies, cost-cutting and amalgamation have not proved to be the engines of outstanding sustainable growth.

That can only be achieved by successful development of brilliant products. Franz Humer, the head of pharmaceuticals at Roche, shrugs off criticisms of its performance, saying that 'we like to set our own benchmarks'. But these benchmarks can be wrong – even with 'the luxury of family ownership'. The meaningful benchmarks are set, not by management, but by markets.

All Europe's major companies face an intimidating set of questions:

1 Are we lagging behind, not leading, global standards?

2 Are we setting the technological pace and keeping to the fore in exploiting the state of the art?

3 Are we exchanging vertical bureaucracy for the new style of horizontal management, which relies on relatively loose associations of managerial groups – many of them transitory?

Very few companies (and Roche is clearly not among them) can honestly say yes to all three of the queries. But new enterprises require the triple strengths. They must be the main source of growing revenue in any industry, let alone pharmaceuticals. The global arena in which Roche has long operated, but which is now becoming everybody's playing field, has become more fluid and less certain. Fragmenting markets means that organizations need to become fluid and highly changeable, and this means taking risks.

The more rigid the organization, and the more set in its ways, the more painful this transition must be. That's especially true of a company like Roche, which for as long as possible used its privacy as a protective screen. Appropriately, its Basle headquarters are hard by the Park of Silence. Back in 972, Roche kept silent even about its turnover: the sales that year, some £650 million, were semi-bared by an unguarded remark from the then president, Dr Adolf Jann. Defending Roche against charges of profiteering, he noted that it spent around £100 million on R&D – some 15 percent of sales.

Since then, Roche has had veil after veil stripped away, partly because governments paying huge drug bills have sought evidence that they are being fairly charged. Certainly Roche reaps a very fair profit. In 1995 it earned $2·7 billion on sales of $11·8 billion, leaving its two Basle rivals, Sandoz and Ciba, far behind. The great bulk of that gusher of wealth, though, sprang from the firm's past willingness to gamble on overcoming the horrendous odds against finding a pharmaceutical goldmine like Valium: its future depends on current promising new drugs.

The contrast between its risk-taking and its deep corporate conservatism was always a paradox. There is another paradox. The risk-taking company is a safer place to be. At all times it checks to ensure that its policies, strategies and tactics are in the vanguard. It continuously evolves to reflect changing conditions and market demands. It responds to demanding financial and non-financial targets, continuously revised as feedback animates the business system. It lives by seizing and creating opportunities.

Whether the key shares are owned by institutions, families or management, the ability to grab those opportunities and capitalize on their potential is crucial. In today's conditions, living off the past is a dangerous game. Given that the future will be still more arduous and competitive, taking carefully calculated risks is mandatory. Anything that deters management from adventure is no luxury: it is an extravagance that even firms as rich as Roche cannot afford.

The rewards of risk

Why do risk-taking companies backslide into conservatism? Manfred Perlitz of the University of Mannheim traces a kind of managerial rake's progress, in which the risk-taking start-up develops through successive stages of maturity until it reaches the ossification from which dwindling

performance and eventual crisis result. Xerox Corporation's progress from
Great Innovator to victim of the Japanese perfectly illustrates the cycle,
but doesn't explain it.

Research cited by Perlitz suggests a potent explanation, however. It
lies in the risk:reward ratio. In academic theory, he points out, managers
confronted with a choice of investments will select the alternative with
the highest probable rate of return. Thus, a straight financial investment
yielding 10 percent will not be chosen if a riskier option has a 25 percent
chance of yielding nothing, but a 75 percent chance of returning 15
percent.

The sums are simple. Multiply the odds by the return, and you get
zero plus (75 x 15) = 11·25 percent. So the safe 10 percent choice should
lose out. When this theory was tested against real-life managers, however,
it collapsed. Offered a choice between a safe 10 percent return on a
financial investment, and a higher but riskier yield on a new product or
new process, managers questioned in a sizeable survey plumped
overwhelmingly for safety. The risk they are dodging is that to their
own careers. The risk they unwittingly run is to the future of their
company.

What happens when the less risky option has unacceptable results?
Now the business is in trouble: continuing with the present policy means
losing 10 percent on investment. The managers are told that a new product, if they are lucky, has a 25 percent chance of yielding a zero return
– but a 75 percent chance of losing 15 percent. The simple sum now
shows that the certainty, a 10 percent loss, is worth more than the risky
option: zero minus (75 x 15) = a probable 11·5 percent loss. Yet the
surveyed managers now overturn the theory in the opposite direction:
less than a third will select the certain loss; all the rest go for risk.

With new processes, as opposed to products, nearly six times as many
managers will take the risk. The worries about their careers have been
swamped by their anxieties over the crisis of the company. In crisis, a
breakeven risk investment seems a better choice than a certain slide
into further losses. As Perlitz argues, the better course is to create crisis
conditions when no crisis exists. Alter the target/reward system in favour
of taking innovatory risks, and more innovation will follow.

Better still, thrust the company into a furnace of technological change
in product and process, fanned by intense competition, and fuelled by
compulsory risk investments. Chipmakers, for instance, are driven by
incipient crisis that demands continuous investment in the next state of
the art. The management responses of companies in such situations have

developed increasing power and speed with experience. Their risk strategies have been annealed in the furnace.

Those fires propel the high-tech company towards achieving the highest technological and commercial standards it can reach – and then going beyond them. The wonderful soprano Emilia Galli-Curci observed that, when she listened to her own recordings, and recalled her musical aspirations, she was 'very humble'. But when she listened to other sopranos, she was 'very proud'. In lesser people – and organizations – pride in outdistancing the competition can overtake the drive to outdistance your own achievements. Another danger is that headlong growth often stretches management and financial resources.

The leading American high-tech companies – Intel, for example – when confronted with these challenges, have emerged as dominant suppliers, not only in the US, but throughout the world. Where have Europe's technological powerhouses been while others were stealing the future? Preserving the *status quo*. Market leaders are understandably reluctant to cannibalize existing technology and disturb existing markets by introducing new-technology products with superior characteristics.

The Perlitz Syndrome applies. The bird in the hand looks far more attractive – in career and corporate terms – than the two or more birds in the bush. Without risk-taking policies today, however, tomorrow's bush may well be birdless. Hold back today and you'll be cannibalized or leapfrogged by somebody else. In more leisurely eras, followers could get away with technological lags. But an age of shortening product life cycles leaves no room for creative delay.

The changes in markets have happened and are happening at a speed which would have been unthinkable in the days when the vertically integrated giants ruled the earth. Miss what C.K. Prahalad of the University of Michigan calls 'industry transformation', and your company gets thrown into the vortex of corporate reconstruction, often too late to save the day.

Perlitz offers an interesting cure for innovatory reluctance syndrome. The onrush of the new, he argues, imposes arithmetical obligations on managers. For example, Germany's global electronics giant, Siemens, claims that half its revenue derives from products introduced in the last five years. The huge turnover represented by those new products is equivalent to the ninth largest company in Germany. However, it follows that, simply to maintain this ratio, Siemens must add 10 percent of turnover every year in new product sales.

In this way, and in every product line, argues Perlitz, life cycles determine innovation targets. If the life cycle is a year or less (as with PCs), the whole product line must be changed annually. With industrial robots, whose average life is 2·5 years, nothing in the product portfolio of 1996 will be marketable before the end of 1999. Microprocessors are on a similar turbocharged treadmill: an industry which rejoiced in the three million transistors of 1992 is proceeding towards a 100-million transistor chip by the year 2000. By then two BIPS (two billion instructions per second) should be achievable.

The technological targets inevitably impose managerial ones. Accelerating the creative process means climbing progressively higher mountains, both technically and financially. In the faster-moving industries, before a new product is even announced, the design teams are already sketching in the next design. As that proceeds towards the market, work on the next miracle must be in hand.

Plainly, a company on this accelerating treadmill doesn't (because it can't afford to) suffer from what Perlitz sees in many cases: corporate constipation, where top management complains that nothing new is coming up and the R&D teams moan that none of their bright ideas are being taken up – because there's a blockage in the middle. The approach of setting specific innovation targets looks highly promising: shifting people's risk focus alters what they see – and therefore what you get.

The managers in the survey reported earlier were risk-averse so long as they thought that failure would endanger their careers. In the traditional Western blame culture it probably would. Failure is treated as a disciplinary offence: one back-firing risk gets a black mark, repetition brings punishment – perhaps dismissal. The blame culture holds that if you leave failure or underperformance unpunished, you undermine the efforts and motivation of others.

Going by this philosophy, only a blithering idiot would adopt the following policies:

> 'If we don't understand why a manager consistently underperforms, we promote him. In 74 percent of cases, performance improves immediately.'

> 'When I find an employee who turns out to be wrong for a job, I feel it is my fault, because I made the decision to hire him. Generally, I would invest in additional training, education, or a change of duty. As a result, he will usually turn out to be an asset in the long run.'

Far from being idiots, the first speaker was Minoru Makihara, the chairman of Mitsubishi, and the second Akio Morita, then chairman of Sony. Both companies depend overwhelmingly on risk-taking investment in new technology and products. The theme of both chairmen is that managerial ability is not an innate constant. How well managers perform is determined, not by nature, but by nurture – by their environment, the tasks they are given and the support they receive.

Sony, for example, has a policy called 'self-promotion' – anybody can look for a project without even telling his supervisor. The PalmTop computer was created by a programmer in home computers. His venture sprang from two years spent (at his own request) in technical support in Britain. The Data Discman was invented by ten men whose boss kept both the project and its costs (simply charged to other projects) secret from his own superiors. There is great wisdom in the Mitsubishi-Sony approach: if you regard underperformance as your fault, not theirs, you are far more likely to turn bad managers into good.

The same responsibility applies to risk-taking. Turn people's focus from risk-aversion to the opposite – so that lack of new ideas is their greatest career hazard – and their behaviour will change accordingly. To take risks with impunity, though, managers need freedom and encouragement. They often receive neither. More commonly, they are obliged to risk their own careers to take intelligent risks.

The examples of big company innovations assembled by authors P. Ranganath Nayak and John M. Ketteringham in *Breakthroughs!*[1] include two instructive European cases (which are, typically enough, heavily outnumbered by the Americans and Japanese).

The first, the EMI brain-scanner, suffered from the same resistance as most of the non-European innovations: many had to be forced through the risk-averse corporate parent whose fortunes they transformed. The other European innovation, SmithKline Beecham's Tagamet anti-ulcer drug, might well have suffered the same fate, had top management known exactly what was going on. Top managements in general intervene and interfere constantly – and their interventions are far more likely to discourage risk than to energize the risk-takers.

Whether written or unwritten, any rules and restrictions have a deadening effect on risk-taking. Companies like Microsoft and Intel would have been stillborn under such leadership. It is unfair, no doubt, to compare these former start-ups, both launched by owner-managers, with the captive employees of a vast multinational like Roche. But the point is that the qualities of the start-up that the giants find hard to develop –

speed, intensity, innovation and tolerance of mistakes – have become inexorable necessities, even for giants.

IBM's sales stagnation followed from neglecting these necessities. Although it invented Reduced Instruction Set Computing, it found no use for this new technology's prowess for years – finally incorporating RISC into advanced engineering workstations three years after Sun Microsystems had shown the way. Not risking RISC was too great a risk for its sponsor and far too frustrating for the RISC creators within the company. Their frustration is typical, not just of IBM, but of most major companies – typical because the prevailing culture of control is deeply averse to that of risk.

David Benjamin, who worked as a researcher on *Breakthroughs!*, has produced some notes based on his researches. He argues that the 'cool, controlled, orderly' process of good management is inimical to the hot, undisciplined, random business of innovation. So 'innovations consistently occur despite management efforts, and very often out of their sight'.

As Benjamin says, when the risk has been well taken, and you have a hit on your hands, like the RISC technology, then you have to follow some highly anarchic rules in dealing with your risk-taking champion, like:

- 'Glorify the son of a bitch. This is once-in-a-lifetime for the company' – and for the individual.

- Be humble and get curious. Don't assume that this thing fits any established pattern.

- If you can't improve it, or vary it, or expand it, just let it run its course and get the hell away from it. Exile it to a separate division and get back to work.

- Don't even think about repeating it or institutionalizing the 'process'.

Those four points delineate the gaping gulf in cultures between risk-takers and controllers. The gap can, however, be bridged by risk-oriented people management, which exploits the potential of devolving authority to individuals and teams and gives them the resources to take decisions and responsibility. The cool, controlled and orderly manager is invaluable in assessing what risks are being run and deciding which are worth the candle.

The idea isn't to let managers make wild bets with the shareholders' money, but to take quick decisions on plans which involve carefully calculated odds, with a suitably high upside potential and an acceptably low downside risk. This equation is seldom improved by procrastination, and often made far worse – which is a convincing argument for delayering. The more numerous the layers of management that come between the risk-takers and the summit, the slower the decision process, and the greater the likelihood that risks will be shunned, for no better reason than their riskiness.

James Champy's ideal is an organization with three layers: top management, executive management, and all the self-managers below, aided by experts in specialist disciplines such as IT. That would greatly limit the potential for risk-averse obstruction and hierarchical time-wasting. It may sound pie-in-the-sky, but Champy's ideal is neither a new principle nor a fantasy: newspapers have long enjoyed such ultra-flat structures, giving the editors direct access to all journalists, and vice versa. The departmental heads act as coordinators of quasi-independent product centres – the individual men and women who fill the paper, and are trusted to do so.

Trust is among the six essentials that true innovators require:

1 *Trust*: the cornerstone of managed risk-taking, the first of its imperatives.

2 *Teamwork*: internal partnership reduces risk by bringing many minds to bear.

3 *Clarity of objectives*: fuzzy aims lead to unacceptable risks.

4 *Clarity of communication*: if higher management knows what's going on, it becomes more likely to provide...

5 *Resources*: right-minded top managers see their risk function as facilitating, not impeding.

6 *Pay for Performance*: all risk and no reward does nobody any good.

These half-dozen simple conditions create the culture of risk exemplified by the great high-tech entrepreneurs. Their managed risk-taking has turned personal visions into great technological and economic achievements. Leading-edge management keeps companies with leading-edge technology thrusting forward past their own best standards towards perfection. That's the pursuit of the unattainable. But in the nineties and beyond, that's what you must keep on seeking to attain.

The gap at Siemens

The lag in European innovation is the most conspicuous, and threatening, sign of economic weakness as the millennium approaches. In microelectronics, as in aerospace, Europe is an also-ran. In consumer hardware, Asian ingenuity is a long-running rebuke to European competitors. In cars – both in design and manufacture – the Japanese have been allowed to set the pace. The list rolls on and on.

The lag was clearly demonstrated by a global innovation survey produced in August 1992 by CHI Research. It ranked nearly 200 top companies on three counts: the number of US patents awarded in 1991; 'high impact' (the relative frequency with which a company's patents get cited); and the median age of its patents. The top 25 consisted of 11 Japanese (taking the first four places), 11 Americans, and only three Europeans: Philips, Siemens and Hoechst, all of which were in the bottom half.

Siemens was one of only three companies (General Motors and IBM being the others) whose research and development spending topped $5 billion in 1994. Where was the reward for all that investment in the future? In that year Siemens earned just over a billion dollars on its $51 billion of sales. The turnover figure was the fourth largest in the electronics/electrical industry worldwide, but the miserable 2 percent net profit left Siemens far behind US rivals like General Electric and Motorola. The former earned 4·7 times the German profits on just a quarter more in sales. Motorola earned half as much again on two-fifths of the Siemens turnover. Even more extraordinary, Britain's GEC, with under a fifth of the sales, lagged Siemens' profits by a mere 18 percent. Under the aegis of Lord Weinstock, true, GEC had often been criticized for underinvestment in R&D. In contrast, the German company Siemens had a cornucopia of technological riches – but why weren't the riches generating more richness?

The number of Siemens' inventions is awesome, second only to Matsushita. The range of Siemens' technology is equally enormous. It ranges from dishwashers to airbag detection systems and fuel cells that operate at record high temperatures, power stations to point-of-sale systems for the English Teddy Bear Company. Maybe the range holds one answer to the question. Immensely proud of its technology, Siemens has tended to cover the waterfront: it hasn't applied a sharp enough focus on those sectors where it can make both breakthroughs and money.

At Siemens, the labs used to come first – even ahead of the customers. This was rammed home to one group of Siemens managers when, at the instigation of their new chief executive, Heinrich von Pierer, they confronted their European customers from Sony. As the complaints poured out, the Germans were shaken out of the complacency which bureaucratic in-breeding always encourages. This is only one of the ways in which Siemens is trying expressly to convert a supertanker into a flotilla of high-speed motor-boats, each trying to outrun the others.

One of these boats has been outpacing the rest: semiconductors. As the sole European manufacturer of DRAMs (Dynamic Random Access Memory chips) for PCs, Siemens has shared in their explosive growth. It is also sharing in partnerships – with IBM and Toshiba, for example – that will advance the technology and market strength of its memory chip interests. But these are now commodity businesses. Siemens (also strong in mobile phone chips) generates greater profitability from custom-made semiconductors of many types. Yet the profits of the entire vast group are only a third of those made by Intel, largely from its near-monopoly of one dominant chip technology, the microprocessor.

Siemens has a direct stake in computing through Siemens-Nixdorf. But this marriage of two failed computer companies never promised more than survival from the start. The company did make a profit in 1994–95, but that was the first in its history – owed, moreover, entirely to its position in selling PCs to business users. Only the overall financial strength of the parent has kept Siemens-Nixdorf viable in a personal computer market where its share outside Germany is insupportably small.

In PCs, this great European corporation simply isn't the size of player justified by its resources, human and otherwise. Siemens hasn't fallen into the too frequent trap of regarding R&D almost as a financial activity: the foolish notion that, if you throw a certain amount of money at the company's technology spectrum, results will certainly follow. But neither has Siemens matched its might to the market. The company has not been spending enough on accelerating and improving its response to customer demands for the right, profitable products.

At the level of the firm, Siemens in some respects mirrors the economic failure of European industry as a whole. The excessive fragmentation of European industries, which means that innovation is spread over too many companies, needn't be decisive. Take cars as a saddening example. Europe's motor industry is no more fragmented than Japan's: each has a full hand of world-class competitors. But Japan has three car firms (Nissan, Mazda and Mitsubishi Motors) among the 15 with the highest-impact patents, Europe none.

Although Detroit also scores zero, that's no consolation. There's a glaringly obvious connection between innovatory lag and Japanese ability to penetrate Western markets. In Siemens' industry, the top ten electronics innovators include no fewer than six Japanese companies, two of which (Hitachi and Matsushita) are significantly larger than Siemens, another, Toshiba, is within close range. Part of the Japanese groups' strength in depth is their closeness to the cutting edge. Their 'technology cycle times' are shorter, which means that their competitive power must be greater. In cars, the three Japanese leaders *average* about four and a half years to develop new models, against six or more for General Motors, in both the US and Europe.

Another aspect of Europe's lag is the heavy non-European presence in European industry. In consequence, American technology has squeezed out much European competition, and the Japanese have repeated the squeeze to even greater effect. Countries with no camera or copier industries aren't going to generate much innovation in copying or photography.

In industry after industry, market after market, Europe has abdicated what were once tenable positions. In computer innovation, as it happens, Europe's technologists – including those at Siemens and Nixdorf – were relatively quick off the mark, faster than IBM. But it did them little good, because Europe's managements were much slower than the technologists. The innovation gap, as Siemens has recognized late in the day, is one of management, not technology.

The missing link is focus. Rosabeth Moss Kanter's famous Four Fs apply generally to management, but are also utterly indispensable in R&D. The innovative effort has to be Friendly (that is, cooperative and collaborative), Focused, Flexible. And very Fast.

Developing prime products

For several years I have talked to students attending an excellent course on New Product Development organized at Oxford by Bill Ramsay, formerly of General Foods. Looking at those mostly eager faces, mostly also young, it's easy to understand why product innovation is the renewing force of any business.

One of Japan's greatest but least celebrated managers, Ryazuburo Kaku, the builder of the modern Canon, used to stress this truth in an unforgettable way. Late in his brilliant career, he still carried in his pocket a graph charting Canon's profits over his decades of service. Against the largely upward curve, Kaku had plotted Canon's new product introductions. As a junior employee in the finance function, Kaku had first spotted that every burst of innovation had coincided with, and undoubtedly caused, a surge in profits.

He concluded that, to achieve sustained advance, new products had to flow, not in the previous fits and starts, but in a steady stream. The logic is inescapable, and Kaku's exploitation of the logic at Canon had exactly the results he foresaw. But translating the theory into practice has some inherent difficulties for most managements.

1 Outside FMHT markets (fast-moving high technology), neither markets nor technology are changing fast enough to engender powerful new products on a regular, rapid basis.

2 Even the best of innovators has a high rate of failure; even though, as Ramsay has pointed out in a paper,[2] the miss ratio is three out of 10, not the 90 percent of mythology, those failures still represent much wasted effort.

3 In most companies, the needs of innovation, with its uncertain results, unpredictable timescales and spiralling costs, are in conflict with the orderly processes of 'ordinary' management, and possibly with financial regularity as well.

4 Kaku's Law hinges on new products achieving high profitability. In many cases, the handsome returns either never come at all, or appear only after an unconscionable delay.

The usual response to these realities is to try to improve the innovatory process: to raise its fertility, elevate the success ratio, erect higher thresholds to ensure better returns on investment, and so on. Above all, companies seek to create a superior innovatory climate, to remove the barriers which hamstring the efforts of those eager young people in new product development (NPD).

But that's not enough: genuine reform should end by terminating NPD as a separate activity. Innovation should be integrated into the company's day-to-day, month-to-month and year-to-year *management*. The ultimate answer can only lie in reorienting the management ethos of the firm away from the tried, trusted and obsolescent and towards the continuous evolution of the new, thrusting and competitive – competitive not only in winning patents, but in applications, scale and profitable growth.

There is an essential parallel here with the current revolution in management itself. The changes are directed at replacing obsolescent hierarchy with new, thrusting, competitive modes. Fully decentralized operations, working in flexible teams to pursue self-defined objectives, are inherently more creative. The Japanese, generally right in these matters, believe that, in the next industrial wave, creativity will be decisive. They are striving to develop further the kind of 'creagement' (their word) that Europe needs even more urgently than Japan.

'Creagement' has to be based on coordinated, strategically sound planning of innovation. These days, companies must deliberately set out to create major positions in technologies which will prove valuable, not only to them, but to many others. Today, no company can hope to anticipate or afford all the technologies it will need. Its own proud possessions in science and engineering, however, are bargaining counters, technologies that can be traded for the missing pieces in the jigsaw.

If the correlation between new product introduction and profitability still holds true (and it surely does), it doesn't follow that the key to success is simply to proliferate the products. This is one area in which Japan sets a bad example. Its generation of new products has been profuse to the point of profligacy: 227 different Walkmans, or one every three weeks, since Sony introduced the product; six dozen distinct Toyota cars since 1979, which equals one every ten weeks. And 2,000 new products have sprung from the Seiko watch company every year, or one per designer every four weeks.

The reality is that profits should in theory improve for companies that are able to lengthen product life cycles and reduce variants. It is perfectly possible to halve the latter, to cut down product ranges by 20 to 30 percent, and to extend life cycles without upsetting the paying customers. If you can add an extra year to a four-year cycle, say, you can hope to get the 'third year' profit twice. Instead of profits peaking in Year Three after amortization, and then dipping in Year Four, the good times roll for another twelve months.

Whether such an approach succeeds depends partly on the causes of the fourth-year dip. How far is it determined by expectation of the model change among the customers and inside the company itself? Is it a self-fulfilling prophecy? Moreover, will all competitors come into line? If not, the stand-outs, with their fresher product lines, must win. Whatever the answer, nobody doubts that new model proliferation in itself accomplishes nothing. Indeed, it may be counterproductive.

The European car industry could be discovering this unpleasant reality the hard way. New models have been pouring out of the car plants, with more lining up. In the 'lower-priced mid-sized segment', for example, *Business Week* lists three head-to-head contenders: the Renault Mégane, Rover 400, and Opel/Vauxhall Vectra. In spring 1996, with sales dull across Europe, the magazine counted 20 newcomers in all: 'it doesn't help that so many new models are having to jockey for position in this anaemic market'.

Much of the multiple birthing can make only a negligible contribution to parental volume, still less profits. Too many models must mean excessive costs, misspent time, a great deal of overlapping, customer confusion and dilution of the brand. Bringing down the time and cost involved in NPD, however brilliantly, is a means, not an end: excellent execution of something better not attempted is still sheer waste.

European manufacturing philosophy, heavily product and production-led, is catnip to engineers. If a new feature can be economically incorporated, they love to change the product, confident that enhanced technical excellence will improve sales. The beneficent process has clearly worked in many markets – but only when truly significant advances were made. A ceaseless spate of innovations hasn't saved even the personal computer market from slowdowns and oversupply.

The Japanese quick-to-market philosophy has won would-be emulators worldwide. But speed and cost aren't the only factors in the final equation. A third factor outweighs either: the broadly defined quality of the new product plainly matters more than the speed of its appearance. If the Mercedes Swatch car succeeds, it won't be the ability to produce the little two-seater fast, and to amortize it on a small production run, that will be decisive. Success will prove that the daring of attacking the sub-mini segment was right as well as imaginative.

Technical development and production abilities are allies for such acts of the imagination. Much of Europe has yet to learn that a product-driven philosophy is out of place when there's no such thing as a product any more. As Rosabeth Moss Kanter stresses, the product is only part of the delivered package of 'customer value'. This stands the old marketing concept on its head. Insurance companies and banks started talking about financial services as products. Now, say the gurus, you should talk about products as services.

Seen in this light, innovation takes on a new aspect. Some crucial questions need asking before embarking on a new idea for a product – or a service:

1 What additional value will this innovation bring to the customer?

2 What rewards will it bring to the supplier in terms of realized price and customer loyalty?

3 How will the customer be made aware of the greater value that's being offered?

The value-led approach assists greatly in deciding which innovatory direction to follow. Now the question becomes: What values would the customer respond to most strongly – if they can be created? This isn't a question that responds to conventional market research, for a well-known reason: you can't expect people to give meaningful opinions about something that doesn't exist. But that is, of course, the vital task of the innovator.

The innovator must focus, not on competition, but on what Edward de Bono calls 'surpetition', which means creating a 'value monopoly'. The tiny Apple had that when it created business computing. The 'surpetitive' innovator enters a race he is certain to win, there being no other runners. In the hierarchy of sources for creating new customer value, surpetitive monopoly comes easily top in potential power. It can be won in several ways – for example, by exploiting:

1 Unfilled need.

2 Disadvantages in existing products.

3 Gaps in otherwise well-served markets.

4 Extensions to, and new formats for, existing lines.

5 Technological breakthroughs.

6 Successful ideas transferable from other markets.

7 More economic ways of satisfying expensively met needs.

Any annual roster of best new products can be matched against this list. Scanning existing product lines and markets on these seven counts will throw up many opportunities. If the search is organized both systematically and creatively, the problem isn't to generate ideas, but to choose among them. That means deciding which proposition offers the most value to the customer *and* the company. In an existing market, that doesn't necessarily mean the product or service that is both better and cheaper than the competition.

Value is a matter of perception, not numbers. Thus, round teabags, which offer no advantage over the square variety, nevertheless found a ready market. The decisive issue is increasingly quality, but not in quality's technical sense of 'conformance to specification'. The relevant meaning lies in the value created for the customer, which requires continuous improvement, using measurable criteria.

To make any sense, that definition plainly must include the existing as well as the brand-new. 'Old product development' is at least as important as new. Courses on the subject would never sell because 'old' is virtually a pejorative word in marketing. My preferred term is 'prime product development', or PPD. In fact, tapping the huge potential of PPD must be the foundation of product development work, not just in sharpening skills and processes, but financially.

This is because PPD generally costs far less, carries significantly lower risks, and produces much higher and faster returns, from which the costlier NPD can be financed. PPD's better performance follows from the fact that, if a product exists at all, it must already have the one essential for all success: customers. Moreover, the company has deep experience of the product, plus broad, long knowledge of the market. Provided that you don't become a prisoner of the past and its assumptions, continuous PPD offers a continuous, golden stream of growth.

The Japanese have demonstrated this truth with overwhelming force. As Kenichi Ohmae, McKinsey's Tokyo head, pointed out in *The Borderless World*,[3] Japanese managers can't acquire other businesses as freely as Westerners, nor change employers so readily, so they are compelled to make the best of what they have. Hence the rapid evolution of products.

European companies have also made PPD the cornerstone of strategy – for example, in generating the exceptional performance of the Guinness hard liquor business. By marketing its old, prime brands with new vigour, and concentrating on prices that matched the value as perceived by the customer, the company achieved a 31 percent margin, and sharply increased profits on static volume. Note, however, that the wonders worked by such a strategy are of limited duration. Sooner or later, the higher prices choke off demand. If prices rise more than perceived value, the customers turn elsewhere – as Guinness discovered to its subsequent cost.

That is one vital caveat. There's another. Don't be misled by the term 'prime product' into developing only the significant few that contribute the bulk of profits. *Any* product that has an established position in a solid market is probably capable of yielding prime profits. It needs examination with the new eye of a greedy entrepreneur. Try:

1 Approaches that nobody has ever tried before.
2 Analogies from other products, business and markets.

3 Customer value not provided by anybody else.

4 Reexamining and challenging the way things have always been done.

5 Looking for problems in use, and solving them.

6 Finding the focus, for in innovation what you want is the surest guide to what you get.

Above all, try the Aladdin's Lamp approach. The summoned genie has given you personally, and absolutely free, this product, with all its acquired brand values, its customers, its hundreds of thousands or millions of cumulative sales. There is only one condition: you are not allowed to dispose of the business. What would you do to capitalize on this gift? The right answer could open up Aladdin's cave.

The corrected blunder of BP

Top managements are never wholly sure what their 'corporate culture' actually is. That doesn't stop them from embarking on costly and disruptive efforts to change that culture to something nearer to their tastes – and perhaps to the company's needs. No culture change programme has been more ambitious than British Petroleum's Project 90. A forceful chief executive, Robert Horton, determined in the later eighties to remake BP by making a complete break with its Imperial past.

Horton had made his reputation running the giant BP subsidiary in the US, and was eager to revamp the parent company in the same dynamic, purposive American-style manner. According to the *Financial Times*, 'layers of bureaucracy' were to be stripped away to make the company 'more responsive to market conditions'. But there were several catches. 'Like all reorganizations', wrote the paper, 'it has left some people very unhappy.'

Critics alleged that removing the middle management layers had 'isolated top management from other employees' and that the company lacked firm direction – the very opposite of what the culture change was presumably meant to achieve. None of this would surprise one sensationally successful manager. He believes that what happened at BP – disaffection and disappointing profits – is an inevitable result of 'the worst thing a corporation can do', but which boards 'insist' on doing. The sin? To reorganize.

The top manager taking this unorthodox view was very well known to British officers sent to the Gulf to liberate Kuwait. Lt. Gen. William 'Gus' Pagonis ran the logistics side of Desert Storm to spectacular effect. He differentiates between reorganization and ensuring that 'the right structure' is in place. Instead of reorganizing in Project 90 style, which produces 'tremendous challenges from within the organization', the Pagonis team only 'tailored'.

Pagonis believes that 'you have to learn to take an existing organization structure and modify it to meet your demands. If you make drastic changes you cannot go back to rely on a lot of other things that you may need later'. In other words, don't throw the baby out with the bathwater. Giant companies tend to reorganize heavily in their times of trouble – but the troubles often only get deeper as a result: in 1993, BP earned only 2 percent on sales and assets, against 5 percent for Royal Dutch-Shell.

Sir David Simon, the prime architect of BP's emergence from this slough, observed later that Project 90 involved his own biggest blunder: being part of a top management that had launched an ambitious change programme without having any clear idea of what business results it was supposed to achieve. The consequent problems, as BP's earnings were crucified by mistaken assumptions about the oil price, convinced the board that change was needed at the top. Simon's promotion to chief executive in 1992 signalled powerful corporate change and the adoption of results-linked strategies.

'The first thing we did,' says Simon, 'was to focus the efforts of everyone – throughout the business – on performance.' This was achieved by a set of 'very simple targets', linking overall group results with objectives for every unit and team. The new priority given to current performance was a culture shock for oilmen reared on a lifetime tradition of long-term planning and investment. But the 'very hard jolt' administered to the culture clarified purpose and process and provided a palpable, potent stimulus.

Performance management and better focus on the business portfolio had a brisk impact on costs and productivity, to the tune of nearly $3 billion over three years. In 1994, the company more than doubled its profits: the 2 percent return on sales and assets had become 5 percent. The next year, there was another 36 percent jump, with cash pouring in, thanks largely to what chief executive John Browne called 'sustained self-help'. In Simon's phrase, 'the right internal dynamic had been created' – and part of that dynamic was personal, as he told MCE's Top Management Forum in June 1996:[4]

> The required behaviour on all sides is a sense of openness, and a willingness to share and to learn – for the benefit of the whole. The quality of learning – and this is something we're still working to understand – is the most important single factor.

Simon and his colleagues used organization structure to align the three elements which he places at the heart of strategy: 'The external reality, an objective assessment of your own capability and . . . the aspirations of the company – the sense of direction and ambition which drives and motivates people.' The cultural and institutional change initiated under Horton continued, and was vital. But the emphasis was now on process and outcomes, on getting from A to B.

Clear authority was given to the 80 heads of business units worldwide: their relationships to head office were 'tailored' to fit the new federal philosophy. That meant cutting down 'the layers of bureaucracy which can so easily grow up between the core functions of head office and the operational teams running the assets'. Planning shifted, too, with a new primary drive: testing performance against objectives, quarter by quarter.

This would all delight Pagonis. The interview he gave to McKinsey's Graham Sharman, published in the consultancy's *Quarterly*, is especially significant, given its author's army background. No organization suffers more than the military from 'the chain of command in the inevitable constraints of a large organization'. But even in the army you can seek to flatten, not the organization, but the way in which it operates.

The type of reorganization the General so strongly criticizes is concerned with procedure, not process: with structure, not conduct. Simon makes a crucial point: 'Without the right behaviour', the structure adopted for BP 'wouldn't work to its full potential'. Those who concentrate on getting the outcomes they require end up with concrete results.

After the new top management determined that it wanted to build on the foundations Horton had laid, there was a rapid improvement in all BP's performance indicators, led by profits. While not so swift a triumph as Desert Storm, BP's comeback is convincing proof that in organization, form should follow content: what you want to achieve should govern how you set about its achievement. Do it the other way, and the content will content nobody.

Dynamizing the system

Acute financial crisis often arises because a company has become stuck in the patterns of past success. It is among the most common causes of the inertia which is endemic in management. The major cause of corporate failure, or lack of relative success, doesn't lie in complex problems whose solutions are unclear or uncertain. As every consultant knows, the prime cause of failure lies in the refusal of managements to implement solutions that are logically and economically compelling, but which are psychologically unacceptable.

'Ert' would be the perfect word to mean the opposite of 'inert': fast, sharp response. It also makes a useful acronym: the 'ert' manager is Energetic, Responsive, and Thinking. The inert executive, in contrast, is well illustrated by a company where corrective action called for reversing the much-trumpeted policies of 'three generations of top management. All three . . . were alive, in town, on the board, and stockholders'.[5]

As Professor Jay W. Forrester of MIT points out, in those circumstances, objections to changing the strategy were 'almost insurmountable'. Pernicious inertia was built into the system. It will infect even executives who are arguing in favour of a policy change. Forrester has found that, if change contradicts established corporate practices, the firm's internal change advocates, faced with a computer game simulating the business system, may not even try their own favoured option.

That's why using the best technical means to propose improvements in the system isn't enough. That's the 'hard' (i.e., objective) part of the job. But you're thrown back on the 'soft' (i.e., subjective) element of human relations. For example, a basic equation in any system is between costs, prices, output rates and profit. Their interactions can be represented rationally. But individual and collective humans are also part of the system: and they may not behave rationally at all.

For instance, who sets the prices? If the answer is whoever controls sales, it's dead wrong. In a manufacturing operation, if the production rate is set by the executive in charge of production, that's also a mistake. Neither executive should have these responsibilities, which are truly crucial. Over-produce or under-produce, and you wreck the short-term results. Under-price or over-price, and you achieve the same grisly effect, but with severe longer-term consequences too.

The most obvious argument against price-fixing by sales people is well-known: they will opt for the price that, in their view, maximizes turnover (and commissions), and will most readily meet quotas. So long as sales are being sustained, they will resist price changes, up or down, for fear of rocking the boat. Similar factors operate with production. If quotas have been set, or if pressures for delivery are intense, production rates will be upped automatically to meet any shortfall, even though the consequences may be a severe and costly cutback later on.

That last sentence points to the underlying and critical truth. Neither sales nor production people are in a position to make these crucial decisions. They don't possess enough information to see the system as a whole. And the correct decision can only be taken within the context of the entire system.

The object is to optimize the performance of that system, which can't be done without a complete understanding of the relationship of its parts. That's exactly what the truly 'ert' business executive possesses. The truth is stressed by the excellent book, *The Fifth Discipline*, by Peter M. Senge, on systems thinking, which was discussed earlier. The author teaches at MIT in Boston, and his views closely reflect those of the great Professor Forrester.

Forrester is the founding father of time-based competition, in which operations are analysed to eliminate wasted time. His thinking is basic to 'system dynamics'. Take the above-mentioned prices and production rates: each fits into a system. The dynamics of pricing 'interact with production rates, field service, quality, profits and product design'. Production rate 'is based on backlog, inventories, production capacity, average past sales, profitability, corporate liquidity, and other considerations'.

The quotes are from a compelling interview in the *McKinsey Quarterly*,[6] which tells graphically what happens if you take fundamental decisions in isolation. Suppose sales are not being maintained, but instead are slumping. Everybody knows how salespeople will react. They will demand price cuts, not least because of the large unofficial reductions which competitors are allegedly offering. Your salespeople will, if allowed, make unofficial cuts themselves, by offering discounts. But what if the diagnosis is wrong? Sales will not improve, and the financial penalties of depressed demand will intensify.

Keep on trying to match competition with price cuts when the real threat is quality and reliability, and you will make matters even worse. Not only will market share continue to slump, but nothing will be done to correct the true causes of decline. As for production, if you can't match output and sales day by day, the next best approach is usually to maintain a steady rate that will balance the system. At the price of an acceptable level of inventory at times of low off-take, that balance will achieve the year-round delivery performance which will delight the customer and optimize the profits.

For experts like Forrester, it is a simple matter to set up the computer model that will correctly determine that steady production rate. But there remains the much more complex problem of persuading people to obey the model's findings. The difficulty is that, while the techniques for establishing where the system needs changing, and how, are proven and highly effective, they are not matched by equal precision (or success) in getting the changes adopted. As Forrester says, 'Education for implementation and getting acceptance of the required policies may be a greater challenge than the design.'

Meeting that challenge is best achieved by shifting the manager and the company permanently from inertia to its opposite – ERTness. The successfully Energetic, Responsive, Thinking business works on the assumption (an inherent part of genuine quality management) that everything can always be done differently and better. It requires asking some penetrating questions:

1 What are the key management attitudes that account for corporate actions and reactions?

2 What are the organizational goals, and how, why and when did they originate?

3 To what extent does past history affect current decisions?

4 What happens when people are overloaded?

5 What are the key internal financial pressures, and how are they applied?

6 What is the true nature of relationships to customers, and how are they maintained?

The thrust of all these questions is directed towards establishing how far the organization is responding to its present and future situation, and how far its behaviour is conditioned by a probably irrelevant past. The past gets crystallized into procedures and manuals which look harmless, but can be deeply pernicious. These static housekeeping methods may be a more powerful influence on performance than the dynamic strategies which top management is attempting to enact.

Pricing proves the point. Many European companies base their charges on adding standard margins to manufacturing costs. Often, these costs are grossly miscalculated (an error which applies both to direct costs and overhead allocation). But the technique is wrong in principle as well as practice, as the Japanese have demonstrated. In Japan price is determined by whatever level is thought appropriate to win the desired share of market. *That* sets the level of cost which can be afforded. Cost is thus constantly challenged.

Commenting on this difference (which has been a winning factor in far too many markets), two academics from the London School of Economics write that, in Japan, 'factors such as desired market share, cycle time, reject rates and innovation are given more weight in managerial decisions, making them calculative exercises about financial viability'. In other words, the Japanese manager, by instinct and training, bases decisions on the entire system, not on single issues seen in isolation.

The Thinking part of ERTness hinges on selecting the interrelated factors which truly determine the success or failure of the organization. In these complex times, the factors in any significant business are unlikely to be few. As a non-executive director of minicomputer maker Digital Equipment, Forrester constructed a model for his personal use. It had no less than 250 variables. The fascinating aspect, though, isn't so much the complexity as the small proportion of tangible, 'hard' items – a mere 5 percent. The rest were intangibles – including those covered in the six questions above.

The model taught Forrester why some growth companies stagnate and others move on to greater heights. He found five key interrelated factors:

> Prices.
> Delivery lead-times.
> Capacity expansion.
> Quality of design.
> Market reputation.

Get any of the five wrong, and you vitiate the others. Get them all right, as the Japanese did in spectacular fashion when attacking key European markets, and each factor reinforces the others.

It is fascinating to speculate whether Forrester's model could (or did) foresee the crisis at Digital Europe. The débâcle (see Chapter 3, p.62) came about because the parent company was over-committed to its minicomputers, whose *prices* had become too high in relation to microprocessor-based alternatives. This produced a gross surplus of *capacity*, which compelled the company to make costly cutbacks that ran against the corporate grain. Digital Europe's new top managers now had to rely on *market reputation* to support them as they sought a future built around the Alpha microprocessor, whose *quality of design* has won high praise: the key factor will be whether the Digital system, with its marvellous customer base (second only to IBM's), can achieve the *delivery lead-times* necessary in an over-supplied and fiercely demanding marketplace.

In any organization, any strategy session worthy of the name must build on critical examination of these five factors. Do they truly conform to present and future market needs? That question demands a sixth factor: ERTness itself. Is the organization capable of *thinking* clearly, looking at the five factors with eyes that aren't misted by the past? Is it *responsive*, reacting quickly to stimulus from inside or outside the organization, and is it ready to change anything until convinced that no further improvements can be made – for the time being?

Finally, is the organization *energetic*? Will it rapidly and effectively make the essential changes that responsive thought has unveiled? This is the sticking point that distinguishes the successes from the failures. It can be defined as the difference between top managers who want to change their companies, and are prepared, for that purpose, to change their own behaviour, and those who aren't.

Many consultants are at work in many companies to assist their clients in creating effective change, despite the frustrating knowledge that, without changes in top management, the assignments won't succeed. The phrase 'changes in top management' is deliberately ambiguous. Some managers will always find it impossible to change the set ways and thinking that cement the existing system. Sadly, there is no alternative but to replace them, at all levels, right up to the top.

Given the external pressures, it is not surprising that, in several large companies, boards of directors have concluded that the sitting chief executives had to be changed – because these bosses couldn't change themselves. The logic is hard to fault. At many other companies, the top chairs became very wobbly, and for the same reason. Persistently bad results, despite repeated efforts to cut costs and improve efficiency, are always clear proof of systemic failure.

It usually takes share price underperformance to stimulate shareholder unrest; but falls in stockmarket value generally reflect falls in the 'real' market. Real, non-financial measures like market share should always be among the key system indicators: anyone who tries to explain away non-financial deterioration should have their arguments treated with grave suspicion. Unless management has deliberately chosen to lose share, relative decline almost always indicates relative failure in the system.

I found this true even in the magazine business, where special deals invalidate the only readily available objective measure of competitive success, the number of advertising pages sold. Experience showed that if the share of volume was declining, even though there was every reason to suppose that share of value was rising, some underlying weakness was always present. And if that weakness went uncorrected, share of value would eventually follow volume downwards.

The systems dynamics approach accepts the presence of underlying weakness as a given. No system can ever be equally strong at all points. But business system engineers aim to elevate the organization to much higher levels of performance by continuously raising standards of effectiveness throughout the system. That won't be achieved without dispelling the forces of inertia through insistence on Energetic Response, guided by the best Thinking of which the combined minds of the organization are capable. ERTness is all.

EIGHT

Mobilizing the Motivators

The bubble-up at Opel

'From Bubble-Up to PAD': what sounds wholly mysterious has a very specific meaning inside General Motors Europe. It refers to the years between the start of a product (when ideas 'bubble up', for instance for a new car like Omega) and the crucial day (22 April 1994 in this case), when customers can at last inspect, admire and order the car: 'Product At Dealer'.

A wider meaning can be attached to 'bubble up'. The Omega programme was one very significant part of profound changes at General Motors. Dramatic developments had made the old GM style of organization as obsolete as the horsedrawn carriage. John Smith, the chief executive appointed in 1991 to reverse decades of decline, knew that well – and he knew that the answers could be found, not in the US, but in Europe. Better solutions, bubbling up from Germany, Britain and Spain, could transform performance in North America.

Smith had made his reputation, after all, at GM Europe, which has taken spectacular strides forward, not just in competitiveness, market share and financial performance, but also (enabling its turnround) towards New Century Management. The advances have been revolutionary by GM standards – although by those of world-class management they came late in the day.

Better late than never. The changes established the basic platform on which motivation can be harnessed throughout the organization. Thus, in the late 1980s, the Omega executive car was the first GM Europe range entrusted to a process where teams represented all ten disciplines, from product engineering and finance to marketing and service, forming product development groups for all thirteen sections of the car. Whether it was seats or wiring harness, bumpers or engines, the multidisciplinary teams worked together to give customers what they wanted, as determined by thorough research. Omega preproduction cars were also the first to be assembled on the shopfloor, allowing production workers to contribute to the final decisions. In making these changes, GM Europe was at least a decade behind the Japanese, but the Omega represented an important breakaway from the top-down, demotivating, hierarchical principles of the past.

The Omega was the first new range where final approval rested, not in Michigan, but with local top executives in Germany and Britain. Team members worked together in a carefully mapped process which emphasized speed less than the desired result: total transformation of the top-end image. Opel and Vauxhall, the GM twins, had been dogged in the past by their reputation as mass-market providers. Although their managements had raised GM to profitable sales parity with Volkswagen, Ford and Fiat by mass-market hits like the Cavalier and Corsa, that wasn't enough.

The task of the marketing arm, from Bubble-Up (or concept initiation) onwards, was to leave the mass-market image behind by developing a range that directly addressed the desires and needs of the executive driver. Bubble-Up and 'Phase Zero' (the period of 'programme development') evolved the concept of merging the strengths of two ranges, Omega's predecessors: the Carlton, thoroughly competent but lacking in charisma, and the 'top-of-line' Senator, excellent, but lacking in sales. The Senator excellences would be packaged within a Carlton wheelbase.

Omega thus bracketed the main competition, supplied by Mercedes, BMW, Rover and Ford Granada/Scipio. Every step towards establishing the car's profile was based on results from careful research. To succeed, Omega had to become a full member in what GM Europe's planners refer to as the ECC – the Executive Car Club. But the executive car market isn't homogenous, either in its customers or its dozen competitors. Omega had to weave a careful path between its rivals.

The spectrum runs from 'The Old Guard' (BMW and Mercedes) to the 'Junior Members' (Scandinavians, Japanese, French and Italians, with much smaller market shares). Omega aimed for the position of 'Associate Member' between and overlapping the two, ranking alongside the top Germans and Rover, but appealing to Junior Member customers. The motif and colour scheme were destined to run through all promotional and other material in all markets: consistent communication of Omega's standards of quality, safety and comfort was intended to achieve and reinforce the car's credibility and sustain it over a long life cycle.

All these strategies were the work, not of top management, but of the Omega teams. As the project came nearer to zero hour (pilot production), retreat and top-level interference became not just difficult but well-nigh impossible. Naturally, the top tier (the chief executive and vice presidents for engineering, finance and marketing) received a final full presentation covering every aspect; but when final approval was granted, some ten months before pilot production, the new car was virtually a *fait accompli*. All the decisions had been taken and executed lower down. The presentation was primarily designed to deliver 'total reassurance': it was known internally as a 'warm feeling document'.

What happened with Omega is part of a global revision of responsibilities which have the same downward motivational drive. For example, GM's product development is based in Germany, at a Technical Design Centre whose 3,500 'crew' are now so imbued with the concepts of 'Design for Manufacturability' – in which quality in its broadest sense is built into the design from the start – that they won a global role. Success in Europe, where GM was once a money-losing also-ran, has brought the Centre worldwide responsibility for the product lines it handles.

Inside Europe, the old national frontiers have vanished in everything except marketing. Vauxhall is GM Europe's marketing and sales arm for the UK, although Britain is also vital to production, both of cars and key components. Omega is imported from Germany, but the top-of-line six-cylinder V-engines are made at Ellesmere Port.

The ultimate bosses in Detroit, led by Smith, had of course approved the delegation of authority involved in the Omega project – and the idea of investing £720 million in its execution. But the whole European success story remained puzzling. GM's Europeans had been able to apply new management principles which its North Americans still resisted. What do other companies have to do to achieve desired and desirable results?

Confounding the corpocracy

Top managements in large and long-established corpocracies are uncomfortably aware that their cultures are antithetical to their desires. They want to be motivational, spontaneous, innovative, adaptable, but their cultures drive them towards rigidity, conservatism, demotivation and immobility. Increasingly, baffled managements are casting envious eyes, not at their direct competitors, but at the breakout companies, the entrepreneurial operations that have won outstanding success.

The Omega project represents a step – not a giant one, but progress nonetheless – towards the philosophy of the breakout business. A small, self-contained group is separated from the body corporate, given a single, clear objective, plus all the powers and resources required to meet that aim, and allowed to proceed to completion with little interference from on high.

Omega highlights some of the foundations of New Century Management.

First, you *design the organization to meet the needs*, never the other way round.

Second, *'rationalize' continually in the true sense of the word* – acting rationally and eliminating unreason.

Third, *build the brand* by offering customers genuine product advantages, for which they will pay accordingly.

Fourth, *benchmark all the time and act on what you find* to match or excel the competition.

Finally, *emphasize opportunities, not problems*. Solving problems creates opportunities – provided that the problems are actually solved.

Though no studies count the score, multidisciplinary breakout teams (the most famous being the Boca Raton group that created the IBM PC) appear to have a remarkable record of distinctive achievement. Yet even within companies whose excellence is widely acknowledged, it has been impossible to transfuse the highly motivated entrepreneurial blood into the corpocratic arteries. The top corpocrats know what needs to be done. Their problem, as ever, is doing it.

The dominant requirements can be readily defined. The large company (like any company) needs to practise the following Seven Goodly Virtues:

Compete – defending and extending profitable market share with passion and commitment.

Lead the Market – on every criterion of importance to the customer.

Think Big – seeking only No. 1 or No. 2 positions in any market.

Be Professional – accepting only Best Practice standards in all activities.

Innovate – forming and embracing new ideas in products and processes ahead of the competition.

Defend Bases – ensuring that core businesses maintain and/or replace core strengths.

Change – recognizing and reacting to developments in the environment and the marketplace by mutating rapidly.

When large companies falter and fade, failures on these criteria are often glaring. Top managements preside complacently over catastrophic drops in shares of market, fall behind on customer service and innovation, conceive their markets too narrowly, are highly unprofessional in areas like allowing costs to run out of hand, miss major innovation opportunities, and fail to defend their bases. When they do try to change, they take so long over the changes that any benefits are frittered away.

Commonly, these defects, despite their blatancy, are not recognized either within top management or by the opinion-formers. The reputation for excellence outlives its withering away, just as the strength of a brand identity outlives its real strength in the marketplace. The truth is easily revealed by questioning customers, employees, suppliers and others. But the management often lacks the will to act on the findings.

The distinctive quality of long-term successes is their readiness – despite (or because of) their excellence – to acknowledge the gap between ambitions and performance, and to act to close it. Using the device of project teams, working parties, or task forces can both improve performance and accomplish the needed blood transfusion.

For Omega, the 13 Product Development Teams represented a logical and sensible approach to seizing the opportunity and solving the many problems which any car project produces. Teamwork is invaluable in problem-solving, even if all members of the team aren't equally well-informed on all aspects of the problem. That relative ignorance, in fact, can be an asset. In the pioneering Omega sessions, asking apparently 'dumb' questions often produced highly intelligent results – and many ideas sprang out of interaction between disciplines.

Sub-corporations like this are 'virtual', working closely with customers and suppliers and reserving for internal supply only what cannot be provided more effectively outside. Second, they are free-standing, not beholden to any other part of the organization. Third, they also recognize another principle that New Century Management has to embrace: you work backwards from what the customer will pay, so price determines cost, not the other way around.

Fourth, in end-century markets, which present a fragmented and fragmenting pattern, such teams understand how a product must be perceived: as different and better. To dedicated project teams, the project is an end in itself. That's a fifth vital principle of the new management, in which *ad hoc* task forces are the key life-forms of shifting organizational structures. In project-based management, the end clearly defines and generates the means, the motivation – and the triumph.

Customer partnership is a sixth basic principle. Seventh, these are usually *crash* programmes, executed in haste. This demands a management approach that became highly fashionable in the nineties – synchronicity, or executing component tasks in parallel, rather than in sequence: the essence of Omega. The eighth essential is to liberate the energies and abilities which the organization will otherwise hide from itself. People plucked from other jobs seize responsibility in their new teams and exercise it with full freedom from the familiar corporate constraints.

Rule nine: it is no garden party. New Century Management is fully as demanding as the most draconian traditional regime. Anybody who can't keep up with the project's demands can't stay. Nor can individualism run riot. New collaborative devices are required – like democratic, informal Saturday morning meetings so that the inner circle can stand clear of day-to-day pressures and pull the project together. There is no time for slow decisions, indecision or second-guessing, either. Wrong decisions are simply corrected.

The contentious style of argument (what Edward de Bono has described as 'I'm Right, You're Wrong') is self-evidently inappropriate. A far more suitable management fashion, and a vital tenth principle, is that of 'consensus'. The most effective demonstration of the group's cohesion, and of an eleventh necessity, speed of reaction, will come when crisis inevitably arrives. As the right leader copes with crisis, he or she shows instinctive mastery of a twelfth new management principle: leadership by example and encouragement.

The true leader knows how to generate the invaluable morale that sustains such endeavours. Enormous energy and power can be let loose by 'turning loose'. Equally, it can quickly be vitiated by 'tightening up'. Task forces that take the form of independent business units are especially vulnerable to this: once successful, can they keep their independence? In large corporations, the power over all significant operations tends to gravitate towards the centre, and managers who go out on a limb often get cut off.

The logic of project-based management doesn't hold with any of that. Today's gurus bless the reorganization of businesses into smaller sub-units, each given the fullest possible decentralized authority by a small, strategic headquarters. But do reorganizing firms obey this logic? At first sight, some intriguing research by Exeter University's Centre for

Management Studies gives an encouraging answer. Of the British subjects (nearly one in three of the sample) which had 'been involved in organizational changes' in the past three years, many had decentralized, in just the way the gurus would specify.

Alas, an equal number of firms surveyed had moved in the opposite direction. Whatever the gurus propose, those who dispose are far less interested in achieving the most motivational and effective structure. If change is needed or wanted, and the business is decentralized, it centralizes; the centralized outfit does the opposite. Top management has no trouble in making persuasive cases for either of the contradictory courses. And under either banner, it can take out whole ranks of management by 'delayering'.

'Delayering' sounds wonderful, and can be. Motivation and effectiveness alike will improve as unnecessary relays, delays and interference are removed. That only applies, however, if management processes are reorganized round the fewer layers. If processes stay unchanged, the layers may vanish, but the duties don't – and the results are demotivating in the extreme. As the Exeter report says:

> . . . the removal of a layer of management which many companies have undertaken has meant that responsibilities from the moved tier have been reallocated to the levels above and below . . . the staff remaining have more responsibility, in some cases too much, which can lead to stress and inefficiency.

Much of this clumsy and counterproductive restructuring has been done in haste to cut short-term costs. The real issue is longer-term: what the company's shape should be in two, five, ten years' time. Fewer layers are only part of the answer. It's doubtful whether the traditional layered hierarchy will make any sense for those futures. By the mid-nineties, all managers stood agreed (in theory, anyway) on the need to break down barriers between departments. But there is a more radical solution: breaking down the departments themselves.

The concept of the decentralized sub-unit is the antithesis of departmentalized management. Why keep large central functions, from marketing and sales to finance, if the organization is subdivided into discrete businesses? There is an extreme alternative. There is no reason why self-managed groups, each with full functional services, shouldn't be the building blocks of the organization, which gains in flexible speed and shared experience what is lost in tidiness.

This essentially develops the task force idea into an organizing principle. At Sherwood Computer Services, a relatively small British firm, each business has full powers: so that one unit, threatened with loss of its market (and thus its existence), itself found and developed another activity to fill the gap. The motivational force was survival. But without the free-standing structure, that motivation could easily have run into the ground.

Organizing businesses along these lines presents a stern challenge to management at the centre. Top management naturally loves to 'manage' (or interfere) – and will always be tempted to hire more staff to help run the interference. At the unit level, the business can be large enough to breed bureaucracies of its own. The critical test of both centre and subdivision is whether the latter's management can find its own ways to buck the centralizing, corpocratic tendencies, and to enshrine the motivational principle in its workings.

In motivational restructuring, the new structure goes hand-in-hand with new management processes that will liberate the talents of the whole organization in new ways. Best practice, not cost-cutting, should be the starting-point of reformation for the millennium. The improvement activity can infiltrate the entire ethos of the business. Successful operations for achieving best practice are led by a non-bureaucratic, non-hierarchical, small central team with full-time colleagues in all major functions and business groupings and part-time activists in sub-units.

These operations are based on collaborative working, both among existing teams and by *ad hoc* groups formed to tackle performance across departmental and functional boundaries. They aim only at achieving measurable, measured and sustained improvements in performance in the areas selected. They are bottom-up as well as top-down – individuals and teams are encouraged to put projects forward. Workshops are widely used to inculcate methods of analysis and implementation, together with the Best Practice philosophy.

Above all, the task force approach to Best Practice becomes a corporate-wide way of life, built into business plans and budgets, marked by presentations and celebrations of special achievement – which, however, is *not* marked by special payments. Best practice stems from best culture in a highly benevolent circle. The cooperative search for best practice, and insistence that nothing less will do, itself creates and reinforces the necessary cultural norms.

In many companies, however, while this methodology is well understood, implementation of the programmes, often formed with high ambitions and high-sounding titles, disappoints or fails completely. The causes are:

1 Top management, while committed verbally, does not lead by example and apply best practice principles to its own functions.

2 Too much effort is dissipated on the insignificant many activities, rather than the significant few.

3 The impact of very marked improvement in specific areas is offset or vitiated by general errors – either strategic or organizational.

4 Possibly because of (3) above, the programme loses momentum and commitment and becomes the flavour of last month.

All this flies in the face of New Century Management. Time and again, it has been proved that part of the corpocratic elephant can dance like Fred Astaire. Unfortunately, success means that the paths of the elephant and the hoofer start to converge fast. The result of their collision can never be in doubt. To get the whole corporation performing like Fred isn't a question of teaching the elephant how to dance but of getting rid of the elephant entirely. Then whole chorus lines of dancers, led and accompanied by brilliant soloists, can produce a corporate choreography for the new century.

The break-out of British Steel

The steel industry in Britain had every reason to be one of the most demotivated in Europe. Out of several major concerns, one remains – British Steel – and that is an epitome of Britain's industrial shrinkage. Where once a quarter of a million people worked on 37 steelmaking sites and in a host of other plants, only 41,000 work today. Steel is now made on only four sites, managed, in effect, as two (Scunthorpe/Teesside and Llanwern/Port Talbot), in order to keep the fixed costs as low as possible. This colossal shakeout has no real parallel in European industry. Yet its payoff has few parallels, either.

To quote one executive, the company is 'world-competitive on costs, world-competitive on quality' and 'world-competitive on technology'. All three claims are astonishing to anybody who knew the old, fragmented, high-cost, low-quality, demoralized industry that was nationalized in 1967. Its resistance to new technology was shared notably and equally painfully by the Americans. By 1995 chairman Sir Brian Moffat could claim 'we're much better than them': using a standard index, US costs were 16 percent higher, Germany's 30 percent, Japan's 42 percent.

What British Steel has accomplished contains no mysteries: the only puzzle is why it wasn't done long before. Simply, Europe's most inefficient steel industry saw that it had to become a low-cost producer. Having done so, the management determined to stay that way. Once the epitome of the production-led mentality, British Steel turned product-led: it now worked back from the market and adapted capacity accordingly, where once its predecessors created capacity and tried to fill it at all costs – often excessive ones.

Now, British Steel seeks to add capacity at minimal outlay. It can easily afford its expansion plans, thanks to a strong balance sheet and £690 million of net cash – the result of encouraging managers to see cash as king. Determined to come through the 1990s recession cash-neutral, Moffat achieved his aim: 'We owe not one penny to the banks.' With that financial foundation in place, Moffat could sensibly envision an 'internationally based steel company. There's no such thing in the world today.'

The global ambitions flow from gains in productivity, manning (with the headcount under continuous pressure) and flexibility. Nothing measures the gulf between old and new, inaction and action, more than the distance travelled on training. Almost unbelievably, the industry once did not educate its men to operate the plants. At a price of 5 percent of employment costs, that has totally changed: today the company educates everybody. Workers who understand the plant and the process, and are backed by on-line diagnostic equipment, can keep mills going without breakdowns.

Such long overdue changes, according to Moffat, are a 'reflection of what the Japanese have helped us with' – not Japan's steelmakers, but automotive and other manufacturers who have become British Steel customers in Britain. Responding to their example and demands, British Steel has ceased to inspect out-quality. Today it builds in quality.' That helps to explain a generally good showing on benchmarking comparisons with other steelmakers round the world. On some counts, the company is equal best or better: across the board, it's in the upper quartile, and (more important) it is still striving to improve.

The enhanced performance underpins the global ambitions. With trading and selling organizations all over the world (14 in Asia Pacific alone), British Steel is getting to understand other markets which should be able to support manufacturing plants. That is an exciting prospect for a business which is already established in the US. Yet the company still comes only midway down the list of the world's 33 largest metals companies: it is 64 percent smaller than Nippon Steel, 60 percent less than

Tyssen. Moreover, the financial picture shows a company that has often run hard up the down escalator.

In the year to end-March 1990, British Steel made record pre-tax profits of £708 million. Earnings collapsed the next year in recession; two loss-making periods followed. In 1993-4 British Steel did produce a rare profit among world steelmakers. But the numbers were still far below respectability – a mere 15 percent of the level achieved four years before, and several miles away from what Moffat defines as viability: 'an operating profit of around 13 percent of sales'. The company was equally far from covering the cost of its capital.

In June 1996, though, British Steel announced a 90 percent boost in its pre-tax profits to a peak £1.1 billion on £7.05 billion of sales. At that point, the highly favourable market conditions which explained that performance were already waning. But the world-class strategy is essentially long-term, and its advance has gone well beyond simply catching up on competition. Further promise lies in management's evident determination to lead, not only in the labs, but in the mills and the marketplace.

Some 900 people operate in R&D and 1,500 others in technology, many in task teams, all working to a powerful philosophy: to develop products with customers, focus on technology and the marketplace, and buy process technology and get more out of it than anybody else. Which markets to serve and how to address them has become the dominant theme, not of a revolution, but an evolution, whose progress lies in the ability of individual British Steel businesses to outdo the competition.

The old image of steel as a monopoly or oligopoly is as obsolete as that of heavy metal and reeking mills. The market is very open to competitors, which, among other benefits, sharpens the managerial reflexes. 'The whole management style has changed,' in Moffat's view. The British industry's renaissance, thanks partly to the relative sluggishness of several European competitors, is neither too little nor too late. Nor is the company smug: 'we're thinking forward in terms of technical change in the product – it's going to be remorseless'.

This sense of forward movement, keeping pace with an industry advancing rapidly on every front, from the severity of customer demands to the challenge of pan-European logistics, permeates British Steel. To emerge as the world's most profitable steel company represents a substantial and encouraging victory over notably difficult circumstances. More than the British industry's own inefficient past had to be overcome to create a highly productive business.

Moffat tends to describe his company's motivation in monetary terms. 'We're motivated by profit, not tonnes. We have a track record of reducing tonnes to make more money.' So far, the financial results are only impressive by the steel industry's abysmally low standards. The will to win the physical improvements which underlie the financials, however, is impressive by any standards. The ability of Moffat's executive team, not only to see what needed to be done, but actually to do it, passing their motivation on to the men, is the main reason for believing that the world-class ambitions are worldly wise and achievable.

Closing the management gap

Managers have become very familiar with the concept of the 'management gap' – meaning the distance between the actual and the ideal. In both operations and strategy, it is the gap between 'where we are' and 'where we want to be'. There's a more important gap still: between knowing what needs to be done and actually doing it. As Peter Drucker has written,[1] the first part (knowing what to do) is relatively easy; why is the second so hard?

Top managers understand that strategic thinking is essential, yet fail either to (a) devise a strategy or (b) communicate the strategy down the line or (c) ensure that it is implemented. They commonly, worse still, believe that they have a clear strategy, clearly grasped by everybody who needs to know, and vigorously pursued, when all three beliefs are unfounded. Such managers get comfort from their illusions, of course, and that may explain much of a yawning motivational gap.

In quality drives, for instance, top management itself won't be disturbed by a programme that concentrates on operational improvement lower down. But a poor quality strategy, devised by top managers, will undermine those operational efforts – there's no virtue in excellent performance of missions that should never have been undertaken. No doubt the Charge of the Light Brigade was quite well executed. But riding into the Valley of Death doesn't win wars – or commercial prizes.

The most conspicuous valley-of-death strategies in recent years have involved mergers and acquisitions, bids and deals and diversifications. As Michael Hammer and James Champy write in *Reengineering the Corporation:*[2]

Some people think companies could cure what ails them by changing their corporate strategies. They should sell one division and buy another, change their markets, get into different businesses. They should juggle assets or restructure with a leveraged buyout . . . This kind of thinking distracts companies from making basic changes in the real work they actually do . . . If they are not succeeding in the business that they are in, it is because their people are not inventing, making, selling and servicing as well as they should.

Real corporate strategy is directed at these organic activities, at pointing innovation in the right direction, at making and selling in more effective ways, at serving the customer with greater perceived success.

That was the essence of the transformation at British Steel. It was also the key to the astonishing turnround at the Dundee plant of NCR. The strength of James Adamson's strategy as boss, and in its implementation, lay, not only in its particulars, but in its origins. This wasn't a strategy imposed from across the Atlantic. The significant role of NCR's owners in Dayton, Ohio, was to impose an either/or ultimatum on Dundee. When automatic teller machines for two of Britain's Big Four banks. When the machines were found to be defective and sent back, the writing was on Dundee's wall – unless its boss, James Adamson, could close the gap. Asked by Adamson to design an ATM twice as reliable as the competition's, the engineers, initially sceptical, ended up by *trebling* the reliability. Simultaneous work on creating a close customer relationship enabled Dundee to quadruple output in four years and to oust IBM from its world market leadership, moving up from ninth position.

Note that the people who made this miracle were seeking their own salvation. Even within the plant, nobody imposed the winning strategy from above. The entire body of employees was enlisted in the effort, and that enlistment, too, was emphatically strategic.

Strategy in this sense is everybody's responsibility, not just that of top management. Corporate wheeling and dealing may have an ancillary role in strengthening or accomplishing the strategy. But the leadership's fundamental task goes beyond devising and revising the overall plans. Good leadership ensures that the makers and sellers, and the innovators (ideally, everybody), are all moving forward, continually closing the gap between the ideal and the actual by turning radical rethinking into conspicuous achievement.

One such miracle showed what can be achieved even in the British motor industry. The Land-Rover Discovery required one of the world's shortest-ever development times (27 months against a 48-month industry norm) to create an off-road vehicle whose sales volume far exceeded expectations. The company did this by forming a multidisciplinary project team, headed by a man – among the youngest involved – who had never led a team before. After initially refusing the job, he only accepted when convinced that the organization would provide full backing for radical solutions. In the event, so much waiting time was eliminated from the processes that the team leader's own leader, Tony Gilroy, deeply impressed, before long had 900 project teams beavering away all over his new company, Perkins Engine, to achieve similar successes.

Phenomenal results can be achieved by rethinking before reworking. In the Dutch bank ING, five units were supplying mortgages which ranged from very simple to highly complicated. Paradoxically, the most complex took the least time (three days) and the simplest the longest (10 days). There were too many checks, for a start. After redesign, accelerated processes were implemented in all five units, and even the quickest learnt from the others. The solution – entrusting the task to one generalist who handles the application from start to finish, instead of a different specialist for each stage – nearly always works in such circumstances. Nothing could better support the thesis of the late W. Edwards Deming that the system, rather than individual effort, determines the outcome of work.

People involved in the mortgage process at ING informed the reformers that 'we could have told you that years ago', a cry that is frequently heard when archaic processes are held up to the light. It is a compelling reason for treating frontline people as frontline consultants when tackling defective process, and using them as a team. ING's mortgage attack team consisted of a quality leader, a process designer, salesmen, product managers, and back-office people.

You don't have to be senior to have superior ideas. At Honeywell, a group of UK sales engineers cracked a familiar hard nut. The problem arises when you're visiting a customer who expresses interest in another product made by the company, but not in your province. If you remember the enquiry at all, you don't know the right contact; even if, with difficulty, you find that contact, the enquiry disappears into what Dennis Kennedy, the UK managing director, calls a 'black hole'. The sales engineers found the answer: link a toll-free line to a central enquiry desk. The call can be made there and then from the customer's office, the desk keeps track of the enquiry, and the messenger gets reports on his message's fate all the way to the end-result: sale or no sale.

Processes can also be reformed by a team of one: one Honeywell customer service man in fluid control components single-handedly pushed through a project which halved inventory, cut obsolete and obsolescent stock by 90 percent, and doubled service levels.

The power available lower down the organization was brought home to me by a manager-led Hammer-Champy example, at Ford Motor. Accounts payable employed more than 500 people in North America. Senior management was enthusiastically pursuing a 20 percent headcount reduction when Ford made a stunning discovery – its associate in Japan, Mazda, needed only five employees for the same function. A far more radical solution was then devised: Ford redesigned its system, not around the invoice, but around the original purchasing order. Confirmation of delivery instantly triggered payment, and the accounts payable activity became redundant.

What struck me about this wasn't the brilliance of the concept, for I had encountered exactly the same revolutionary introduction of new logic in Bristol, at National Westminster Life, just a week before: only this time the discovery had been made, not by senior insurance executives, but by a quality improvement team of very junior people in the finance department. It was their own solution, reached without any knowledge of what was happening at US Ford, or anywhere else. You couldn't ask for more convincing proof of the great untapped powers that reside down the line, in groups more than individuals, in all organizations.

Yet Ford was stumbling into deep macro-economic trouble at the time when these micro-miracles were being achieved, which brings me back to my starting point: both gaps have to be closed. Both the strategic framework *and* the operational processes have to be reengineered if either is to achieve its maximum benefit. Otherwise it is all too easy to fall into the trap described by Gary Hamel and C.K. Prahalad in 1989 in the *Harvard Business Review*:

> Too many companies are expending enormous energy simply to reproduce the cost and quality advantages that global competitors already have . . . assessing the current tactical advantages of known competitors will not help you understand the resolution, stamina and inventiveness of potential competitors.

I would put that even more positively. Strategy and its implementation are the ultimate test of your own resolution, stamina and inventiveness: of how far you dare to be different, and how effectively you capitalize on that difference. To use again the concept of management thinker Robert Fritz, it is the distinction between 'resolving behaviour', which takes the organization from the current to the desired state, and 'oscillating behaviour', in which (as at Ford) everybody runs very fast to stay in exactly the same space.

The Fritz formulation dovetails neatly with the ideas of Deming (that you can only raise individual performance by elevating that of the entire system) and Peter Senge (however hard you push, the system pushes back harder). You want to achieve the double-whammy effect of radically and dramatically improving performance of components in a system which is itself being radically and dramatically transformed.

A chief executive who has achieved this combination offers a confident explanation: 'Because we're a company that listens to our customers and are not afraid to change . . . When the traditional thinkers tell you your goal is far-fetched, you're probably on to something big . . . when they stop telling you it's far-fetched, you've probably already lost the war.' But his first, utterly basic point had three vital words missing. You need a company that 'listens to our customers *and our employees*'.

Read most accounts of management miracles, and the process of proactive listening – hearing and acting on what you hear – dominates all others. It is powerfully motivating – witness what happened at Dundee when NCR's engineers, challenged to double reliability, went 50 percent better.

Proactive listening has to work both ways. For instance, another management, having devolved full project authority to an *ad hoc* team, didn't like part of the design. In the old days, the bosses would have simply ordered a change. What action could, or should, they take under the new dispensation? The team was strongly against any alteration because of the high cost, for it was their devolved responsibility to meet their targets. When their seniors continued to stress the defects of the design, the team went back to the drawing board and found a way to introduce an improved feature at a quarter of the cost.

This anecdote is consistent with Hammer and Champy's eminently practical guide to closing the management gap. An especially valuable checklist addresses the central problem, which is the high failure rate of would-be gap-closers. The list of 19 items is 'a catalogue of the most common errors that lead companies to fail . . . Avoid them, and you almost can't help but get it right.' Turn the eight most important Don'ts upside down, and you get the vital eight Do's:

1 Change the process – don't just try to fix it (i.e., tackle the whole system).

2 Focus on business processes (i.e., don't have task forces on 'issues' like empowerment, teamwork, innovation, and customer service).

3 Recognize that successful reform of business processes will trigger radical changes elsewhere in the business system.

4 Involve people, their values and beliefs and their reward and recognition in the change.

5 Go for big prizes; it's not worth making a big effort for minor results.

6 Keep right on to the end of the road: quit too early, and you've wasted your time.

7 Have no constraints on the definition of the problem and the scope of the reengineering effort – you're almost certain to find problems you never knew existed.

8 Kick existing corporate cultures and management attitudes out of the way.

The last Do is the hardest. Managers resist change instinctively, because they fear their last state may be worse than their first. Unless the top people are all marching to the same tune, transformation and remotivation can't be taken all the way down the company. That top alignment had to be resolved before Honeywell UK started on the road to Total Quality Management with a 1988 launch under the heading 'Taking First Steps'. Year by year, it moved on from 'securing management commitment' to 'building the foundations', 'experiencing measured improvement', 'working to achieve "right first time"', 'understanding the business quality challenge', and 'responding to our customers' (in 1994). At that point, 'seeing the difference' and 'customer confirmation' lay beyond.

These stages emphasize that closing the gap is a long-haul journey that never ends. Therefore, don't even start on the road unless you're fully committed. That commitment has to start with the chief executive, but can't end there. Any change effort must go far beyond being identified with a particular leader. Whatever title you use for radical and dramatic reform, it won't succeed unless a radical spirit, focused on achievement, runs throughout the company.

It is the business equivalent of the old Latin tag, *mens sana in corpore sano*, a healthy mind in a healthy body, a motivated workforce in a motivational environment. As NCR demonstrated at Dundee, redesigned processes within a redesigned strategy will bring health to an ailing corporate body. As Honeywell showed at Newhouse and in the whole UK business, they will also regenerate bodies that are already wealthy and healthy and wise. And as British Steel proved, they can save an entire failing industry.

The megamergers of Europe

Mergers are highly motivating for top managers. They love the thrill of the chase, the enlargement of power that comes with fruition, the overnight achievement of growth, the publicity and the plaudits. The motivation is seldom shared by the workforce, primarily because mergers so often result in job losses. That, however, must always be a powerful demotivator, especially in an industry used to fast organic growth – like pharmaceuticals.

As noted earlier, the union of Glaxo and Wellcome alone cost 7,500 jobs. But it isn't just the lost jobs that worry employees, right up to middle management and beyond. Often they have no understanding of the rationale behind the deal. In that they are not alone. If a drug industry leader like Hakan Mogren 'cannot understand why some of these mergers have been done', why should less well-placed workers be any less baffled?

Megadeals have radically reshaped pharmaceuticals. Mogren's own company, Astra, may well have helped precipitate the Glaxo-Wellcome alliance: Losec, the Swedish company's anti-ulcer drug, has eaten into Glaxo's Zantac sales and profits. In general, though, the move to merge has more powerful and broader motives: witness the cross-border deals that created groups like SmithKline Beecham (SB), joined Pharmacia with Upjohn (a union which soon ran into unhappiness); and brought Sandoz and Ciba to the altar.

Mogren suspects that low-growth, high-cost operators will 'mix old problems with new problems and get drowned'. Losec sales, negligible in 1989, soared past $3 billion in 1996, and Mogren believes that 'If you are growing at high speed, you can't do mergers and acquisitions at the same time.' That's one part of the case against the megamerger wave, which is sweeping across many other European industries: that managements are seeking to compensate for inadequate organic growth by purchasing expansion.

The issue is whether they will succeed. The evidence is not encouraging. You will not find a study anywhere that supports the case for mergers

– especially megadeals: as a *Business Week* headline once said, 'Most Big Deals Don't Deliver.' A study of 150 deals valued at $500 million or more showed that 30 percent had substantially eroded shareholder returns, 20 percent had eroded them to some extent, and 33 percent had created only marginal returns – which left a mere 17 percent as substantial successes.

Naturally, every chief executive (defying the odds) believes that his mega-deal will join the 17 percent club. That is even less likely if the deal crosses borders. The $848 million BMW purchase of Rover, for instance, halved the purchaser's already inadequate returns on sales. The Rover workforce's morale and motivation, once among Britain's lowest, had soared remarkably as enlightened management borrowed techniques from its partner, Honda, and made quality its motivating theme. The sharp post-merger criticisms uttered by the new German owners must have reversed the forward thrust.

The demotivating trend is more marked with transnational takeovers like BMW-Rover than with purely national deals. Among the pitfalls of foreign buying listed by *Business Week* were 'Differences of language and culture aggravate integration of two management teams' and 'Employees tend to be even more frightened of new management if bosses are from another country.' Add the fact that 'Vertical integration is much harder in cross-border deals' and you have a potent recipe for brewing up poisonous trouble.

There is an antidote: draw on the strengths of the different nationalities. That is what happened at the Franco-Italian SGS-THOMSON – and chief executive Jan Leschly describes the same process at SmithKline Beecham: 'Two cultures created an extraordinary new company and forced two nationalities to adapt to each other.' From 1989 to 1995, sales of SB's continuing operations rose by a third, and net profit after tax nearly eightfold. This wasn't only the result of blending nationalities: SB took care to blend top managers into a team 'working as a whole, with joint understanding and a joint strategy'.

Understanding and participation are crucial to motivation. Where Europe's megamergers possess intelligently conceived objectives that go beyond cost-cutting economies, where the motives surpass mere fear of other agglomerations, where employees at all levels share the thinking of the strategic team – then even cross-border marriages have strong chances of success. Where the strategy is misplaced, so is the corporate wedlock.

It follows that merger-makers should be doubly or trebly careful about which strategies they select. But that's the middle of a management process which starts with methodology – who initiates the strategic discussion, and on what basis? The third phase, after the actual choice, is execution – who implements the strategy, and how? That process can take many forms, but in practice the programme is (1) chief executive initiates (2) *and* decides (3) *and* drives the execution.

At SB, Leschly is on far firmer ground in advocating the team approach: many minds improve the broth. Just as important, the chief executive's colleagues and subordinates have a personal stake in the strategy: their jobs depend on its success just as much as the chief executive's. If he bets the company, their careers are also being placed on the line. Large-scale mergers and acquisitions, whether or not they involve the sacrifice of one-time corporate cores, can be painful for individuals as well as risky for the company.

It is important that the odds be tilted in favour of the megadeals, for many of the merger-hungry managements are trying to generate, not just financial or industrial aggrandizement, but a new kind of company for a new world. Making sense of the Single European Market means making sense of all its major markets. Nor can the cross-border drive stop within the European Union. With competition pouring in from outside, Europeans must raise their horizons to global markets.

The trans-European, global corporation needs to be very different in character from a German, French or British business confined to its own national frontiers. But motivation crosses all languages. Without the willing cooperation of the workforce, satisfying results won't flow. With such a flow, cooperation is far easier to win. Astra's Mogren is right. The megamergers risk being a bet too far. They don't have to be.

Acquisitions of advantage

Mismanaged mergers demotivate two workforces: acquirers and acquired suffer alike. Companies which (like the pharmaceutical giants) long shun takeovers, then finally take the plunge, are more than likely to bungle. The errors committed won't be unique in character, nor are they confined to first-time buyers. Most acquisitions, by both experienced and inexperienced buyers, fail for reasons that are common to other calamitous 'strategic' moves:

1 Some strategic grand design becomes a 'must', which by definition excludes all other possibilities.

2 The strategy is not subjected to continuous review – and plans are not promptly modified or scrapped if events contradict them.

3 The strategy plays, not to the buyer's strengths, but to its weaknesses.

4 The initial risk exposure is increased by unplanned post-acquisition initiatives by management.

5 External and internal approval of the strategic stroke is taken as confirming its rightness – and Cassandras, internal or external, are ignored.

6 Top-level strategies are not rigorously examined at lower levels, and top management over-commits to the deal.

7 Accepted rules and routines are applied – without being checked for relevance.

8 Messengers are discouraged from bringing bad news – and corrective reaction to bad news is dangerously delayed.

9 Failure is not admitted; rather, it is denied.

The whole nine-point pattern is an exercise in demotivation – especially the ninth point. The price of failure is magnified if it is not recognized. Failure to admit error and thus learn from the mistake, the unforgiveable management sin, is no way to make a success of the next acquisition – if there is one. Indeed, that's one of the more valuable lessons of failure. There's an easy way to avoid the pitfalls of acquiring: don't do it.

Yet there is one corporate breed that does it all the time. Financially oriented conglomerates (FOGs) have made acquisition a way of life. Moreover, they have a better record in general, and in making acquisitions pay, in particular, than companies which are motivated by grander strategies. FOGs begin with a powerful advantage. They don't overpay, for a start; bargains are their meat and drink. Acquisitions work out financially with most ease if value is bought inexpensively. That sounds just as trite, but is just as true, as Bernard Baruch's famous stock market tip: buy cheap and sell dear.

The conglomerates, however, claim to go beyond mere bargain-hunting. They and their friends argue that these activities represent a revitalizing force in the economy. FOG buys are supposedly transferred from weak hands to strong. To reawaken their buys, and reap their own profits, the FOGs apply a management formula which sounds convincing and coherent. Their methodology is the antithesis of the strategic fumbling enumerated above. Instead of falling between two or more stools, the conglomerate goes straight to the point:

1 There is no grand design; the deal is strictly opportunistic; disposals of unwanted assets are briskly made.

2 The business strategy is therefore highly flexible, and, after disposals, largely left to operating management.

3 The purchaser is only interested in the buy's strengths, and acts swiftly to eradicate weaknesses and weak operations.

4 Post-acquisition management follows a highly developed model and is designed to narrow the already small risks.

5 The acquirer is only interested in external and internal approval to the extent that they help or hinder the capture of the target.

6 Top management is committed only to the financial success of the deal.

7 The rules and routines applied to the new situation have worked in many takeovers and situations.

8 Bad news produces immediate and effective correction.

9 Failure is not allowed; the acquisition has to meet the purchaser's simple, clear and comprehensive purpose: to make money.

Because of that purpose, all decisions are financially based, and all managers are financially judged. Motivation operates on the simplest possible basis with these people. If they meet or surpass targets, they are rewarded. If they fail, they are thrown overboard. Spurred by the whip and the carrot, easily monitored through financial reports, the managers of the acquired businesses seem to have the motivating conditions for super-performance: responsible independence under demanding control. In reality, they are caught in a system as rigid as any corpocracy: the regime demands certain behaviours and allows no others.

That's no way to motivate people, in or out of mergers. The frequent results of such tactics are demonstrated by Hanson's experience with EverReady in Britain. To Hanson management, this ranked as a splendid success. The battery group cost £95 million. Of that, £40 million was recouped by sell-offs which severed most of the international assets. In its last 21 months of ownership alone, Hanson stripped £37 million in pre-tax profit from EverReady: £132 million more arrived when Ralston Purina, owner of US EverReady, bought the British business.

What was left to buy? That has been documented by David Bowen, writing in the *Independent on Sunday*. Before Hanson took hold, in the late 1970s, EverReady's factory near Consett made over three million batteries a day. After treatment, Hanson handed over a plant making a mere half million units daily with a workforce reduced by 87 percent. The market share of a once-great brand had dropped from over 80 percent to 30 percent by value.

Before Hanson, classic underinvestment had affected the technology, the brand, and the factories. The irony is that Hanson management, with its very different motives, repeated the same pattern of decline that had created so cheap a takeover target. The old management had a vast sunk investment in the old zinc-carbon battery technology. The new alkaline batteries were a threat that management chose to ignore, even to wish away, because of the damage that conversion to alkaline would inflict on the company's profits.

But technology won't stop for anybody. The price has to be paid at some point. Either you pay now, in lost profit on obsolescent lines, or you pay later, in lost business. Either way you lose. Diehard management simply makes a present to competitors, which is what EverReady obligingly provided for Duracell. Low Pre-Hanson spending on R&D (a miserable 1 percent of sales) was a down-payment on a cemetery plot. Curiously, though, a successful product emerged from this myopia.

Starting alkaline production too late to save the day, the old management sought to avert that day's evil with a technology that used the existing plant: zinc-chloride. This stop-gap 'Silver Seal' was no answer to the basic loss of competitive power to alkaline brands, and the plant making EverReady's own Gold Seal alkaline batteries was much too small. Hanson faced a choice: heavy expenditure on the winning technology, or a far smaller, £4 million investment in Silver Seal to hold the fort – until the white flag might have to be sent up the pole.

The £4 million choice, naturally, was trumpeted forth as proof that Hanson didn't strip assets, but enhanced them. As noted, however, the FOG had stripped EverReady of its international assets (save in the protected South African market). The acquisition was thus turned into a single-country battery maker with no future. 'Efficiently managed decline' thereupon became the only option.

The books, which show that Hanson shareholders recouped their investment many times, don't show the fish that may have got away. If a truly restored EverReady had retained the old market share for Hanson, the shareholder value created would have far exceeded £132 million. True, strict financially-oriented management, with its mercenary bent, could never have created that value. Not that there's anything wrong intellectually (as opposed to morally) with being mercenary, but it doesn't build a business. That demands taking a long view, which may mean paying a short-term price in higher expenditure and lower profits.

The philosophy of financial orientation revolves around lower spending and higher profits. That can damage a business just as effectively as misguided strategists have ever done. You can't create value by undermining it. The corollary is that the true object of acquisition isn't to add value for the acquiring shareholders, but rather to the *acquired business*.

You can understand why targets, threatened with being strategized or EverReadied, are motivated to resist takeover so desperately. But is there a middle way? Can you strike a happy medium between the poor strategic buy, which subjugates the acquisition to misplaced master strategy, and the rapacious deal which robs Peter (the acquisition) to pay Paul (the acquirer)? The middle way does exist, but only if you imitate the predators' initial thrust: the price paid will determine the upside potential of the purchase. Buy too dear, and you will never see the colour of your money again.

The concept of Economic Value Added (Chapter 5, page 111) applies. Unless profit covers the cost of capital expended, the purchase must destroy value. If equity is involved, the hurdle becomes higher, not lower, because the true cost of equity capital is greater than that of debt. In theory, an acquirer can surmount the financial hurdle without clearing the cost of capital, but that marvel only materializes if the capital value of the purchased business can be sufficiently enhanced.

Rupert Murdoch managed that after buying TV stations and Twentieth-Century-Fox from two ferociously demanding sellers, respectively John Kluge and Marvin Davis. Note that a precise purpose, the creation of a fourth TV network, lay behind the purchases. The chances of success are far higher where the buyer has a defined strategy which stays close to the mainstream of the existing business.

This is especially true if the purchase is of assets, rather than an entire company. Purchased assets must be slotted into the existing organization; no other home is available. With whole companies, the option exists of allowing the buy to continue in its own sweet (or sour) way. That isn't usually a sensible alternative. The FOGs get this general principle right, too. Being interested only in the assets, and never mind the culture, they stamp their brand on the acquired management from day one.

As noted, the conglomerate stamp may well be the wrong brand for the long-term future of the herd, but that doesn't diminish the power of the principle. It can, however, be applied in different, more motivational and more productive ways. The principle itself, moreover, needs careful definition. The objective is to ensure that the acquisition achieves the highly specific, clearly understood business purposes sought by the acquirer and achieves those ends as effectively and fast as possible.

That doesn't necessitate either obliteration of the acquisition's identity, or massive interference. In a business which the buyer doesn't know, interference is on balance likely to be harmful. Second-guessing and misunderstanding on unfamiliar ground will offset the benefits of any better disciplines installed by the buyer. Misunderstanding shouldn't arise when buyer and bought are in the same business, but that has never stopped less intelligent buyers from throwing their weight – and their acquisitions – around.

Too often, acquirers trap themselves into a baby-and-bathwater dilemma. A complete hands-off policy guarantees preservation of the acquired culture: the baby will stay in the bath. But all acquisitions (like all companies) can be improved, sometimes radically. So hands-off means accepting some degree of unacceptable underperformance. That may be eliminated by placing hands on: but then, will the baby get thrown out with the dirty water?

In this dilemma, fundamentally a conflict between the parent's culture and that of the acquired business, *the parent culture always wins*. What's the solution? Don't create the dilemma in the first place. It reflects defects in the purchaser rather than the purchased. If a company already has a tolerant attitude towards variations between people and businesses, adding another culture will provide an equally comfortable fit. That internal tolerance is one of the keys to motivation: if it doesn't exist, the company will face problems of mounting intensity, with or without acquisitions.

The ability to embrace and encourage cultural diversity within the firm, and to combine different strengths to achieve unified progress, has become a driving force of modern motivation. The organizational pressures, however, work in the opposite direction, towards uniformity. The question of whose uniformity, though, arises urgently. Successful marriage is more achievable by far if the governing partner recognizes that it is a partner, and that a new entrant by its very entry changes the group, and must also – indeed, has the right to – influence its nature and destiny.

That destiny is the starting-point of all successful acquisition: those highly specific, clearly understood business purposes already mentioned.

The purchaser knows exactly what it's doing, why, and how. Too often, that's far from the case. Buyers invariably set about financial research with 'due diligence' (but often get deceived); very few are anything like as diligent about non-financial researches, which are far less likely to result in deception.

The buying company can always find out the crucial non-financial truths by talking to customers, competitors, analysts, market researchers, former employees, journalists, and so on. Without such research, you cannot complete the following catechism – short and simple, but rashly omitted, time after time:

1 Have you firmly established your own true strengths – and weaknesses?

2 Do you know everything possible about the target's activities and its strengths – and weaknesses?

3 Does the purchase make sense in relation to the mutual strengths and weaknesses, and in its own right?

4 Are you ready and able to take a rapid hold on the purchased business and its management?

5 Can you blend the two cultures effectively and swiftly into a new, mutual, lasting way of life?

Many companies have thrived without ever feeling an itch to acquire or merge. For those where combination is a viable, perhaps a highly desirable, option, there is only one imperative: to answer the above catechism with Yes five times over. Do that, and a motivated, united and productive deal will easily out-Hanson Hanson – even with a multinational megamerger.

NINE

Making Teamworking Work

The super-quirks of Quinn

Only a few businessmen, in Europe or anywhere else, have established a sound line in management advice, based on the way they run their own firms. Ireland's answer to Ricardo Semler, the Brazilian entrepreneur who turned his Semco engineering business into a laboratory of heretical management, is Feargal Quinn. His Superquinn supermarkets in Dublin have made him (like Semler) a star on the international guru circuit.

Like Semler, the Irishman believes in 'putting people first'. The key people are customers, but that proposition has a twist – you put *employees* first to put customers first. Julian Richer, a Briton whose personal fame, built in similar style, far exceeds the importance of his modestly-sized privately owned business, believes the same. An American businessman-guru, Hal Rosenbluth, actually entitled his book on customer service *The Customer Comes Second*.

You wouldn't think that from the quirky ways in which Quinn pampers his customers (quirky only by the conventional standards of other supermarket operators). Quinn learns what housewives want by the simple device of asking them, through permanent customer panels – and he acts on their advice. He provides children with signs saying 'I'm shopping for my mum', so they won't get shoved aside by adults. He locates store managers by the enquiries desk, so that customers (and employees) have easy access. He stages parties for customers after hours.

Quinn not only involves employees deeply in his customer service philosophy, he enlists suppliers: their colour photographs are displayed above the displays of the fresh produce grown on their farms. The Irishman has sought to create a holistic company, in which every part reinforces the whole. Like Semler, whose *Maverick!*[1] is a highly stimulating account of experimental management, Quinn has written about his practices: *Crowning the Customer*[2] is a better guide to what customer service really means than many weightier tomes.

Richer is another author. His book, *The Richer Way*,[3] describes how he turns employees in his hi-fi shops into agents of excellent customer service. His approach works well enough to give one small shop, near London Bridge, a world-record turnover of £17,000 per square foot. Each member of staff has a plastic folder containing six small cards bearing simple admonitions like 'provide second-to-none service and value for money to our customers'; 'provide ourselves with secure, well-paid jobs, working in a stimulating equal opportunities environment'; 'be profitable to ensure our long-term growth and survival'.

Richer is hardly alone in believing that 'if customer service is the top goal' the company will find that 'long-term revenue and profitability will follow'. Any bigtime corporate manager will echo the sentiments. What distinguishes the mavericks, though, is that their actions suit the words. This isn't MBLS (management by lip-service), but management by service. In Richer's case, MBS involves a multiplicity of techniques. For instance, 'mystery shoppers' test the level of service, while authentic shoppers are asked to rate the service received and return the ratings to Richer personally.

Crucially, a reward system reinforces the goals. Employees receive bonus payments for high customer appraisals, but get fined for complaints. Like Quinn's lollipop signs for kids, the Richer fines are a quirky feature. So are the very special bonuses for the monthly champions emerging from the customer appraisals: driving a mouthwatering car belonging to Richer himself.

Managers of Richer's stamp make little distinction between the two ends of what's known as the Herzberg seesaw. The basic job provisions that Frederick Herzberg called 'hygiene factors' and what he identified as 'motivational forces' merge into generous and stimulating conditions of employment. The generosity extends to sharing profit. Like Semler, Richer pays a percentage of profits to staff: the Brazilian's figure, 23 percent, is the bigger – Richer pays 15 percent. The latter can afford his percentage: profits have been growing fast, rising ten times in 1990–95 as sales trebled.

Creating enough profits to spread around the staff naturally rests on firm business foundations in the first place. Quinn bases a strong appeal on the quality and freshness of produce. Richer specializes in buying obsolescent hi-fi equipment and selling at low prices which still yield high margins on a turnover that exceeds £21 million. Another of his secrets lies in taking small premises in unfavourable locations, which keeps the ratio of rental costs to sales to a fifth that of major rivals.

But it is the customer aspects of his formula that have made Richer popular with large companies – like the Halifax Building Society and the Asda supermarket chain – who believe that his ideas will help them win their competitive wars. He has nothing to teach them on store layout or design: Richer stores, festooned with posters and cluttered with equipment, are nobody's model. But in a hi-fi market whose customers are generally ill-served, Richer has shown that a business really can be designed backwards from the delighted purchaser.

Quinn has shown the same in a supermarket industry that too easily gets dominated by margins. The way that some far larger rivals react to margin pressure is to compromise on quality and cut staff numbers. Both courses have a severely adverse knock-on effect with the customers. In many aspects of their operations, the big companies' systems are superior to Quinn's, just as Richer's shops are outshone on shop-fitting standards. But excellent customer service can't be achieved by efficiency alone. It can only be achieved by constant attention, renewal – and experiment.

All organizations are laboratories for management thought in action, but the testing of new concepts is seldom deliberate. It is probably no coincidence that Semler, Quinn, Rosenbluth and Richer run private companies. They are in a better position to exploit a vital truth: that profits and growth are not an end in themselves, and that these financial benefits follow from success in non-financial areas – above all, in customer service and employee 'service' – which is the only source from which customer delight can spring.

Power to the empowered

Which interest group should a management put first? Shareholders, customers, or employees? Ask the question in different countries, and you'll get different answers. In the US, investors would get the vote maybe nine times out of ten. British managers are more likely than not to agree with the Americans. In Germany, and most of the Continent, the shareholder would rank last of the three – and the same would be true in Japan.

Since the German and Japanese economies have been notably more successful than the Anglo-Saxons over the whole post-war span, putting investors first doesn't appear, at first glance, to be the best policy. But which of the other two should take priority? One audience of senior German managers plumped overwhelmingly for the customer. Their choice is the conventional wisdom: even shareholder-first companies will often swear their undying devotion to the cause of satisfying the customer. But 'customer-first' can be misleading – as demonstrated by Ricardo Semler, Feargal Quinn, Julian Richer and Hal Rosenbluth, poor service has a cause. Studies in retail chains show that the lower the staff turnover – which is a clearer indicator of satisfaction or dissatisfaction than any employee attitude survey – the higher the profitability.

There is a chicken-and-egg argument here: which came first, the staff satisfaction or the profitability? People are generally happier in an atmosphere of success. Whether the service chicken or the profit egg comes first hardly matters from the investor's point of view. Over the long term, companies which give equal priority to shareholders, employees and customers far outperform investor-first firms. And 'employees' means all the employees, not just those in the front line. Studies in factories have shown that shopfloor productivity rises faster if non-production workers share in bonus schemes linked to output.

So customer first equals people first. But managers express a deep ambivalence about this simple equation. Asked 'can workers be empowered?', the assembled German senior managers already mentioned were unanimous that it could be done. But when asked if the pursuit of customer satisfaction could drive the organization – as the gurus recommend – not a hand rose. How can that be reconciled with the group's overwhelming decision in favour of the customer-first philosophy?

The object of empowering employees is partly to set them free to use their own initiatives to improve service to the customer. That implies working back from the customer's needs to drive the business processes, using the employees' skills and contribution to optimize those processes. If that truly is impossible, much of the expert management advice currently being lavished on companies, however full of good intentions, is short on practical value.

The two questions that generated schizophrenia in those German minds were part of a list of nine, designed to test how far an organization's top management has accepted the ideas of the management consensus. The consensus holds that a new breed of company can be born – not only customer-driven, but customer-leading: that is, highly innovative and dynamized by progressive ideas, aiming not just to anticipate the market, but to shape its development in profitable ways. The full list is:

1 Can organizations become more creative?

2 Can corporate cultures be changed?

3 Can workers be empowered?

4 Can resistance to change be overcome?

5 Can customer satisfaction drive the organization?

6 Can better management style produce better results?

7 Can markets be led by smaller players?

8 Can quality of management be improved?

9 Can organic growth be planned?

That particular German audience was very sure, as noted, that workers can be empowered. It also thought that better management style can generate better performance. The managers were fairly confident about the possibilities of raising creativity and overcoming resistance to change. Leading markets in respects other than size and planning organic growth were apparently thought less feasible. And nobody thought that corporate cultures could be changed – which helps explain the group's similar certainty that the customer-driven organization is a figment of the gurus' imagination.

Of course, the answers to all nine questions should be yes – if, that is, you want to build a new and better brand of company. But most employees, from the top downwards, actually want no such thing. Unless the company is in poor condition, and sometimes even when it is, they want the security of familiar surroundings. No doubt that is why these managers all thought you couldn't change a company culture. They liked the culture of their business – a well-managed one in a comfortably rich industry. They didn't want to change what they liked.

It is a relevant choice. A German cigarette boss speaks admiringly of the economics of the 'money machine' created by the Hanson management at Imperial Tobacco. 'Lean and mean' in the extreme, equipped with the very latest machinery, the factories in Bristol and Nottingham poured forth cigarettes and profits with minimal overheads. After initially losing market share, the company regained its position, and the managers reaped very high rewards from the Hanson system of paying cascaded bonuses linked to performance against profit targets.

But the legend goes that after taking over Imperial (in a bitterly contested battle) Hanson took a robust attitude to the tall landmark office block in Bristol. Starting at the top of the HQ building, a whole floor was cleared out every month until nobody was left but the core management – working in the basement. The conference room was windowless: the half-dozen people in the marketing department, squeezed into a small room, could hardly be seen behind the piles of files.

That German competitor, while admiring the business results, made it very clear that he wouldn't have liked to work at Imperial. The investor-customer-employee issue raises a fundamental question. Can you have a successful business with unsuccessful, unempowered human relations? If so, for how long? To repeat, economic success can be achieved by a business that's fun to work in, humane, happy, and employee-driven – indeed, these may be the conditions of lasting success.

Research by behavioural psychologists confirms the commonsense view that people perform best when they most enjoy their work. So the money machines might even generate more surplus wealth if their people liked working inside them. This goes against the harder-nosed culture, which suggests that people are like machines: that, so long as they do what they're told, their happiness is irrelevant.

It is far more logical to assume that good employees are just like good managers. Managers like to believe that they are dedicated to producing excellent work, and that they are great team players: I've yet to meet a company which doesn't (often with scant justification) boast of the excellence of its management team. Bosses also regard themselves as creative, loyal and honest, and this self-view is generally right: but most other people are also creative, loyal and honest, too – given the chance.

That opportunity depends on their managers. The latter can't themselves manage without being prepared to take responsibility. But in many companies today responsibility has ceased to be a prerogative of the managing class. The key to major progress – as in Semco, Superquinn, Richer Sounds and Rosenbluth – has been the readiness to give people far down the line total responsibility for an entire operation. While the people concerned will remark on the extra pressure involved, nobody at life assurance company Sun Life, to cite one typical example, has ever wanted to return to the old system.

That's hardly surprising. How can managers possibly suppose that they can achieve transformation without transforming the way people work together? Obviously, the two processes must go hand-in-hand. But you can't transform the way people feel about the business and each other without establishing a base. The fundamental principle of Total Quality Management, business process reengineering, or any other corporate medicine is to discover that base – to find out where you are now so that, having determined where you want to go, you can decide how to reach that destination.

There's a big jump between the standard corporate culture and the ideal: an open, cooperative company with no internal politics, which isn't ruled by fear or blame, has high ambitions and expectations of performance, and trusts and empowers its people to perform. How many companies fit this description? Quite apart from other issues, changes in management personnel and positions are so frequent in the typical large business that there's no opportunity to develop effective working relationships – let alone a culture that can perpetuate them.

Two opposing trends appear to be at work in Europe. One is the effort to develop and deploy 'human resources' to the best possible advantage in the ways described above. The other is the drive to cut costs by forcing down numbers employed – which can be expressed more positively as the drive to raise output per man. But that can be accomplished in two ways – by increasing sales without a concomitant increase in manpower (the highly positive approach); or (negatively) cutting employment by more than the output trend: in theory, you can increase productivity on falling sales.

It is truly difficult, though, to combine the more negative 'downsizing' strategy with a positive policy on people. Economist Stephen S. Roach in mid-1996 was wrongly assailed as an ardent downsizer who had suddenly recanted. In fact, he had argued much earlier that employment cutbacks were counterproductive – that is, if you measure true productivity as willing, sustainable effort. He wrote in the *Herald Tribune* that 'Many of these work force reductions reflect an overdue pruning of corporate bureaucracies,' but also noted that, if fewer people are managing an unchanged process, the strains could prove very damaging.

The pressures have already shown up in longer actual working hours for blue-collar workers. White-collar employees are feeling a different kind of strain. Consolidation and automation of work have reduced clerical jobs in many industries – notably banking – and middle managers have been superseded in some roles by computer networks. But laptops, cellular phones, wireless modems and home fax machines have had a paradoxical effect for higher-level managers. Roach argues that in the labour-intensive, intellectually-driven work of planning and directing a company, the capacity of the human mind sets the work-rate. All the machines have done is to extend the executive day: on train or plane, in car or home, the office accompanies the manager. He or she thus joins the factory hand in an unpleasant situation: these people are over-stretched, delivering more only because they are working more.

The whole thrust of empowerment is towards working smarter rather than harder. That is the essence of the philosophies of W. Edwards Deming and Peter Drucker, and it is the secret of success at SGS-

THOMSON, which cites the following list of results from adopting the steering committee approach, working through consensus rather than coercion:

1 Sense of ownership and self-worth is manifested.
2 Productivity increases in groups.
3 Dissatisfaction among members is reduced.
4 Goals and job needs are defined in a clearer manner.
5 All the results are achieved without any sense of being overworked.

All this, note well, should and can be accomplished without special reward for the achievements. That is a basic principle of total quality which the older-fashioned school of management finds hard to understand. Surely special effort deserves special reward? The answer hinges on the word 'special'. Working with optimal effectiveness shouldn't be special. The immortal words of Taichi Ohno, the inventor of the Toyota Production System, apply: 'The word work refers to the production of perfect goods only. If a machine isn't producing perfect goods, it isn't working.'

The same concept, as Ohno was quick to recognize, applies to people. They are paid to produce perfect work. Perfection being unattainable, they are paid for continuous improvement. That in turn depends overwhelmingly on management's ability to provide the right environment, the appropriate system. TQM is one method – and probably the most effective – of providing a system which encourages and enables people to perform at their best.

As Deming memorably taught: 'Workers work within a system that – try as they might – is beyond their control. It is the system, not their individual skills, that determines how they perform.' He went on to say: 'Only management can change the system' – but that statement needs heavy qualification. As countless examples show, self-managing groups can change the immediate system. But, of course, higher management has to allow the self-managers to manage in order to achieve optimum performance and to meet corporate goals.

But are those goals truly 'corporate'? Or are they only the goals of top management? Whatever the size of the company, a key principle applies; the more closely involved people are in both decisions and their execution, the better the results will be. The instinctive response is to suppose that large companies are more difficult to change in this respect than small. But that depends on the approach. If you start by believing that a big business can't be changed quickly and comprehensively, the belief will become a self-fulfilling prophecy.

Without change, the triple priority – ranking investors, customers and suppliers equally – won't be satisfied, and the nine questions listed earlier won't get the right answers or action. Of the three groups, investors are the easiest to satisfy. They don't demand exceptional performance, only a return that's greater than the true cost of capital. Customers are far more difficult, because of the multiplicity and complexity of their demands – and the eternal impossibility of achieving perfect service. But employees, traditionally the toughest nuts to crack, shouldn't be so hard – after all, management and employees can be in daily, even hourly contact.

The difficulties are those inherent in all relationships between human beings, as individuals and in groups. The starting point is to have clear objectives for what you want from people and a clear understanding of what they want from their jobs. As with managers, so with others: there will be mismatches. But humane policies can be just as hard-nosed as those of the Hanson-style money machine. And in the long run, the empowered people machines will always win.

The knock-on at Nokia

In at least one sector of the microelectronics revolution two European companies can stand comparison with any in the world. Oddly, the pair don't come from the heartlands of the European Community, but from the Nordic fringes – Sweden and Finland. The latter's Nokia isn't the actual world leader, but it has been gaining on the champion, Motorola: in early 1996, Nokia's global share was 25 percent versus the American company's 36 percent.

Considering that Nokia, at $8 billion of sales, enjoys under a third of Motorola's total turnover, that's a remarkable achievement, built on the foundation of fast-to-market processes for highly innovative products. Only Ericsson, Europe's other top contender, can make a cellular phone for less money than Nokia. Yet the Finnish company was near to heading downhill in 1992 before chief executive Jorma Ollila and cellular phones saved its day.

The gadgets made Ericsson's day, too. The Swedes, who once relied on selling telephone exchanges to the world, are ahead of Nokia in another way – they lead the market in supplying the infrastructure for mobile phones. In 1995, orders booked by Ericsson for infrastructure and phones themselves soared by 75 percent in US dollars as the number of mobile subscribers worldwide grew by 61 percent to 85.3 million. By 2000, it is predicted, Nokia and Ericsson will be battening off a market of 350 million users.

That is so gigantic a boom, and one so obvious in its inevitability, that it raises some fundamental issues. Why was it the Nordic fringe that produced these evidently attractive, world-winning products? Why did mainstream Europe's technological giants lag so far behind? As the *Financial Times* commented as late as early 1996, 'competing products from the likes of Alcatel and Siemens have been slow to appear'.

What can these lagging European companies learn from the two Nordic exemplars?

The first factor is that, since their home markets were too small by far to support great ambitions, both companies felt compelled to think, plan and act in global terms. Second, they were forced by limited resources to concentrate, to pick markets where they could secure global positions. For Nokia's Ollila, that meant abandoning paper, tyres, metals, electronics (including PCs), cables and finally TV sets. Nothing was left to divert attention from telecoms.

The European tendency – demonstrated by Nokia's previous bizarre spread – is to operate in too many markets. That dissipates resources, complicates management, and makes it difficult to set the technological pace. The key to modern markets lies in constantly upping the technological ante. What Intel does in microprocessors, Nokia achieves in mobiles. The 1610, for instance, with seven hours of talking time and 200 hours of standby, had the best performance on the market in early 1996. At the CeBit computer fair held then, Nokia ventured still further ahead with a digital phone that also has computing power – complete with keyboard and E-mail capability.

Nokia will no more be alone in this 'smartphone' market than it is in mobiles. Ericsson, of course, is competing – though it hadn't by then gone as far as Nokia. Its new product, however, was a line of digital phones with *four* times the data transmission speed of current lines. Both companies are betting heavily that digital users will employ their phones for both voice communication and information services.

To help tap this putative market, Nokia has turned to a Californian company, Geoworks, Inc., for its software requirements. The West Coast company's president, Gordon Mayer, is supremely confident about the powerful application of 'the combo of a cell phone and E-mail and Internet – not to browse, but to deliver services like stock quotes or restaurant guides'. Nokia holds some 8 percent of Geoworks, which is further evidence of the globalism on which Nokia and Ericsson partly depend; indeed, Ericsson has also licensed the Geoworks technology.

But the pair also depend totally on one paramount internal resource – the ability to manage and harness technological development. Men from both companies were among the corporate invitees, leaders among Europe's big R&D spenders, assembled in early 1996 by the Arthur D. Little consultancy to discuss this very issue. Kaj Linden, senior vice president of Nokia's technology, stressed the pressure faced by investors in new wonders: 'The long term in our minds has almost disappeared. Two to three years is the longest we think ahead.' Linden's *vis-à-vis* at Ericsson, Jorma Mobrin, added that 'we need to have a way of planning for the unexpected'. In other words, in rapidly changing times, with a rising degree of uncertainty, companies need a higher standard of strategic management of technology.

The need was plainly felt just as strongly by the other 12 companies represented at Little's Geneva get-together. Yet, while the dozen are all heavily committed to research, none can point to global successes as marked as the unexpected gains of Nokia and Ericsson. Companies like Siemens and Philips have had difficulty in matching the commercial outcomes of their research to the scale of the scientific effort – and management, not science, appears to be at the root of the difficulty.

Writing in the *Financial Times*, Vanessa Houlder discerned 'three closely interwoven themes' that emerged from the R&D colloquium. First, companies need to build a seamless innovation process, breaking down departmental barriers and building teams for new product development on which all relevant functions are represented. Second, that has to be accompanied by changing the mind-set of the R&D specialists, who need to have a strong sense of the commercial and economic consequences and purposes of their labours. But the most important of the trio is strategic management – and here the R&D effort is being ill-served by European employers.

The stategic issues are complex. Nobody at Nokia and Ericsson, for instance, can be sure that the smartphone will provide the new, massive impetus to profits that will one day be required. The need for new impetus arises because the original mobile phone market is maturing rapidly, and prices are coming under pressure as growth slows and competition increases. In 1995, Nokia suffered a 43 percent drop in earnings, which continued into 1996 (with a 70 percent first quarter slump) and sent a tremor through both the stock market and the industry. Ericsson, however, raised profits by 36 percent in 1995; and Nokia bounced back.

The problems at Nokia, according to Ollila, were the result of short-term mismanagement, rather than long-term problems. Whatever the truth, the setbacks cast an inevitable query over the Scandinavian breakthroughs. Undoubtedly, deep-rooted difficulties will emerge unless superior technology again enables the Nordic duo to break free of the pack with a new generation of premium products. They can't afford to make the wrong decision about the balance between long-term strategic needs and short-term financial pressures.

In many European companies, that balance has tilted sharply towards the short term. Ron Jonash, a vice president at Little, warns that North American companies have trodden this path before – focusing on the short term and cutting longer-term technical development. 'Now, all of a sudden, every CEO in every company in the US is talking about longer-term R&D, asking "what are the new ideas?"'

This is a lesson that Europe's managers must take to heart. In light of that necessity, you couldn't have a more ominous phrase than that used by one vice president of corporate R&D: 'There is a reluctance to take risks in these short-term, profit-driven times.' His employer is Siemens. With that risk-averse mind-set, Nokia and Ericsson could never have got moving in mobiles – and certainly couldn't have moved so fast. Unless the rest of Europe moves with equal speed, and in many more technologies, the race is already over – and lost.

Managing the creators

The clear fact that conventional risk-limitation approaches can't meet present needs places unprecedented pressures on management. The pressures aren't confined to those corporations that are actually in crisis. Their critical problems are shared by businesses far removed from present trouble. The ground is shifting beneath managers' feet as markets and methods change, and as the emphasis shifts from sustaining established positions to winning new growth by seizing organic opportunities.

The secret of the high-growth companies which set the pace is to sustain the emphasis on individuality and originality by stress on youth, recruitment, technical challenge and initiative. Communication and results are far more important to these managements than lines of command and bureaucracy. Likewise, monetary reward is not determined by some bureaucratic system of scales and set bonuses, but flows irregularly from achievement itself: the better you do, the more you make.

Personal identification is very strong – with the organization's leadership, with the individual's work, and with clearly defined missions. Ethos is vital: not 'the way we do things around here', but 'the spirit in which we do them'. For all the eccentricity often found at highly creative companies (with their in-house jargon and high-jinks junkets), the management forces at work in these firms are plainly going to affect every organization.

New Century Management needs all these features:

1 Defined, homogenous missions that are known to and shared by all employees.

2 Vigorous recruitment policies aimed at providing a steady flow of the brightest and best talent available.

3 Rapid deployment of talented people into mission tasks that will stretch and develop their abilities.

4 Provision of electronic communications, preferably full networking of PCs, that are freely available to all.

5 Deliberate opening of loopholes and bypasses so that individuals are not confined within the system.

6 Loose methods of payment that relate reward to results rather than hierarchy.

7 Personalized management – encouraging ownership of business groups by long-term leaders, so that they become personally identified with the product or project.

8 Keeping such groups to controllable size.

9 Becoming 'customer-led' – in the sense of concentrating efforts on improving and innovating products and services that will increase customer satisfaction.

10 Finding informal ways of ensuring that everybody, including top management, knows what's going on – above all, what's new.

The blueprint is for a *thinking* company: one that is capable of thinking, not only about its products and their purposes, but about itself. If ideas are going to make the crucial difference in new century markets, New Century Management must be built around the generation and realization of ideas. That demands a deep understanding of intellectual processes and the rejection of elements which stultify intellect.

As David Benjamin noted, innovators are iconoclastic to a 'fiendish' extent, have a threatening tendency to steal resources, and live up to the conclusion of John Jewkes in the 1950s: that 'innovation is an individual enterprise – egocentric, fanatic, conspiratorial'. What right-minded management would knowingly saddle itself with colleagues who fit that description – people who, in a phrase, cannot be managed? There, is however, no alternative to accepting the disorderly conduct of the innovation process and its agents.

If you study the systems of unusually creative companies, you find that the inventiveness hinges on allowing an appropriate degree of disorder within a reasonably orderly framework. That's where management has a most potent role. In the first place, it must select or approve the areas to be explored. Second, it selects the innovators – or appoints their selector. Third, it must make the go/no go decisions, and finance the 'gos' adequately and effectively. Fourth, when success has been achieved, it must turn the innovation into marketable reality. That's where the rational processes of good management come into their full and potentially glorious own, and where the battle is finally won – or lost.

In any of these four departments, fateful choices must be made. ICI lost the prospect of discovering Tagamet by deciding that the innovator, Sir James Black, had no realistic chance of creating another breakthrough as important as his beta-blockers. SmithKline decided to concentrate on ulcer therapies, let Black pick his team, bet its all on the discovery, put a worldwide sales organization together at top speed – and, after generating billions of dollars, lost leadership by losing concentration just when powerful competition appeared from Glaxo.

As noted earlier, Glaxo managed its innovation superbly by riding on the back of Hoffman La Roche to crack the US market, charging a premium for Zantac (instead of undercutting the market leader) and intensifying its marketing expenditure after breaking through (instead of following the industry norm, and spending less). That stresses the basic truth: to manage creativity to superb effect, management must be creative itself.

The levels of talent in management, therefore, need to equal those in the labs. But what is talent? Like quality and innovation, the word suffers from multiple meanings. At a basic level, it refers, as in 'graduate talent' or 'talent pool', to educated recruits who will provide future leaders. At the opposite extreme, as in 'managing talent', it usually implies the handling, always tricky, of research scientists, development engineers, creative personnel – anybody whose divine spark is more valuable than their daily grind. The management use of talent in the second sense is what distinguishes innovators from corpocracies. Since the latter can't afford to allow that distinction to continue, they must cease being corpocratic or fail.

Already, in many companies, people are working in far more creative patterns, coming together in free-standing groups outside formal, fixed hierarchies; being rewarded for strategic and innovative contributions, not just for coming to work; using computerized networks to exchange data and ideas and to create effective, achievable, consensus-driven plans. The Microsofts and the Sonys prove that creation is as responsive to organized thought as any other work. That is their key strength.

Irreversible global changes have put a premium on creative brainpower, on the acquisition and use of knowledge: and on its management. Success may well depend on the degree to which organizations become 'talent-intensive', and on their ability to find people with the desirable attributes in which talent-hunting human resources directors rejoice: 'is extremely good at communication; has a "winner's mentality"; has drive; is able to operate in an ambiguous environment; has not just intelligence, but social intelligence . . . can take initiative and sensible risks'.

The quotation comes from *Managing Talent*, by Philip Sadler,[4] who derived several such lists from his researches into the world of talent-spotting. There, two quite different problems arise. One is making the most of people's ability through maintaining an environment that encourages natural talents and, most important, develops others which are *unnatural* – as in the ever-popular courses on 'finance for the non-financial manager'. The second problem has already been mentioned: employing successfully the mavericks, one-offs, iconoclasts, and creators.

These 'laws-unto-themselves' can unleash uncovenanted success. Michael J. Kami warns his audiences about talented and creative people: they are '9D'. That stands for 'difficult, demanding, disagreeable, disobedient, dislikeable, disorganized, disputing, disrespectful, discordant'. He advises that you shouldn't expect anything original from an echo, but should 'tolerate talented gorillas' and reward them in any way they want and you can afford.

There's obviously much truth in what Kami says: easygoing, undemanding, obedient, cooperative and charming bundles of creative talent do exist – but don't count on finding them. Often great talents either cannot be 'managed', or are not managed. In the transformation of SmithKline Beecham by Tagamet, Black did and spent more or less as he pleased, working outside the control of his American paymasters. They totally shared his objective: to find a new wonder-drug that would successfully treat stomach ulcers. And he did.

That is the crucial point. Talent is without value unless it delivers – and delivers something that's wanted. Superbly talented individuals who won't perform are worthless; average people who perform to the best of their ability are worth plenty. So are those who can lead them to that achievement. Another Sadler-quoted authority numbers no less than twenty-one 'qualities or traits' associated with 'the leadership of people engaged in creative activity'. The list ends with 'resistance to stress' and 'sense of humour', after starting with 'effective intelligence', defined as 'ability to solve problems in a way which leads to practical action'.

To repeat, solutions that don't lead to action have solved nothing. In the Japanese language, the word 'creation' breaks down into two parts, meaning 'first make'. Creative management is about being first, not necessarily into the market or the technology, but into the latter's most successful manifestation. The crucial talent is the ability to perform – to do the right things in the right way at the right time. Helping people to rise to that achievement (above all, by the training and exercise on which even champions and maestros depend) outweighs initial selection every time.

The book *Strategy for Creation*, published by Nomura Research,[5] contains the acronym FINDS for the 'development of what is truly needed': it stands for 'Fulfilment, Intelligence, Nourishment, Discovery and Sensibility'. Without applying FINDS to creative management as a corporate priority, even inspired recruitment and good businesses will fail. Yet in all but four cases, fifty chief executives contacted by Sadler for his research into managing talent referred the enquiry to their company's human resources functions: a very bad omen.

Bosses who don't understand that their own chief job is 'managing talent' won't make the best use of any talents they employ, including their own. They have no role more important than that of encouraging, facilitating and rewarding the generation of ideas. That means using all available means of creating the teaching, thinking company. That is the reinvented life-form towards which all Europe's managements have to strive.

The happy teams at Heineken

Very few European companies can claim to be the largest in a world industry. RTZ in mining is one – and Heineken in beer is another, although the statistics appear to place the Dutch company second to America's Anheuser-Busch. The latter brewed 88 million barrels in 1994, far ahead of Heineken's 51 million. But the vast bulk of the American's sales are in the US, like those of the number three, the Miller subsidiary of Philip Morris. In world markets, it is no contest – Heineken is half as big again as the Belgian/Canadian combination of Interbrew and Labatt.

Heineken's superiority rests on three pillars: the unique international strength of its global lager brand (available in 150-plus countries), its successful purchase of national brewery investments (like the Moretti deal which gave the Dutch over 40 percent of the Italian market), and its remarkable corporate culture.

There is nothing accidental about the cultural strengths. When Gérard Van Schaik took over as chief executive in 1989, he realized explicitly that:

1 There is a relationship between an organization's culture and its performance.

2 The best culture for an organization is a strong team culture.

3 Any large organization is a team of teams – and people who have to work together as a team must also think together as a team.

4 All large organizations therefore have a team-thinking culture to some extent.

5 The critical questions are (a) to what degree and (b) *how* can that culture be strengthened?

To get the right answers to those two questions, and implement the findings, Van Schaik turned for assistance to Ben Heirs and his Geneva-based consultancy, Heirs Associates International. The preliminary finding was that Heineken's team-thinking strengths on a scale of 0–100 were 50: far ahead of the doomed Maxwell Organization, but far behind the Japanese car industry, scored at 90. For all its market strength, Heineken faced what Heirs calls 'serious management issues that needed to be urgently addressed' – especially since the Dutch press had been making morale-sapping criticisms.

Early in 1991, Van Schaik issued what could well stand as a manifesto for New Century Management. 'We should move towards clear, transparent, fact-based decision-making.' That meant clarifying definitions, simplifying reporting, and clearly setting out objectives and the 'hurdles that have to be overcome'. He promised that 'There will be less hierarchy, and life will be more demanding on everybody's ability to work with others. Professionalism and team performance will play a greater role.'

Communication was one key to turning these aspirations into reality: Heineken commissioned Video Arts to make a training film on team-thinking, starring John Cleese and Robert Lindsay. *Think or Sink* has been translated into five languages and shown many times to over 1,000 Heineken managers. The management cadre was also subjected to 'Team-Thinking Profiling'. Not surprisingly, this showed that low-performing and problem teams had leaders with weak team-thinking profiles, and vice versa. Heirs says that 'this proved to be true throughout Europe'.

The profiles are similar in spirit to the 360-degree appraisal which emerged as a new management fashion in America and has spread to some European companies. The Profile asks individual managers to assess themselves on a scale ranging from 5 to –5 as (a) individual thinkers (b) members of a team of thinkers and (c) leaders of the thinking team. The Combined Profile sets this assessment against that of the manager's own leader. The Reverse Profile adds the assessment of subordinates – again on all three counts.

More than 75 management teams and over 400 managers at Heineken went through this scoring in six European countries. Coaching, training and mentoring recommendations followed. Each team leader was expected to coach all managers in order to improve team-thinking performance, and six-monthly reviews were ordained 'to determine what progress had been made and what more needed to be done'. Profiles were updated annually for the same purpose. In late 1991 and early 1992, moreover, all key managers attended seminars on team work and team culture led by London Business School Professor John Hunt.

You can't repeat important messages too often. Van Schaik used every opportunity to ram home what he called 'the new Heineken Spirit' and the need 'to create a strong teamworking culture throughout our whole organization'. The message was underlined by Heineken's success during 1989–92, when both profits and market capitalization more than doubled. The management reckoned that the company's team-thinking strength had risen by 40 percent over the period.

That left a distance to go, but Van Shaik's successors declared their intention to get there. Their manifesto for 'professional team-thinking' was translated into seven languages:

1 The aim is to reach the best decision, not just a hasty conclusion or an easy consensus. The team leader always has the ultimate responsibility for the quality of the decision taken – and therefore, for the quality of the team-thinking effort that has led up to the decision.

2 To produce the best professional team-thinking, the team leader must ensure that ego-trips, petty office politics and not-invented-here rigidity are explicitly avoided. There should be competition between ideas – not between individual members of the team.

3 The team-thinking effort must first ensure that the best question to be answered is clearly and completely formulated.

4 The team-thinking process is iterative – not linear. Therefore, the question may have to be altered later and the process repeated.

5 The team leader is responsible for seeing that sufficient alternatives and their predicted consequences have been developed for evaluation by the team.

6 The team leader will thus ask 'what are our alternatives?' – and not just 'what is the answer?'.

7 The team leader also recognizes that it is wiser to seek and listen to the ideas of the team before expressing his or her own ideas and preferences.

8 In any professional team-thinking effort, more ideas will have to be created than used. But any idea that is rejected will be rejected with courtesy and with a clear explanation as to why it is being rejected. To behave in this way is not naive, it is just decent and smart.

9 A risk/reward equation and a probability of success calculation will be made explicitly before any important decision is taken.

10 Once a decision is made professionally, the team must implement it professionally.

11 When you think, think. When you act, act.

Arguing with any of these eleven points is absurd.

Heirs believes that the Heineken brew is the only culture that meets the 'needs of the mind, the individual and the team, as well as the complex competitive thinking demands' of a turbulent age. The methodical creation and sustaining of that culture is 'one of the most profound and enduring challenges now facing the leadership of any large organization'. Today, 'a strong, autocratic, bureaucratic, compromise-driven culture' has no friends. It doesn't deserve any.

Virtuous circle companies

The team-thinking at Heineken demonstrates what former Air Force General Bill Creech enjoins on companies as 'the power of decentralized team management'. In theory, that organizational approach has won centre stage: centralization has few friends in the nineties. In practice, Creech proved its power at Tactical Air Command. The absolute air supremacy achieved in the Gulf War was founded on remarkable results won back in the States, including an 80 percent rise in productivity and doubling of strike capability achieved with no more money and no more men.

Every successful independent project team adds further proof of Creech's point. The decentralized team, though, is highly vulnerable: any step towards centralizing their operation must be a step backwards – and a stride towards failure. The leader often has to fight desperately to defend his team against corpocratic attack. That is only one of the leader's vital roles.

If teamwork is what wins, why should the leader make much difference?

The first answer is that the world of business management is changing, which must push change management to the fore. Leadership is needed to help tomorrow's manager (and increasingly today's) to operate in flatter and looser structures, on a global stage, in conditions of great uncertainty, under unremitting competitive pressure. That applies at all levels and to every one of the groups or teams which are the focal points of the new leadership.

Teams, even small ones, need leaders as much as autocracies and corpocracies, but the brand of leadership is necessarily different. The new leadership demands the ability to handle complexity and multiplicity, and that involves disparate humans as well as complicated machines and chaotic markets. The old leadership was often called a lonely task. Walking alone is now ruled out by complexity, although too many still attempt the impossible.

A common theme of recent boardroom putsches is that the deposed boss led too prominently from the front, with too little success. In all these cases the deposed managers didn't obey the messages which come under new names like the Learning Organization, Organizational Architecture, the Virtual Corporation, and so on. The messages are not all new, by any means; indeed, they revolve around a Holy Trinity so aged that Claus Møller, the Danish founder of the TMI consultancy, calls them 'evergreens'.

The test of the new team leadership, according to him, is its success on three interrelated scores:

Productivity comes first because the difference between inputs and outputs determines the strength of the organization – any organization, public or private, small group or major company. Every operation should have a plan for reducing inputs as a proportion of outputs, which should be easier to achieve if output is rising. But that perfect outcome of mounting productivity can't be managed (in either sense of 'managed' – that is, run or achieved) unless *relationships* between people and groups of people are excellent.

Both productivity and relationships are intensely involved with *quality*. The underlying business system connects all three. Rising productivity is achieved by good working relationships, which result in rising quality of products and service, which raises customer satisfaction and demand and hence boosts productivity, which improves relationships, which enhances quality, and so on.

You can see that virtuous circle in the introduction of many blockbuster products. As the circle turns, good team relationships, even under intense time pressures, achieve quality which attracts such powerful demand that productivity soars. The team seems to have done everything right – but only if you include in that definition (as you should) rapidly correcting each and every mistake as soon as it appears.

The flexible style that capitalizes even on failures to create successes is the engine of mega-growth: the style is usually charismatic, loose-limbed, improvisational, lean, concentrated. The contrast between the old management and the new is acute. In New Century Management, action takes precedence over everything else. Teams no longer have to wade through the layers upon layers of bureaucracy that arise from having vertical, specialized jobs. Vertical systems allow neither individuals, nor any individual group, to have clear visibility or a clear view of their work and its consequences. The 'evergreens' can't interlock – and that interlocking is crucial to the business system, which must be treated as a whole system.

The TMI logic is inescapable. Push for higher productivity at all costs, and you damage quality. Concentrate on quality at all costs, and you damage productivity. Concentrate on relationships at all costs, and you damage the company's economic purpose. Lay off thousands of workers to boost productivity, and you destroy relationships – and quality as well. You may be applauded for the cost-cutting, but the cheers won't last. Anyway, customers are not impressed by draconian actions taken by companies in deep financial trouble.

The point is well made by Regis McKenna. Chapter 6 (page 146) referred to his book *Relationship Marketing*, with its stress on the crucial importance of 'dynamic positioning' and its three aspects: *product positioning, market positioning,* and *corporate positioning*. It is the latter which leads him to point out that 'when a company's profits slip, [its] position is tarnished. People are reluctant to buy from companies in financial trouble.'

McKenna draws product, market and corporate positioning as three intersecting circles, with the customer as the hub at the point where the circles intersect. That's precisely how Møller illustrates his threefold elements (productivity, relationships and quality), with the customer replaced at the hub by 'employeeship'. The two diagrams could be super-imposed on each other, for they cover most of the critical aspects of any organization.

Team leadership is responsible in both cases for keeping the three rings revolving in a virtuous rather than a vicious circle. But the point of 'employeeship', in Møller's view, is that responsible leaders can also rightly ask the employee, what about you? What's your responsibility? The exercise of good employeeship involves employees feeling responsible for the overall results of the organization – a responsibility from which they can never escape.

The essence of teamworking, by the same token, is that all members are responsible for the results of the team – but this principle in no way absolves the leadership in cases of disaster. When a previously successful team runs into colossal setback, that team that has been doing everything right suddenly seems to get everything wrong. Critical errors are allowed to run riot. The virtuous circle has turned vicious. Why?

The buck, at its simplest, stops at the boss's door: the leader may simply have been outgrown by the task. It is one of the oldest truisms in management. The leader who is supremely the right choice for launching a new enterprise is the wrong person to lead the business into maturity, especially if words start parting company with deeds. The following words of one champion venturer, taken from a house magazine, have the resounding ring of the glory days: 'Our management style is geared to eliminating overheads, unnecessary meetings and discussion; to operating with lower cost, fewer people and shorter development cycles.' Alas, even when this hero wrote those words, his division was adding cost, people and time in exponential increases.

A large contribution to such divisional calamities usually comes from top management, which is rarely inclined to allow successful independent business units to stay independent. More managers, more disciplines, more policies and procedures, more reviews are guaranteed to kill drive and sheer energy as the corpocrats move in. Productivity, quality and relationships – Møller's evergreens – thus all deteriorate profoundly in a very short time.

One of the essential elements of keeping the evergreens green is to cut back on 'reporting to'. Managers can't manage even an old-fashioned operation effectively if much of their time is spent on the road 'reporting to': not travelling to establish rapport with customers (which might well be valuable), but voyaging to explain their actions to second-guessing superiors who are vainly trying to control the uncontrollable.

Today, fewer managers are trying the impossible. Conditions – not least, the necessity for team leadership itself – are forcing managers to adopt the preaching of the gurus. As teamwork becomes a fact of corporate life, managers have to accept the need to change roles. They become facilitators rather than commanders, leading by encouragement and coaching, not *diktat*, and 'frequently' discussing with subordinates the way they do their jobs, and suggesting improvements.

That was the excellent practice, so they said, of three-quarters of senior managers of information technology staff surveyed by Ashridge Management Research Group in 1993. Less excellently, two-thirds of their staff reported otherwise: that they had *never* discussed either their jobs or how to improve those jobs with their leaders – let alone frequently.

That survey was one of eighteen areas of management research presented by Ashridge in a fascinating day-long programme entitled *2001: A Research Odyssey*. Time and again, the researchers reported on yawning gaps between preaching and practice, on the failure of top-down initiatives on customer service, quality and values to make any progress on any of these three counts. As one researcher noted, the top-down leaders talk about fundamental change, when they only mean *improvement*. The latter doesn't threaten their power, while the former involves its redistribution. No radical change, no real improvement. In contrast, the new leaders are concerned with potential, not power – with releasing and combining all the abilities and resources in the firm.

Decentralized teamworking is a potentially marvellous method for doing precisely that. But it forces many 'leaders' up against a painful truth that they prefer to dodge: that their companies are not geared to accepting new ideas and initiatives from below the summit. If leadership isn't shared, it can't be exercised. That is the uncomfortable aspect of genuine group working. It faces managers with the need to change their ways. Often, they won't. That is bad leadership in the mid-nineties, and it spells disaster for 2010.

The way to avoid disaster isn't complex. To achieve Bill Creech's 'power of decentralized team management' . . .

1 Eliminate bureaucray and hierarchy.

2 Devolve authority to autonomous teams.

3 Use networked PCs as the universal management tool.

4 Do all this for the sake of speed, quality and customer satisfaction.

5 Train, develop – and learn.

Those five points echo the wisdom dispensed by David A. Nadler and Marc S. Gerstein in *Organizational Architecture: Designs for Changing Organizations*.[6] They argue that an organization should be designed like a building. You decide on its purpose, consider what structural materials are available to solve the problem of achieving that purpose, create a style that marries the two, and employ collateral technology (like air-conditioning) to produce the final solution.

The metaphor is applied to a company in this way: today's *purpose* is to replace 'bureaucratic control' with quality, speed, customer responsiveness and the ability to learn. The new *structural materials* are the tools of information technology and telecommunications. They enable the new *style* that throws out 'the traditional hierarchical organization' and substitutes 'more decentralized companies where self-managed teams have end-to-end responsibility for satisfying customer requirements'.

As for the *collateral technologies*, they still have to be invented: 'new methods for selecting, training, evaluating and rewarding people consistent with the greater autonomy, responsibility and continuous change inherent in the new design'. They had better be invented quickly, for the pressures on organizational architecture are those of an increasingly demanding marketplace. Ignore the new management demands, and you won't be able to meet those of the customers. And if you can't do that, you're out of business.

TEN

Total Quality of Management

The way to get it right

Imagine that an unkind fate has put you in command of any or all of the following companies. Each faces tough problems, some terrible ones – the difficulties are all quite typical of the pressures crowding in on end-century management. Tempting though it might be to run away from such situations, there's no place to hide.

Company A used to have a monopoly in its market, supplying office equipment. Your company's share has fallen to 17 percent in the face of powerful competition, and is still falling. Your indirect/direct cost ratio is double that of your toughest competitor; you use nine times as many suppliers; your rejects are ten times higher; product lead-times are twice as long; you have seven times as many defects per 100 products. What do you do?

Company B has No. 1 positions in nearly all markets, mainly for industrial products, but you are determined to stay on top – and you suspect that performance could be radically improved in the factory (where overheads are nearly three times direct labour costs) and in sales and service. What do you do?

Company C is an engineering maintenance operation. After a history of strikes, constant friction and fights over every pay deal, management has firmly asserted the right to manage: the shop floor is now under firm discipline. But the parent's profits are falling fast, and you are under pressure to cut costs. What do you do?

Company D, a very large service business, has lost its monopoly. You face new regulations and regulators, new shareholders and new technology (a massive change). Also, by your own admission, you're providing some of the worst service in the Western world. What do you do?

Company E runs a service business in the consumer field that has been growing rapidly, thanks to an excellent concept, backed up by heavy advertising on TV. But the feedback from customers is unsatisfactory, which is a threat to future expansion. What do you do?

Company F is in high technology, but it has a difficult history of mergers, changing ownership, losses, product overlaps and poor competitive performance in a business dominated by a single rival. Customers have a low opinion of your performance, and the market is changing radically from the tied-customer relationship you have always enjoyed. What do you do?

Company G is a service business which has turned itself around effectively from losses by cutting costs, raising prices and curbing some of its services. But the customers are all unhappy. You think that you're providing 85 percent on one key dimension of performance. Your biggest customers say it's only 70 percent. What do you do?

Company H will drop out of its high-tech business unless it can meet increasingly exacting demands from customers and partners. The company has only recently been created by merger. One of the pre-merger cultures is very used to meeting rigorous standards, the other less so. You have to achieve the same levels throughout – and raise them. What do you do?

Company I has been given less than 18 months to set up a major new entrant in a big, sales-driven financial services market. In that time, you must hire and train 600 people, create an entire product line, install all the necessary systems and convert sales agents from their traditional methods to your own philosophy and practices. What do you do?

Company J is No. 12 in a science-based components market where the top competition is vastly more powerful. The business is a recent cross-frontier merger which has successfully improved its technical performance. But the business cycle turns down and catches you unprepared: you lose money and have to face major job cuts. What do you do?

The answers provided in all ten cases were identical. The ten companies adopted the same philosophy, Total Quality Management, as the solution to their very different problems.

Company A is Rank Xerox, which has won back market share from the Japanese while rising remarkably on the customer satisfaction score – from first in five markets on only nine parameters out of 75 (1989) to first on 60 of the counts (1992).

Company B, Honeywell (UK), cut the overhead element from 270 percent of direct labour costs to 100 percent while growing turnover and profits through severe recession. At BA Engineering (C), the *first-year* payoff was £38 million, with £50 million more achieved in Year Two.

British Telecom (D) surmounted enormous challenges of change on its way towards a target of 90 percent reduction in service failures. American Express (E), with Europe contributing powerfully in 1996 generated a high 11 percent return on sales from its more contented customers.

Company G, Royal Mail, now delivers nearly all first-class letters by the next day, and ranks as the best postal service in Europe – where once it was the worst. The Italian aerospace group Alenia (H) has won the vital quality commendation of customer/partners like Boeing. Company I, the financial services start-up, National Westminster Life, has been spectacular: the launch was completed on time and on budget, and a business with a market value of over £1 billion was created on total capital of £200 million.

Company J, SGS-THOMSON, has been raising productivity, crudely but meaningfully measured, by 15 percent annually in the demanding global business of semiconductors. That leaves only one relative failure: Groupe Bull (F), where a marked rise in customer satisfaction and two years of profit were not enough to turn a very difficult corner. The successes, and many other European cases, however, are emphatic evidence that Total Quality Management delivers – you can't argue with the results. Yet disillusion with the quality movement is widely expressed. Why?

What management quality means

The backlash against Total Quality Management was bound to come. No technique has ever spread so far so fast – or so wide. As the Nine Who Got It Right show, examples of total quality success range from great companies in high-tech industries to start-ups in life insurance. Beyond these large firms, relatively small businesses in activities ranging from smokestacks to services have also Got It Right.

As usual, though, serious investigation of the benefits, if any, has lagged behind the adoption of the new marvel – and several of the probes, just as typically, have found performance lagging behind practice. 'TQM PROGRAMMES CAN BE COUNTER-PRODUCTIVE, CLAIMS NEW RESEARCH', was the press release headline to an Economist Intelligence Unit report.[1] The underlying research was done by Ashridge Management College: the study's leader commented that such 'programmes – company-wide, training-led, add-ons to existing jobs – are at best, ineffective. At worst, they inoculate the organization against real change'.

Critical writers promptly seized on this critique as damning the useful-ness of quality out of hand. Yet the title of the study was 'Making Quality Work' – implying that it truly can be effective. This contradiction reflects the confusion in the marketplace, which results partly from inflated claims and unrealistic explanations, partly from fundamental misunder-standing of what total quality means, partly from unsound implementa-tion and partly from corporate regression.

Often, all or some of these causes are present at the same time. For instance, understanding total quality means understanding that it is continuous – you never reach a pitch of such perfection that the quality drive can safely be halted. If you relax the effort, regression is inevitable; indeed, it occurs even if you *don't* relax. Both these observations embody age-old management truths: the most vulnerable moment for any organ-ization is the acme of its success. That is when the financial numbers, internal self-conceit and outside reputation conspire to blind eyes to mis-takes and mismanagement.

Without question, these sins will be damaging the star company's performance right there and then, not to mention setting up the failures that will jeopardize the future. One area of error that's certain to exist in all companies is systemic degradation. In other words, systems back-slide into inefficiency either through slackness or because conditions have changed and the systems haven't.

Federal Express is an example. This was the first service company to win America's Malcolm Baldrige prize for quality, the second most prestigious after the Deming Awards in Japan (Europe's award is only six years old). The company's relatively poor financial performance was highlighted by the *Harvard Business Review* as it questioned, critically but inconclusively, the effectiveness or otherwise of winning the Baldrige.

The lag in earnings growth and other measurements at Fedex implied that, if its service quality was truly excellent, then its quality of manage-ment had to be inferior. That view was confirmed when the business gave a new meaning to the phrase 'overnight despatch' by abruptly firing all the people employed in its failed intra-European services. That failure arose from poor strategy compounded by inept execution.

You could argue that the quality operation was highly successful, but the patient died. The management technique was not linked to the strength of business intelligence and control on which a hard-nosed businessman would have insisted. But would such a character have understood the necessity and value of a quality programme in the first place? That's the point where managing and business meet, or should. The professional manager should be able to demonstrate, first, that 'quality is free'.

That resounding statement is the title of a famous book by Philip Crosby.[2] Ideally, the costs of quality programmes should be absorbed (or better) by the savings from eliminating waste and rejects, with the marketing benefits flowing through as a large bonus. To make such savings permanent and continuous (which is one objective of true quality programmes), the processes and behaviour of the organization have to be changed from top to bottom, and back again.

Top-level commitment is essential, but the words must be accompanied by deeds. Boards of directors expect practical action from everybody else, and demand continuous improvement in every process, after they develop enthusiasm for TQM – every process, that is, except, all too often, their own. The shaping of strategy is just as susceptible to practical improvement as the purchasing process. The difference is that a failed strategic process can vitiate all other quality achievements – and maybe jeopardize the entire future of the firm.

One conversation with a Swiss enthusiast for quality, whose period as chief executive had seen marked quality improvements in many areas, makes the point. Had the top management, I asked, changed its own methods of working in line with TQM principles? The answer was no: the executive committee had evolved a collegiate style of working over many years that had proved highly effective, and its members took a close interest in the quality work down below, but no. In other words, the top echelon saw no need for itself to improve or change.

Other leaders have recognized that this is a fundamental error. The quality of the top management – how it works and what it works on – should be the starting point of comprehensive corporate reform. If you leave the process of selecting and attacking acquisition targets, say, to unreformed processes, you can hardly complain if the result is the usual mess. The larger the issue, the greater 'the benefits, in terms of competitive edge and profitability, that real quality improvement can bring', to quote the Ashridge/EIU study.

Though presented as an attack on TQM, the study actually argues for its adoption. The authors warmly recommend:

1 Leadership which makes quality the number one, non-negotiable priority.

2 Empowering employees to experiment and make mistakes and find their own ways of improving quality.

3 Building quality into the responsibilities of all managers.

4 *Not* making quality the responsibility of a specific department.

5 Providing training on a 'just-in-time' basis, developing skills and knowledge as needed.

A sixth point relates back to the hard-nosed businessman mentioned above: *The whole quality effort should be dedicated to and judged by hard results.* That's why there is so close a fit between TQM philosophy and what Ben Tregoe and T. Quinn Spitzer, when respectively chairman and chief executive of the Kepner-Tregoe consultancy, called 'the seven principles of cost management'.

The definition of the latter sounds very much like one of total quality. It makes 'adding value and containing costs' something 'integral to everything an organization does, from setting strategy to training its people to putting the very best products and services in the hands of its customers'. And, if you read 'quality' for the italicized words *cost management* below, the seven principles make equal sense:

1 *Know your true cost.* Do you know the real costs in all aspects of your business: products and services, markets and customers, suppliers, parts manufactured in-house and inventoried items? Unless you have this information – and it's amazing how many organizations don't – you can't . . .

2 *Continuously reduce costs.* Assuming that the true costs are known, can – and do – your employees, as standard operating procedure, constantly identify opportunities for eliminating, reducing or better managing low-value work? If people are to carry out that invaluable process, you must . . .

3 *Provide the tools to manage costs.* Are your employees being given the decision-making, team-building, problem-solving and other thinking skills which are required to control costs, improve quality and productivity, and enhance performance? The powerfully educative nature of this training is what enables you to . . .

4 *Involve employees in decision-making.* Do you ask employees for their advice on potential *cost management* areas and thus forge commitment to *cost management* initiatives which 'belong' to them? Do they understand, and have they helped to frame, the organization's objectives?

5 *Reduce complexity.* Do you constantly question why work is done and

determine if it is important? If so, do you constantly question how it can be done more efficiently? The 'Rule of 50/5' is a close relative of Pareto's Law: it says that 50 percent of a company's activities produces less than 5 percent of its value added. Just as the Paretoist seeks out the 20 percent of customers who contribute 80 percent of sales, and adjusts his marketing plans accordingly, so the Fifty-Fiver relentlessly weeds out the non-contributing activities. The easiest way to improve an inessential activity is to abandon same: which, because it is inessential, can do no harm in either the long term or the short.

6 *Change the performance system.* Do your employees know that they are responsible for *cost management*? Do they have the skills to manage costs? Do they receive positive reinforcement for *cost management* activities? Do they get timely feedback on the results? While you don't reward people directly for managing costs down (because it's part of their normal work), you place every emphasis possible on encouraging and recognizing their achievements.

7 *Use your strategy.* This is the crunch item. In cost-cutting and quality alike, the actions taken must relate to the overall strategy of the company. A crucial aspect of true quality lies in developing an understood, agreed, effective and appropriate business strategy.

As Tregoe and Spitzer note, tough times create a temptation to rush into cutting costs without thinking carefully about the long-term future of the organization. Cost management and quality alike start with the long-term future. 'The first question the true cost [quality] manager asks is: "What does our strategy say about making the tough choices on products, markets and resources?"'

Making improvements, continuous or otherwise, in the wrong area is a hopeless exercise. Doing the right thing right is the real game. Doing the wrong thing, rightly or wrongly, is the reason why only a minority of companies that have ventured into TQM declare that their competitive prowess has improved as a result; or that their TQM programmes have increased market share, or customer satisfaction, and so on. However, the thrust even of those writers reporting so much disappointment isn't against total quality, but strongly in favour.

My own research into twenty TQM organizations in Europe found example after example of brilliant, effective ideas that couldn't help but improve performance. There is one proviso. They must be applied within a context of commitment to the basic TQM philosophy:

1 Start with the customer: accurately measure current performance in serving customers – from their point of view – and establish the gap (generally vast) between their ideal wants and your actual work.

2 Embody those ideal wants, and embed plans for closing that gap, in a clear statement of policy that everybody in the organization can understand and use.

3 Expose top managers to the full disciplines of fact-based management and to the testing of their own performance, on all counts, against measurable objectives.

4 Then expose them to fellow-employees at all levels to discover what obstacles prevent people from making their fullest possible contribution to meeting the policy objectives.

5 Remove the obstacles and improve the operations continuously through work by trained teams which both select and execute the improvement projects.

6 Avoid bureaucracy at all costs, but align budgeting, appraisal and reward systems with the total quality objectives – and always celebrate success.

7 Never rest on your laurels. Go out and win some more prizes – every day, week and year.

The prizes are plentiful. A study by Ernst & Young and the American Quality Foundation looked at 580 companies in North America, Germany, and Japan. The investigation concluded that huge gains in return on assets (ROA) and value added per employee (VAE) are indeed within reach – but won't be captured unless you relate the quality philosophy to your current levels of performance. That builds on the useful fact that, the worse you are, the better the early gains must be.

A company with low return on assets (under 2 percent), which is adding very little value ($47,000 maximum per employee), is forced to go back to basics. You look for the processes that add most value, simplify them, and quicken responses to customers and the market. That should produce gains so large that they don't need to be measured (even though they should be). They'll catapult you into the next league (return up to 6.9 percent, value added $73,999).

Now you meticulously document gains, and further refine practices to improve speed-to-market and delight the customers. All this time, you've been building up team abilities by training and by sending authority down the line. Now you're ready to benchmark: you measure everything you do against the best standards in the world (not necessarily in your own industry) and set out to match or beat them.

McKinsey has calculated what this means in one area which occupies every company – buying in supplies. The typical company spends 3.3 percent of purchase costs on the purchasing activity itself; the world-class company spends 0.8 percent. Late deliveries of 33 percent compare with 2 percent – and so on. Against that background, you can understand how successful TQM practitioners have won real and large returns from their quality investments.

The backlash against TQM has nothing to do with its efficacy. Rather, it is the defensive reaction of managements which lack the stomach for such wholehearted and long-lasting commitment to very demanding work and to a far-reaching change in philosophy. The criticisms are also used as excuses by managements who have mismanaged their efforts. Returns like those above are the reward for getting quality programmes right. If they aren't right, they have nothing to do with quality.

The birthright of Bosch

In March 1996 General Motors was hit by a 17-day strike at two Ohio plants that brought the entire North American manufacturing apparatus to a juddering halt. The issue was something new: for GM was asserting its right to purchase components – in this case antilock braking systems – wherever it wished, not just from its own plants. The chosen supplier in this instance, moreover, wasn't American, but European: Robert Bosch of Germany.

The choice was highly appropriate, for Bosch had pioneered the product developments which led to GM's decision. In selecting Bosch ABS systems for the 1998 Camaro and Firebird models, GM was opting for a firm of proven reliability and quality. Founded in 1886 as a 'Workshop for Precision and Electro-Mechanics', Bosch had made itself indispensable through both innovation (a tradition that ran from spark plugs to fuel injection) and meticulous attention to detail.

Before anybody had thought of Total Quality Management, Robert Bosch practised many of its principles. His credo was founded on quality: 'it has always been an intolerable thought to me that someone should inspect one of my products and find it inferior. I have therefore always tried to ensure that only such work goes out as is superior in all respects.' He cottoned on to a basic TQM principle, which is that the supplier must be part of the quality chain: 'A good supplier is more important to me than a good customer.'

Consequently one of the dozen quality principles given to all Bosch staff today (and translated into all the many languages spoken by its employees) concerns suppliers: 'Demand the highest quality from our suppliers and support them in adhering to our mutual quality goals.' Old Robert Bosch had set the standard for the whole German components industry. Its reputation for high quality had helped to build that of Germany's luxury cars. This industry at least was exempt from damaging comparisions with the Japanese – or was it?

In February 1996, the *Wall Street Journal Europe* reported that a third of Germany's 3,000 companies making automotive parts were losing money. All wasn't lost, however: these manufacturers 'can survive – if they cut away *many years' accumulation of corporate fat and inefficiency*'. The italics are mine. The Germans have kept their technological edge (witness the ABS systems at the heart of the GM dispute), while losing their competitiveness on the factory floor.

One plant at Edenkoben, belonging to Walker Gillett Europe, carried over twice the inventory it needed, took over six times as long as necessary for a simple die-changing operation, and was so inefficient at moving parts between stages that at one station a 42 percent reduction in time so spent was achieved – without investment. That saving, moreover, was accomplished inside a week, along with a 40 percent rise in production.

The method used to make the savings wasn't exactly revolutionary. The German company simply applied an element of all Total Quality programmes – *kaizen*, the time-honoured Japanese term for continuous improvement. Thanks to this common sense approach, adopted across the whole business, a 15 percent increase in output returned Walker Gillett to profit in 1995 after two years of losses. Without that financial pressure (no doubt intensified by clamour from its American owners, Tenneco), the company might have persevered with its inefficiencies.

Like Walker Gillett, other component suppliers had been far too slow to accept that their methods could be improved – not just by small amounts, but dramatically. Their customers, not only Germany's own vehicle manufacturers, but the latter's rivals elsewhere in the West, have been forced by demanding markets to raise quality and productivity standards towards Japanese levels. That can't be done without exacting similar standards from suppliers.

The car companies have also seen the wisdom of cutting down on the number of suppliers – and thus getting the benefits of closer cooperation and lower costs. Reacting to this pressure, suppliers are joining forces: Bosch itself, by merging with its American brake systems competitor, Bendix, provided the impetus for Varity and Lucas Industries to do likewise. For all these reasons, the writing is on the wall for the weaker performers. Since old-style German productivity and quality comes too expensive, they have to find better ways – or perish.

When your biggest local customer (Volkswagen) has put its people through 14,000 *kaizen* courses, you can't lag behind indefinitely. Robert Bosch, true to its birthright, had signed up when the Kaizen Institute, based in Zurich, opened its doors to spread the cause of continuous improvement around Europe. Many other German companies, though, are ill-constituted to adapt to fundamental challenge.

For instance, at VW the fierce drive to reduce supplier numbers and prices has been partly hampered by political pressure. The return of some parts for uneconomic manufacture in-house became necessary to compensate for jobs lost elsewhere in the company, thus placating unionists and politicians (both represented on the supervisory board). Then, many of the car industry's local suppliers are still controlled by families whose dominant conservative traditions militate against today's requirements for world-class competitive powers.

Robert Bosch has no such ownership problems. The founder vested control in a foundation which devotes its dividends exclusively to public and social purposes. Social ownership at Bosch has been an asset, not least in the drive for quality. The underlying principle of *kaizen* is that the true source of continuous improvement is cooperative, collaborative work by people committed to the cause and the company.

Other German engineering companies could always have turned to this decades-old legacy of Robert Bosch to find the true way forward. The $25 billion sales chalked up by Bosch in 1995 made it the world's largest supplier of automotive components: though the tiny profit margin (1 percent of sales) only underlines the German problem. Quality, innovation and collaboration are the triple keys to the future. With its handicaps of high local costs, German industry desperately needs to be in the forefront of the management revolution, not bringing up the rear. But that truth applies to Europe as a whole: and, as those 1,000 money-losing component firms must know, time is not on Europe's side.

Deploying the policies

The challenge to German companies – and to many others in Europe – is typically presented as that of cutting jobs sufficiently to become competitive. In early 1996, for example, Volkswagen had perhaps 30,000 more workers than required, costing $1.5 billion a year. Once the group got its model line-up properly together, cutting its car platforms from an indefensible 16 to four, still more workers would be surplus to requirement. Any cutbacks will be welcomed by the pundits. But taking out production costs by removing workers is a beginning, not an end.

It's not a happy beginning, either. There's a depressing roll-call of companies whose bosses swore total devotion to their people while busily laying them off. In *Fortune*, author Thomas Stewart acerbically summed up the result: 'your former CEO gave you a superb reference [in the annual report]. He called you skilled/talented/ expert . . . dedicated . . . hard-working . . . motivated . . . confidence inspiring . . . outstanding/the best . . . committed . . . creative . . . bright . . . loyal'.

These are, of course, the very qualities that modern 'human resources management' is supposed to promote. The lost jobs contradict the people policies – and often maim the overall strategy. This is the heart of the issue. What is the business trying to achieve? What policies offer the best promise of reaching those objectives?

The Sema Group lists 'key competitive factors' which translate into four powerful questions:

1 How do we achieve superior customer relationships?
2 What are we really good at, and how can we obtain the utmost mileage from that excellence?
3 How can we share the rewards among those who created the achievement?
4 How can we respond flexibly to the political, economic, sociological and technological environment?

The actual words used by Sema for the second question are 'highly leveraged core competence' – a perfect piece of consultancy jargon. Reduced to simple terms, the idea sounds trite. But there's nothing wrong with simplicity. To quote Jack Welch, the CEO of General Electric, 'For a large organization to be effective, it must be simple.' Welch continues: 'For a large organization to be simple, its people must have self-confidence and intellectual self-assurance. Insecure managers create complexity' – which is another argument against the large-scale redundancies that have made managers as insecure as their subordinates.

To reduce complexity, GE favours 'The Flat Organization' – one of seven Big Ideas which the management consultants at Price Waterhouse put forward in 1992 as answers to the question, What's going on in organizations? In addition to being Flat, you could choose between The Benchmarking Organization (with Rank Xerox as examplar), The Innovative Organization (3M), Business Process Redesign (Ford), The Networking Organization (BP), The Learning Organization (Rover) and The Hollow Organization (Benetton).

All these, said Price Waterhouse, were 'striking ways in which organizations are transforming themselves to keep pace with their competitive environment.' The passing years have provided an interesting test of the validity of the approaches. The two US groups, GE and 3M, have broadly sustained their performance. The results may speak well, respectively, for flat structures and giving the organizational priority to innovation. But both giants can also thank their pragmatic attachment to backing whatever works and dropping whatever doesn't.

Among the Europeans, the US-controlled Rank Xerox has maintained its recovery from the Pearl Harbor-style impact of the Japanese, but has neither approached its previous market strength nor kept pace with the astonishing leaps forward of the IT industry. Nor, for all its efforts to encourage learning, and despite the real improvements obtained in productivity and quality during its association with Honda, has Rover broken fully clear of its past. This was highlighted by critical comments from the new German owners, BMW. Worse still, reporting on a year when Rover thought it had made £91 million of profit, the Germans otherwise. Their stricter standards of valuation turned that profit into a loss of £161 million. Rover's managers were deceiving themselves about the extent of their achievement.

What is true of profit also applies to production: when identical cars were being made on adjacent assembly lines at Cowley, the Britons assembling cars for Rover couldn't quite achieve the quality standards of the Britons working for Honda. Part of the explanation is that the Japanese company's far greater worldwide volumes gave it stronger bargaining power *vis-à-vis* its out-sourced suppliers. Whatever improvements Rover achieved in detail were offset by the fact that too small an output was being spread over too many models.

Similarly, the 'Big Idea' business reengineering case at Ford, however wonderful its outcome in local productivity, couldn't contribute much to the overall performance of a multinational giant.

This is the case reported earlier, in which Ford found that it was using hundreds of accounts payable clerks where Mazda, its Japanese associate, needed only a handful: three-quarters of the clerks lost their jobs. The solution was basically simple: since all invoices ultimately derive from purchase orders, the latter could automatically generate payment instructions, which would be triggered by confirmation of receipt. But the consequent saving to Ford was a drop in the Pacific compared to the damage suffered from over-pricing the new Ford Taurus in the US or failing to match GM's overall advances in Europe.

As for BP, Chapter 7 (page 178) told how the oil colossus suffered a violent hiccough, culminating in the departure of its chief executive, Bob Horton, because its effort to embrace collaborative working ran foul of unclear business objectives and unfavourable business economics (the oil price was much lower than BP had anticipated). Once the new top management had decided clearly on its business priorities, it abandoned matrix structure for a simpler set of operational responsibilities. That paid off handsomely – BP's performance has since been outstanding.

That leaves the Hollow Corporation, Benetton. Its performance has deteriorated since 1992, when Price Waterhouse was deeply impressed by 'sales growth from nothing to $1 billion in twenty years . . . competitive superiority in flexibility, costs, customer service and feedback links . . . strong global brand image and reputation'. Growth has slowed down, and both American and German franchisees have been complaining loudly and litigiously. The formula of 'direct control of purchasing, design and marketing only' still works, but not so marvellously that it can offset errors like tasteless advertising or proliferation of franchisees.

The trouble is that riding high deceives both management and external admirers, even consultants who have been close to the corporate heart. The self-deception gives rise to the myth of the Big Idea. The hero company's success sanctifies the Idea: when success turns to relative failure, by the same token, the Big Idea is rubbished – as has happened to both Total Quality Management and Business Process Reengineering. The truth is that you can major on one or two elements, but unless all the elements are in place, the business results must eventually disappoint.

The Sema consultancy has a neat model which lists six elements surrounding the core of strategy. The six are people, processes, money, information, technology and time. In any such model, the strength of the whole is that of its weakest part. The Price Waterhouse approaches are also interdependent – and management needs all six. The organization must be a Flat Network that Learns, Innovates and Benchmarks as it continuously improves its Processes. As for out-sourcing, the winning organization is only Hollow to the extent that outsiders improve its ability to achieve business objectives.

Unless those are also human objectives, they won't be achieved in anything beyond the short run. Circumstances may conspire to force companies to reduce the input of labour in relation to a desired level of output. But the higher that output, the better able the company is to find new employment for its people. They should have been recruited with care, trained with skill and motivated to make the business succeed. To follow all that by dispensing with their services is a ridiculous waste of resources.

That won't happen if the company can find a way to link the purposes of the people and the business – and such a way does exist. It starts with changing the mind-set that bedevilled the automotive business, not only in Germany, but in the rest of Europe. The mind-set consists of:

1 The *idée fixe*, a preconception that can't be budged.

2 Appeal to false consensus ('everybody says . . .')

3 Wishfully discounting contrary evidence ('you just don't understand this industry/company').

4 Unsupported denial of unpleasant conclusions (Lewis Carroll's Bellman Theory: 'What I tell you three times is true').

No manager, no human being, is immune to the cycle of *idée fixe*, false consensus, wishful thinking, and unsupported denial. It is a defence mechanism. But what is under attack? The mechanism prevents users from having to change, abandoning present behaviour and moving to a new mode. Moves are inherently risky. You are stepping away from known ground. Even if the existing ground is slipping from under your feet, you may prefer present danger to future uncertainty.

In business, the defence mechanism is triggered by money. If your competitor appears likely to steal your markets by superior technology and more efficient plants, you have two choices: spend heavily and quickly in a catch-up operation, or bow to the inevitable. When Ira Magaziner, working for Volkswagen, sought to discover what Japanese car firms were planning in the US, he immediately hit the *idée fixe*. As he relates in *The Silent War* (written with Mark Patinkin),[3] Japan didn't exist – the Japanese couldn't make good cars, because of inferior plant technology. Even if they discovered how, they couldn't make cars suitable for a US market they would never understand. VW fell for this self-delusion no less heavily than the Americans who had reacted so late and ineffectively to the rise of the Beetle to become the fourth largest brand in the market. Led by Toyota, the Japanese, fed by car factories which were actually more modern than any in the US and Europe, stole the small car market that VW had pioneered: the German company's American sales fell by 90 percent in the process. The adverse signs were simply ignored.

Revamping plants, embracing new construction methods and introducing new small cars would have cost Volkswagen dear. Deferring this essential expenditure, though, meant that profits weren't made at all. The account has to be settled in the end, with much greater expense and much lower chances of success – witness the later miserable experiences of the Wolfsburg giant.

Launch a programme to remake the company from top to bottom, however, and even a headlong decline in market share can be replaced, even a Japanese tide reversed. And there is only one way in which it can be done: from top to bottom.

Once upon a time, there was a highly popular nostrum called Management by Objectives which used precisely that approach. It promised perfection. Top management decided on an overall target for the corporation, and each division produced its plan for helping to achieve that target. Each sub-unit in each division did likewise, and the cascade continued down to the individual managers. They all had their individual targets, agreed with their superiors, and linked arithmetically to their remuneration.

Attracted by the carrot, and driven by the stick (wielded by superiors who were defending their own interests, too), the individuals would all meet their targets. Inevitably, so would their units, and so would the divisions, and so would the entire business. MBO only had one defect: it didn't work. No matter how much care had been taken in formulating the objectives, drawing up the plans and involving all the managers, the corporate targets were almost invariably missed.

So the technique passed away as one more fashionable management theory, defeated by the refusal of reality to conform to the plan.

More than the memory has lingered on, however. Many companies practise systems which have strong elements of MBO. But nobody now believes in, or promulgates, MBO as an entire management system. Or do they?

The following definition sounds remarkably familiar: '. . . a fully integrated top-down, bottom-up management system through which the two or three critical breakthrough targets and means are identified and implemented with the full participation and alignment of all managers' – and even all staff. This system cascades down, too: from 'theme to objective, to target, to measures, to means'. The definitions come from the British PA Consulting and refer, not to MBO, but PD: Policy Deployment. Derived from what is known in Japan as *hoshin kanri*, it is the ultimate in the process of Total Quality Management. The approach differs decisively from MBO in several ways: in overall aims (where MBO concentrates on management control), objectives (TQM is 'quality first', MBO 'cost first'), style ('flexibility' versus 'political') and focus.

Getting results through tight target-setting is MBO. Getting them through improved processes is PD. New Century Management must come down heavily in favour of PD's emphasis on processes. But what the two approaches have in common is just as important as their differences. The common aim is to blend individual motivation with that of the organization in order to improve the quality performance of both.

Professor Kasra Ferdows of Washington University has established a pattern which shows that, with quality as the base, a hierarchy of capabilities begins to form:

1 Quality, which leads to . . .
2 dependability, which leads to . . .
3 speed, and finally to . . .
4 cost-efficiency.

Once again, the principle of interdependence or interlocking comes into play. You must keep investing in the quality base to obtain wider and wider benefits from the other strata of this pyramid. In other words, the contribution of quality to the bottom line isn't simply direct, but works its full wonders through its impact on other non-financial measures – reliable performance and rapid response. Those in turn come through to the bottom line.

The issue is whether you need the full programme of PD to reach that destination. The PD process begins with a vision of where the company is heading over the next five years. Next, you select your business priorities – what PA Consulting describes as 'breakthrough improvement themes'. Those priorities set the scene for the deployment of objectives, from which plans are deployed in turn. Implementation follows, with its results reviewed every month, leading up to the annual review, when the whole process begins all over again.

The real issue isn't whether PD is right or wrong. You have to implement every stage, even if you aren't using PD. In one form or another, the stages take place in any organization. The choice is only between haphazard and controlled occurrence. Put that way there is no choice. The label on the package doesn't matter. The contents do. And so does another essential: the package must be transparent. Everybody must be able to see what's inside.

The first step is to analyse and cost your own processes (which usually generates immediate ideas for improvement). Then you study other people to compare their costs and processes to establish which costs are lowest and which processes best. Above all, you change methods and continue until your data match, or better, the best: even then, you don't stop. Just as *kaizen* demands, the cycle of Plan, Do, Check, Act circles continuously – or will do, if nobody throws a monkey-wrench into the works.

In a financially driven group like Rank Xerox, profit pressures have sometimes had that effect, which makes it far from easy to protect quality investments. Squeezed operating managements find cutbacks in quality an easy short-term expedient. Defending the long-term interests of the business against short-term economies 'is a permanent conflict', says chief executive Bernard Fournier. 'A few companies' in Xerox 'stopped the quality drive, and the indicators went down', a result that was predictable, and unacceptable.

The object of PD isn't Total Quality Management: it is Total Quality *of* Management, which takes in every activity in the firm. That isn't achieved by exhortation, but by action. If that action cascades down the organization, binding together all levels, and all the elements of the business system, the name of the process doesn't matter. The result will be continuous reinvention.

The shake-up at Shell

If one company had to be chosen to epitomize the basic economic power of a transnational Europe, Royal Dutch-Shell would surely get the palm. No other long-established group could earn this praise: 'a model multi-national: a loose federation of operating companies with a well-trained cadre of mobile managers and a light touch from central offices'. So nothing symbolizes the change in the nature of all management more vividly than the restructuring on which Shell embarked in the spring of 1995. Out went the alleged looseness. In came a tighter, more centralized regime.

In truth, the old Shell never fitted the above description from *Business Week*. For all its efforts to throw off the avuncular 'Joe Shell' image, which began with massive reconstruction (and large job losses) in the mid-sixties, the group had retained an introverted, bureaucratic culture. The matrix system made that inevitable. Shell might pride itself on its mastery of the matrix, but one operating manager still had three bosses: his country boss, his functional chief and his business leader.

The reporting lines – and the dotted ones connecting up the matrix – crisscrossed the globe. 'So much bureaucracy had built up, we couldn't change it unless we got rid of it,' one Shell executive told the magazine. For years Shell had ignored the silting up: after all, huge profits rolled in ($6.9 billion in 1995, 11 percent up on the previous year) on gigantic sales of $110 billion. Other oil giants, led by Exxon, had reformed their ways earlier, probably because they were first to feel the pain of low oil prices in a more competitive climate. Shell was restrained by another factor – the very culture it is now seeking to change.

The top management consequently wanted more than a new structure. This involved swapping the tripartite matrix for single lines of business (exploration and production, say, or chemicals). The responsibility was vested in business committees of senior operating managers: departments and regions were to become history. But Shell Man (and Woman) proved unexpectedly resistant: according to the *Financial Times*, the restructuring 'proved more difficult to carry through and "sell" internally than management expected' – the deadline had to be extended twice as a result.

In other words, Shell also needed a new breed of manager. Instead of the traditional lifers, the new era needed people capable of thinking new thoughts and doing new deeds – people like Chris Finlayson and American Alex Kulpecz, who told the paper, 'I'm an outsider with the reputation of a maverick.' The pair, both in their thirties, were given the task of rethinking the exploration and production division. They looked at other companies: ABB, General Electric, Merck, Mobil. Perhaps even more important, they found out how Shell was perceived by the outside world.

'Difficult to work with, slow-moving, arrogant and high-cost,' was the answer. They would have found much the same answer from their own contemporaries inside Shell. You can see why from the delays to the restructuring: 'The planning was secretive, which created a distinction between insiders and outsiders, which created resentment.' Even the Kulpecz-Finlayson exercise ran into similar problems, despite its intelligence and effectiveness – seven or eight layers of management cut to three, no geographical reporting, all units measured according to business results.

The reforms apparently had brilliant outcomes – Kulpecz claims that decisions which took a month and a committee of 20 people now require one man and a day. Yet, for all their common sense, the 'changes encountered hostility from staff who felt they had been excluded from the planning process'. They had every reason for their feelings: they *had* been excluded, and 300 jobs were to go. The Shell culture had conditioned even the 30-something mavericks.

The company's *modus operandi* is still light-years away from the attitudes highlighted in the US outpost of France's Thomson electronics giant, which has 'a successful high-end line of TVs' called Pro-Scan. Each member of a crossfunctional team (from design, marketing, engineering and manufacturing) took turns as Pro-Scan team leader, while continuing to perform in their normal jobs: 'all the team members subsequently moved on to bigger and better things. Says [one], "It made us all better generalists."'

Such anecdotes should always be taken with a grain of salt, in the sense that somebody else's experience is never as valuable as your own. But the pattern of this new approach to management – and its difference from Shell's – is clear enough. The task is to make people offers they can't refuse, because they want to accept – and this will markedly improve the behaviour of individuals and groups. Managers are ceasing to function as part of an order-and-obey chain, and becoming instead links in a much more voluntary process.

The distinction between the old and new manager drawn by *Fortune* magazine notes that the latter 'invites others to join in decision-making', while the former 'makes most decisions alone'. The one shares information, the other hoards. The *passé* manager is bound up (often almost literally) with the chains of command. The new style non-manager 'deals with anyone necessary to get the job done'. That means colleagues, people in other departments, and people in traditionally lower spheres – like the 'workers'.

As work demands more intelligence, so the distinction between the worker and the manager (who presumably is also a worker) becomes even harder to sustain. Workers have long been known as untapped sources of valuable knowledge – like the Milliken textile man whose new European boss mentioned a costly, long-standing technical problem. The veteran suggested a solution, which worked out fine. When had the brainwave occurred? Long years before . . .

Tapping an operative's skill and experience makes indisputable sense, but 'non-managers' go further. Like managers at BA Engineering, whose astonishing cost savings were mentioned earlier in this section, they ask operatives what help they need to perform better. This isn't namby-pamby stuff: the targets for improvement are (and must be) pitched high and taken dead seriously. But the changed approach changes attitudes and takes the first step towards long-term and lasting betterment.

This isn't Utopia: rather, it is the hard-headed reality of some hard-nosed companies. The new concept can be approached from the angle of teamwork. Many companies are now proliferating team projects. These can't be managed by order-and-obey methods; yet somebody has to keep the projects on track and on target. The management contribution is vital, but 'facilitator' is a better description of a role which is by definition temporary.

The 'manager' job, in this and other ways, is becoming less fixed and more flexible, which is just as well in volatile times. But what if your company (like most companies) is far away from this new culture, and persists in the set organizational ways that can be summarized as 'large-company disease' – which Honda's president once identified in his own business? His remedy is one that (alas) must also be used with managers who can't adjust to non-managing in a new-style company: 'For those who are inflexible and refuse to do what they have to do, the only option is to fire them.'

In a company that is inflexible and refuses to do what has to be done, the individual manager can try to fire it in the sense of ignition – but if that doesn't work, the only option is to fire the company as an employer. Non-managers won't stay where they can't non-manage. But more and more, that is the way organizations are being run – and soon there won't be any option, whether the company is a Shell or a small fish. Non-manage, or else.

Reinventing the manager

Everybody knows about the manager of the future. Every guru has been painting much the same portrait for years. Whether the path to the vision leads through total quality, or business process reengineering, or modern manufacturing, or the search for competitive advantage, or leadership, or anything else, the final picture remains the same: an apparently undeniable formula for twenty-first century success.

Manager 2000 will practice cooperation and collaboration with everybody, inside and outside the firm, from colleagues and subordinates to customers and suppliers. He/she will be a tolerant teamworker, tolerant of different and new ideas, forgiving of errors made in the cause of progress, putting the objectives of the team above the ambitions of the person. The environment will encourage these behaviours by devolution of power and delegation of duties – right down to the empowered, self-managing worker near the top of the inverted pyramid.

The inversion of the traditional hierarchy places the top management at the base, and the customer at the summit. Thus, the whole management process will be geared to the non-stop search for competitive advantage, which in turn will be dedicated to providing the customer (who always comes first) with the best in quality and service. That is the vision. It is everybody's ideal, and practicable enough. But it has a huge drawback. Hardly anybody is doing it – yet.

Certainly top managements in Europe are aware of the need for change. As noted earlier in this chapter, Shell is an instructive example. Its top Dutchman, Cornelius A.J. Herkströter, saw the need to change a system 'designed for a different era, for a different world'. Aiming to raise the return on capital by a fifth to 12 percent, Shell needed to break away from its baronies. They were duly swept aside, but the same barons all bobbed up again on the new business committees. In a new era and a new world, playing musical chairs is not an adequate response to the challenge.

The probability is that, as the next decade develops, managements will either adopt their own versions of the new mode, or their organizations will founder in the competitive tide.

There is a powerful analogy. In 1990 I published a book called *Culture Shock*, which pointed out that developments in information technology, especially those revolving round the networked personal computer, were going to change management processes radically – and that was before the Internet intensified the revolution so amazingly. Like the tools and techniques of the management reinvention described above, this IT revolution wasn't state-of-the-art: it was already off-the-shelf. I soon found that the reactionaries far outnumbered the revolutionaries. That may still be true. All the same, the networks are proliferating at an unstoppable pace. By early next century only the greybeards will have desks free from keyboards; or briefcases lacking laptops, notebooks or palmtops; or files over-stuffed with non-electronic communications. Much better information will be available much faster, and shared much more widely.

IT is the enabling mechanism of the management ideal. But plainly the doomed resistance, both to the computer and to the new management modes, has deep roots. Most managers have not yet come to terms with fundamental change in their worlds as the horizontal principle displaces the vertical right across the board. The outcomes of business processes are becoming all-important, while procedures and rituals are receding into the past. Innovation, like quality, has moved from the realms of lip-service into those of necessity.

That must have profound effects on the allocation of the power and the glory, which have long been driving forces in management, as in politics. I once wrote that power, like hot air (and often accompanied by it), rises to the top. The general attitude of the powerful is to approve that rise heartily; but their approval has lately been tempered by much talk of 'empowerment' of those lower down. That only perpetuates the fallacy. Remember, empowered people aren't being 'given' power that doesn't belong to them; they are simply having less power taken away.

Every piece of research confirms that what is more properly called 'enablement' produces better results for the individual and the firm. The issue isn't one of giving people the ability to manage or work more effectively: it's about ceasing to thwart them. But management reinvention has to start at the top. The roles of the chairman, the chief executive (who shouldn't be one and the same by 2000), the board, the executive management – all these have to change before any other lasting changes are possible. And that change is beginning to happen.

In previous chapters I have described some of the many and varied ways in which management is being reinvented. For instance, at Rank Xerox, managing director Bernard Fournier, who is no shrinking violet, submits to twice-yearly feedback from his own direct reports. The same goes for them. Like everybody else in the company, each of these top managers has a 'Blue Book' which sets out the company goals, objectives and strategy, and also lays down their 'vital few actions'. Everybody knows specifically what is expected of them, their departments and the whole company, and everybody is involved in deciding what they have to do.

Whether you call this 'policy deployment' or not, what's afoot is simply a different method of managing. It is mandated not by whim, but by the exigencies of competition. Competitive pressures also explain why youthfully-led project teams in well-run car companies now have total responsibility for new models, from start to finish; and why even towering chief executive egos can't override them.

Reinvented managers, at any level, are similarly concerned with unleashing potential all around them and all the way down. Leaders who don't hear the messages from below, which should come all the way up, won't be listened to themselves. And that will be fatal to their only real authority, which is their ability to enable organizational success.

Old-style, fixed authority is a framework for establishing and keeping the rules. That framework must crumble in an age when progress depends on breaking the rules – if that's the way to optimize the outcomes (as it usually is). The right principle is demonstrated in Total Quality Management and similar approaches. The wisest and best TQM programmes start, as noted, with analysing and improving the work of the board, not with the all too common first step: encouraging frontline staff to smile at the customers.

Moreover, quality initiatives, customer service programmes and any other efforts at improvement (and such efforts are mandatory) will fail unless they are comprehensive. Time and again, as I have observed, marvellous gains in productivity or customer satisfaction are reported in parts of companies whose overall results bear no relation to these splendid achievements: the star players, so to speak, are locked into a team whose tactics and strategy drain away their skills.

Of course, the Augean stables syndrome is universal: no company is ever perfect in every respect. But unless the organization is seen as a system, in which every part relates to every other part, managers won't be able to manage effectively in the new century. One response to the syndrome is to cut down on the system's components, to farm out as much 'non-core' activity as possible. This does produce simpler internal systems, and is, anyway, a trend enforced in many industries by the developing technology of both product and process.

The business system as a whole, though, is unchanged in purpose by the subcontracting. The demands for performance are just as intense. But managers will be spending a lot more time working intimately with colleagues who are employees of other companies – or maybe not employees at all. In an era dominated by outcomes, those who can achieve results will be hired for that ability, not for their willingness to occupy the same desk in the same building every day. The consultancy mode and the manager mode are getting closer all the time and will eventually become interchangeable.

These developments should one day mean an end to one of the least attractive and least sensible management features of the 1990s: the major 'restructurings' as crisis-torn corporations 'reinvent' themselves. Often, the state they reach is worse than the one they left. The restructured business, shorn of key capacities and morale by the cost-cutting, goes on losing jobs without repairing the lost profits and stagnant performance that precipitated the crisis.

A kind of corporate *kaizen* – continuous management reinvention – is the only answer. It is evolving under various names. As I have emphasized, they all mean broadly the same thing. In its fullest sense 'business process reengineering' means looking at customer requirements with totally fresh eyes, and reshaping the entire corporation, right back down the supply chain, in order to meet the redefined customer need. The 'virtual corporation' lives by the same credo, seeking to meet those needs in the shortest possible time by continual adaptation.

As a virtual reengineer, the New Century manager can't expect his or her own job to be static; rather, the business process will determine what's expected at any given time. Since horizontal business processes are all multifunctional and multidisciplinary, the manager is being led in similar directions. Crossfunctional, synergistic and interdepartmental working is unavoidable now; so are task-specific teams. That is all to the good, because the reduction of hierarchical layers (itself a result of the information technology revolution and improvement in management processes) is cutting the number of possible promotions.

Managers will have to advance in prestige and pay by moving from one successful assignment to the next, not by exchanging one title for another. This kind of career progression will be a great deal more enjoyable than playing corporate politics. The idea that jobs should be enjoyed (at all levels in the organization) is inseparable from psychological theories about people's behaviour at work. Though old-established, these ideas are now coming truly into their own. They run like a bloodstream through all the developments discussed in this book.

Theory Y, with its basic belief that work is as natural as play, will dominate New Century Management as organizations seek to tap people's own motivation by genuine involvement – by liberating their energies and rewarding their initiatives. These sound like 'soft' values – but, like the idea of shared corporate values itself, they are far more commonly aired these days than the 'hard' disciplines. Management badly needs both, though, for the 'hard' work of TQM or reengineering is the fastest route to 'soft' improvements – and to excellent results.

At companies in technological or market-driven transition (which takes in nearly everybody), values do provide a steady guide through upheaval. The notably hard-headed strategic consultants at Kepner-Tregoe believe that strategy development must be built around values to be wholly effective. Managers in all businesses will have to come to terms with value statements that actually mean something, and with 'living the vision' by demonstrably acting in accordance with the fine phrases.

That in no way lessens the demand for hard performance. Nor can that demand ever dwindle. On the contrary, new understanding of performance measures, financial and non-financial, is toughening the targets. Traditional bottom-line measures simply tell too little about past performance – and nothing whatever about the future. Many managers already have their bonus payments linked to a shopping basket of factors, which include items like customer satisfaction.

Without question, some of these baskets will include appraisal from below as well as above. That is perfectly logical. Ricardo Semler, the maverick boss of the small but revolutionary Brazilian engineering firm mentioned in Chapter 9 (page 213), has it right. Semco managers who are rated below 70 percent are in danger of dismissal, not because their subordinates dislike them, but because they are losing the authority to manage. They can't get things done: they can't achieve the necessary outcomes.

The real task is to encourage effective, thinking self-management in people who mostly want nothing more than that encouragement. It's no dream. Honeywell (UK) is only one of several companies where self-managed manufacturing cells have taken full responsibility for product lines under a completely changed style of supervision. This company is an affiliate of an American multinational: its initiatives are its own. Its best managers, though, are winning top responsibilities in the US.

Europeans or managers with high-level European experience now occupy the top positions in a considerable assortment of US companies, from General Motors to Compaq, from Ford to Salomon. But Europe badly needs to keep its own top talent and exploit it to the full – preferably people with American and other outside experience, for global markets need global managers. Already, management teams in Europe, including

American affiliates, are likely to include several nationalities, people to whom the boundaries between nations mean no more than those between departments.

The boundaries between firms will also have much less meaning, not only because of the evolving change in supplier relationships from adversary to ally, but because of the fast-growing number of other strategic alliances. In an age when no company is an island, no manager can be insular. The key to the more open organization must be the more open manager – open to new ideas and markets, open to others, and open to instruction: because new processes demand new knowledge and know-how.

The portrait of the reinvented manager is thus clear and complete. An excellent start towards that reinvention is to involve all managers in contributing towards forming the strategies they will have to implement – not least because that forces companies to develop and communicate sound strategies in the first place. Many don't, which is one measure of the great distance management in general has still to travel. But already, in today's world, you can feel the pulse of the forward movement in both strategy and tactics – and that beat is powerful.

In tomorrow's world, those who resist the forward momentum will be swept aside, or overrun, along with their organizations. That's a doubly sad outcome, because the changes under way bring a new vibrancy to the age-old task of mobilizing collective human powers. That task has never offered more viable alternatives, more excitement, or more potential for brilliant success – for the organization, and for the individual, liberated, invigorated, reinvented manager.

NOTES

Introduction

1. Thomas J. Peters & Robert Waterman, *In Search of Excellence: Lessons from America's Best-Run Companies* (Harper & Row, New York, 1982).
2. Robert H. Waterman Jr, *The Frontiers of Excellence: Learning from Companies that Put People First* (Nicholas Brealey Publishing, London, 1994).

1. The Devolution of Leadership

1. James Moore, *The Death of Competition: Leadership and Strategy in the Age of Business Systems* (John Wiley, London, 1996).
2. *Best Practices Report*, Ernst & Young and The American Quality Foundation (1992).
3. Harold J. Leavitt and Jean Lipman-Blumen, 'Hot groups', *Harvard Business Review*, July-August 1995.
4. Masaaki Imai, *Kaizen: Key to Japan's Competitive Success* (McGraw-Hill, London, 1989).
5. Robert Baumann, 'Starting a new job', *Business Strategy Review* (London Business School) 1995:4.

2. Driving Radical Change

1. Robert Heller, *The State of Industry* (BBC Books, London, 1987).
2. William H. Davidow and Michael S. Malone, *The Virtual Corporation* (Edward Burlingame Books/HarperCollins, New York, 1992).
3. Peter D. Wickens, 'The total quality of change', in Robert Heller (Ed.), *Managing 1993: The European Challenge* (Sterling Publications, London, 1993).

3. Reshaping the Culture

1. John Parnaby, 'Organization of manufacturing', in Robert Heller (Ed.), *The Complete Guide to Modern Management* (Harrap, London, 1988).
2. David Harvey, *Re-engineering: The Critical Success Factors* (Management Today and Business Intelligence, London, 1995).
3. Michael Hammer and James Champy, *Re-engineering the Corporation* (Nicholas Brealey Publishing, London, 1993).
4. David Harvey, *op. cit.*
5. Nitin Nohria and Rakesh Khurana, 'The effects of CEO turnover on large industrial corporations', *Harvard Business Review*, Jan-Feb 1997.
6. Charles M. Farkas and Philippe de Backer, *Maximum Leadership: The World's Top Business Leaders Discuss How They Add Value to Their Companies* (Orion, London, 1995).
7. Ingersoll Engineers, 'The way we work: Organisation and processes to meet customer needs in manufacturing industry', Nov 1996.
8. Arie de Geus, 'The living company', *Harvard Business Review*, Mar-Apr 1997.
9. Thomas S. Robertson, 'Corporate graffiti', *Business Strategy Review* (London Business School) 1995:1.

4. Dividing to Rule

1. Peter McColough, speech to New York Society of Security Analysts, March 1970.
2. Zafer Achi et al., 'The paradox of

fast-growth tigers', *The McKinsey Quarterly*, 1995:3.

3. The Price Waterhouse Change Integration Team, *The Paradox Principles* (Irwin, Chicago, 1996).

4. Charles Kiefer, 'Executive Team Leadership', in Peter M. Senge (Ed.) et al., *The Fifth Discipline Fieldbook* (Nicholas Brealey Publishing, London, 1994).

5. Peter M. Senge (Ed.) et al., id.

6. Geoffrey Owen and Trevor Harrison, 'Why ICI chose to demerge', *Harvard Business Review*, Mar-Apr 1995.

7. Michael Goold, Andrew Campbell and Marcus Alexander, *Corporate-Level Strategy*, (John Wiley & Sons, Chichester, 1994).

8. Constantinos Markides, 'Corporate Refocusing', *Business Strategy Review* (London Business School) 1993:1.

9. H. Igor Ansoff, *Corporate Strategy* (McGraw-Hill, New York, 1965. Also published as a revised edition by Penguin Books, London, 1987).

5. Exploiting the Organization

1. Adrian J. Slywotzky and Benson P. Shapiro, 'Leveraging to beat the odds: The new marketing mind-set', *Harvard Business Review*, Sept-Oct 1993.

2. Robert S. Kaplan and David P. Norton, 'Using the balanced scorecard as a strategic management system', *Harvard Business Review*, Jan-Feb 1996.

3. Sir Derek Birkin, 'Leading a global mining company into the 1990s', speech to the American Mining Congress, RTZ, London, autumn 1989.

4. Peter M. Senge, *The Fifth Discipline* (Century Business, London, 1992).

5. Ibid.

6. Robert Heller, *TQM: The Quality Makers* (Norden Publishing House, St Gallen, Switzerland, 1993).

7. Sema Group, 'Transforming the IT of Manufacturing Systems (conference, Birmingham, 1996).

8. Robert Heller, *The Super Chiefs* (Hodder & Stoughton, London, 1989).

6. Keeping the Competitive Edge

1. Helen Bloom, Roland Calori and Philippe de Woot, *Euromanagement* (Kogan Page, London, 1994).

2. Douglas McGregor, *The Human Side of Enterprise* (McGraw-Hill, New York, 1960).

3. Regis McKenna, *Relationship Marketing* (Century Business, London, 1992).

4. Michael Gershman, *Getting It Right the Second Time* (Addison-Wesley, Reading, USA, 1990).

5. William H. Whyte Jr, *The Organization Man* (New York, 1956).

6. William H. Davidow and Michael S. Malone, *The Virtual Corporation*, (Edward Burlingame Books/ HarperCollins, New York, 1992).

7. Rosabeth Moss Kanter, *When Giants Learn to Dance: Mastering the Challenges of Strategy, Management and Careers in the 1990s* (Simon & Schuster, London, 1989).

7. Achieving Constant Renewal

1. P. Ranganath Nayak and John M. Ketteringham, *Breakthroughs!* (Mercury Books, London, 1987).

2. Bill Ramsay, speech to Esomar Conference, Barcelona, Nov 1990.

3. Kenichi Ohmae, *The Borderless World* (HarperCollins, London, 1990).

4. Sir David Simon, speech to the Top Management Forum, Management Centre Europe, London, June 1996.

5. Jay W. Forrester, interview with Mark Keough and Andrew Doman in the *McKinsey Quarterly*, 1992:2.

6. Ibid.

8. Mobilizing the Motivators

1. Peter Drucker, *Post-Capitalist Society* (Butterworth-Heinemann, Oxford, 1993).

2. Michael Hammer and James Champy, *Reengineering the Corporation* (Nicholas Brealey Publishing, London, 1993).

9. Making Teamworking Work

1. Ricardo Semler, *Maverick!* (Century, London, 1993).
2. Feargal Quinn, *Crowning the Customer: How to Become Customer Driven* (O'Brien Press, Dublin, 1990).
3. Julian Richer, *The Richer Way* (Emap Business Communications, London, 1996).
4. Philip Sadler, *Managing Talent* (Century Business and The Economist Books Ltd, London, 1993).
5. T. Murakami and T. Nishiwaki, *Strategy for Creation* (Woodhead Publishing, Cambridge, 1991).
6. David A. Nadler and Marc S. Gerstein, *Organizational Architecture: Designs for Changing Organizations* (Jossey-Bass, USA).

10. Total Quality of Management

1. George Binney, *Making Quality Work: Lessons from Europe's Leading Companies* (Economist Intelligence Unit, Nov 1992).
2. Philip Crosby, *Quality Is Free: The Art of Making Quality Certain* (McGraw-Hill, London, 1978).
3. Ira Magaziner and Mark Patinkin, *The Silent War* (Vintage Books, New York, 1989).

INDEX

In Search of Excellence

Lessons from America's Best-Run Companies

TOM PETERS AND ROBERT H. WATERMAN JR

The international bestseller

American know-how is alive and well and growing stronger daily. *In Search of Excellence* distills the art and science of management used by leading companies with records of long-term profitability and continuing innovation. No-one concerned with international business today can afford not to read what makes leading US corporations successful.

'One of those rare books on management'   *New York Wall Street Journal*

'Required reading'   *International Management Magazine*

'Receiving serious attention in business schools and corporate boardrooms'
Washington Post

0 00 638402 1

Focus

The Future of Your Company Depends On It
AL RIES

Co-author of *The 22 Immutable Laws of Marketing*

IBM had $65 billion in revenues and was still losing money. PepsiCo has almost twice the sales and assets of Coca-Cola, but its stock is worth less than half. What is their problem, shared by hundreds of other businesses world-wide?

Focus has the answer. With practical, no-nonsense advice, Al Ries guides managers back on track and explains why companies that focus on core products and get rid of extraneous, resource-wasting areas are the most successful.

With hard examples from a wide variety of industries, Ries analyses corporations that are focused, and many that are not. He predicts the kind of corporate thinking that is destined to fail, and looks at companies such as Volvo, Blockbuster, Federal Express, Toys 'R' US, American Express and many more.

In today's cut-throat markets, the 'refocusing' issue can make or break a company. This book is vital to chief executives, entrepreneurs, marketing managers and managers of all divisions.

0 00 638735 7

HarperCollins Business

The Tao of Coaching

Boost Your Effectiveness at Work by Inspiring
and Developing Those Around You

MAX LANDSBERG

Coaching is *the* key to unlocking the potential of your people, your organization and, ultimately, yourself.

The good news is that becoming a great coach requires nurturing just a few simple skills and habits.

Max Landsberg, responsible for professional development programmes at McKinsey & Co in the UK, takes you through the stages needed to master and implement coaching to maximum effect. He shows how to:

• nurture an environment where coaching can flourish

• develop a team of people who relish working with you

• enhance the effectiveness of others through learning

• create more time for yourself through efficient delegation

By investing small amounts of time to provide constructive feedback, mentoring and encouragement, managers can substantially boost both their colleagues and their own performance.

With the current emphasis on helping individual employees to realize and deliver their full potential, the techniques of coaching are fast becoming essential tools for managers and other professionals. This is the first book which, in a highly entertaining and practical way, shows how to go about it.

'I'm making this useful guide required reading for my executive team'
GEORGE FARR, VICE-CHAIRMAN, American Express Company

'Practical, readable and relevant'
ARCHIE NORMAN, CHAIRMAN, Asda Group plc

0 00 638811 6

Jamming

The Art and Discipline of Business Creativity

JOHN KAO

No corporate asset is at once so prized and yet so poorly managed as the imagination and creativity of a company's people. In today's competitive environment, companies who understand how to manage creativity, how to organize for creative results and who willingly implement new ideas will triumph.

John Kao, who teaches creativity at the Harvard Business School, offers an approach that demystifies a topic traditionally confounding to business people everywhere. Drawing an analogy, Kao illustrates that creativity, like the musical discipline of jazz, has a vocabulary and a grammar. He explains how creativity needs a particular environment in which to blossom and grow. Like musicians in a jam session, a group of business people can take an idea, challenge one another's imagination, and produce an entirely new set of possibilities.

Jamming reveals how managers can stimulate creativity in their employees, free them of constraints and preconceptions, and guide them instead to a chosen goal where imagination is transformed into competitive supremacy. Using specific examples from a wide range of companies – including Coca-Cola, DreamWorks SKG and Sony – *Jamming* is a fascinating study of the shape and relevance of this most valued commodity in the workplace of the future.

'No matter how much you've downsized, or reengineered your company, all those efforts don't mean a thing if you ain't got that zing . . . *Jamming* serves as a primer on how to nurture talented workers . . . Kao's message is sound'

Fortune

0 00 638682 2

Co-opetition

Two leading business thinkers use game theory to rewrite business strategy

BARRY J. NALEBUFF AND
ADAM M. BRANDENBURGER

The game of business changes constantly. So should your business strategy.

This is the first book to adapt game theory to the needs of CEOs, managers and entrepreneurs. *Co-opetition* offers a new mindset for business: a strategic way of thinking that combines competition and cooperation.

Though often compared to games like chess or poker, business is different – people are free to change the rules, the players, the boundaries, even the game itself. The essence of business success lies in making sure you are in the *right* game. Actively shaping which game you play, and how you play it, is the core of the innovative business strategy laid out in *Co-opetition*.

Barry Nalebuff and Adam Brandenburger, professors at Yale and Harvard, are pioneers in the practice of applying the science of game theory to the art of corporate strategy. They have devised a practice-oriented model to help you break out of the traditional win-lose or lose-lose situations, and dozens of companies – including Intel, Nintendo, American Express and Nutrasweet – have been using the strategies of co-opetition to change their game to enjoy the benefits of win-win opportunities.

Co-opetition will revolutionize the way you play the game of business.

'Seize on *Co-opetition*'

Economist

'A terrific book'

TOM PETERS

0 00 638724 1

The Fish Rots from the Head

The Crisis in Our Boardrooms:
Developing the Crucial Skills of the Competent Director

BOB GARRATT

An organization's success or failure depends on the performance of its board – an ancient Chinese saying is that 'the fish rots from the head'. Yet the vast majority of directors admit that they have had no training for their role and are not sure what it entails.

As boards' activities are made more and more transparent under national and international law, there is an urgent need for a transformation in the way directors' competencies are developed.

Bob Garratt argues that directors need to learn new thinking skills to apply to the intellectual activities of direction-giving and implementing strategy. They need to develop a broader mindset to deal with the uncertainty of higher-level issues such as policy formulation, strategic thinking, supervision of management and accountability.

The Fish Rots from the Head is the first book to clarify and integrate the roles and tasks of the director and provide a programme of learning. As the tide of regulation swells, no board director can afford to ignore it.

'An important contribution to the corporate governance debate and clear and intelligent advice on how to improve the performance of a board'
TIM MELVILLE-ROSS, INSITUTE OF DIRECTORS, London

'This clear, very readable book should ensure that many more fish swim rather than rot'
SIR MICHAEL BETT, CHAIRMAN, Cellnet plc

0 00 638670 9

Microsoft Secrets

How the World's Most Powerful Software Company Creates Technology,
Shapes Markets and Manages People

MICHAEL A. CUSUMANO & RICHARD W. SELBY

Beyond the unquestioned genius and vision of CEO Bill Gates, what accounts for Microsoft's astounding success?

Microsoft commands the high ground of the information superhighway by owning the operating systems and basic applications programs that run on the world's 170 million computers.

Drawing on two years of unrestricted access to confidential documents and project data, eminent technology-scientists Cusumano and Selby reveal, for the first time, many of Microsoft's innermost secrets.

Forty in-depth interviews with employees enabled the authors to identify seven key strategies which demonstrate exactly how Microsoft competes and operates. They reveal a style of leadership, organization, competition and product development which is both consistent with the company's loosely structured 'programmer' culture and remarkably effective for mass-market production of software.

Managers in many different industries will discover hundreds of invaluable lessons in this superbly readable book.

'A fascinating book about a fascinating company'
PETER SENGE, author of *The Fifth Discipline*

'Anyone intending to approach their bank manager to fund their own software company should make this book the centre of their business plan'   *Computer Weekly*

'A unique glimpse into the company's inner workings'   *Daily Telegraph*

0 00 638778 0

The B

Po

the

Kenichi Ohmae

'A must for all globally-minded people'   AKIO MORITA

Kenichi Ohmae's *The Borderless World* has changed the way managers view the world and their businesses, and how they invent, commercialize and compete. It vividly shows the increasing dominance of consumers over companies and countries, and the resultant melting away of national economic borders to create a global market.

Ohmae's timely advice has enabled major Japanese companies to capture new markets across the world. You too can profit from his proven wisdom.

'Any manager who doesn't read this book may well be at a competitive disadvantage in the 1990s'

JAMES D. ROBINSON III, Chairman,
American Express Company

ISBN: 00 638364 5

Brand Warriors

Corporate Leaders Share Their Winning Strategies

EDITED BY FIONA GILMORE

The companies rated by marketers as the rising stars for the future are those with very clearly positioned, confident corporate brands.

Yet not all companies these days consider it important enough to nurture their brands. Instead they spend their resources in the losing battle against increasing costs and decreasing margins.

With people more brand conscious than ever, what's going on?

Brand Warriors brings together some of the top brand custodians in the business to talk about the strategies they employ to put their brands in the lead and keep them there. Archie Norman of Asda, Bob Ayling of British Airways, Robert Holloway of Levi's, Alain Evrard of L'Oréal and C.H. Tung of OOCL are just some of the high-profile contributors who, in a series of revealing chapters, discuss the crucial aspects of:

- effective brand architecture

- the feel-good factor

- the economic value of brands

- powerful brand positioning and corporate communication programmes

- building loyalty – nurturing soft values alongside hard

- global marketing – the new paradigms

- corporate reputation

- the ability to recognize and handle change

- the importance of being not just a caring brand, but a caring employer

Championing the brand is at the heart of winning business strategies. Nothing is as important if a company is to prosper. These highly readable perspectives, written from the frontline, provide penetrating insights – based on proven success – that no business leader can afford to ignore.

0 00 255867 X